THE SPARK AND THE LIGHT: THE LEO ADLER STORY

BY ADAIR LAW

THE LEO ADLER TRUST
Boise, Idaho

Front cover photograph: Viewfinders NW/Bruce Forster
These wagon ruts are just outside Baker City, Oregon. They were formed by wagons following the route of the Oregon Trail.

Back cover: Upper right, Leo Adler and his dog, Prince, ca. 1905. Lower left, a birthday celebration for Leo Adler, 1989. Photo by Gerry Steele.

Cover design and book design by Jeanne E. Galick, Graphic Design

First edition
Copyright ©2004 The Leo Adler Trust

The Leo Adler Trust
U.S. Bank, Trustee
P.O. Box 7928
Boise, ID 83707

To order copies of this book, contact:
Baker County Public Library
2400 Resort St.
Baker City, OR 97814
Phone: 541-523-6419
Fax: 541-523-9088
E-mail: accounts@bakercountylibrary.org

Library of Congress Control Number: 2004096918
ISBN 0-9765100-0-X, paperback
ISBN 0-9765100-1-8, hardback

All rights reserved. No part of this publication may be reproduced or transmitted in any form or by any means, electronic or mechanical, including photocopying, recording or any information storage or retrieval system, without the permission in writing from the publisher.

Printed in the United States of America.

The paper used in this publication meets the minimum requirements of American National Standard for Information Sciences Permanence of Paper for Printed Library Materials.

Contents

Acknowledgements v
Introduction ix
Coming to America 1
Building the Crystal Palace 21
Making a Home in Baker City 47
Magazine Specialist 75
Opening New Territory 85
Becoming Mr. Baker 105
The War Years 123
Finding the New Normal 141
Airplanes, Fire and an Ambulance 161
Leo and Baseball: An Enduring Love 185
Closing the Circle 209
Bright Twilight 229
Afterword 247
Endnotes 256
Bibliography 271
Index 273

Acknowledgments

In putting together the puzzle pieces of Leo Adler's long life, I was fortunate to have the assistance of many students, researchers, scholars and people who knew and enjoyed Leo.

The Oregon Jewish Museum in Portland was an invaluable resource in terms of helping me understand the Jewish diaspora in Oregon and the threads of its connection throughout the state. It is the repository for oral histories of members of the state's far-flung Jewish community that were conducted by Shirley Tanzer in the 1970s. It is likely through her work that many early documents of the Adler family were preserved. Museum Director Judy Margles, curator Anne Levant-Prahl and Rebecca Patchett were generous with their time and space, both at a premium in their small and wonderful museum. Judy Margles connected me with Friderike Heuer, who assisted me with translation of various German family documents. When Friderike was unable to make her way through some of the more dense penmanship found in several Adler family letters, she connected me with Sabine Lenthe at Angebot Transkription in Bremen, Germany.

Liisa Penner of the Clatsop County Historical Society was very generous with the resources she shared about Astoria's history and Carl Adler's time there. She also pointed me toward especially good resources on the Astoria fire. The photographic and microfilm resources of the Oregon Historical Society were of great help as were the electronic resources of the Multnomah County Library. I also appreciate the time that Thomas Vaughan, director emeritus of the Oregon Historical Society, and Gerry Frank took to speak with me about their memories of Leo.

So many people in Baker made me feel welcome and assisted me greatly in my research. There were several Adler Scholars who started research through the Baker papers in 2000, finding the many articles that talked about Leo during his long lifetime. I would like to thank some of those scholars: Casey Boothby, Lisa Britton, Luke Burton, Beth Frantum, Kathryn Gornick, Stacy Hofmann, J.R. Johnson, Nick Taylor, Courtney Warner, and Melissa Wheeler for the thorough work they did. Chary Mires of the Baker County Historical Museum allowed my extended access to the document and photo collections in the Adler House Museum. She was also very generous with her time in explaining the process of the renovation that turned Leo Adler's home into the beautiful Adler House Museum. Thanks also go to Lois Cavallo, Sister Kay Marie Duncan, Johannah Fleetwood, Ralph and Norma Giles, Pearl Jones, Mary Levinger, Sister Martha Joseph Rooney, Barbara Anne Sturgill and Bob Young for sharing their memories of Leo Adler and aspects of Baker history with me. Aletha Bonebrake and her staff made me feel welcome at the Baker County Library during my visits there, even when I was monopolizing the copy machine. Kari Borgen, publisher of the Baker *City Herald* put me in touch with Kathy Orr, who scanned many of the photos that came from Baker City. I thank them for the time and attention they gave this project. Ron Brinton of the Baker *Record-Courier* helped connect me with Gary Holman, who graciously gave permission to use work from the Holman Studios and work done by Carl F. Holman.

Many thanks to the people who have helped take this book from a pile of pages to a book you can hold in your hands. Amy Stephenson edited the book, Jeanne Galick designed it and Amy Platt indexed it. Bob Smith of BookPrinters Network took care of printing and binding.

I want to extend my thanks to Chet Orloff, former director of the Oregon Historical Society who let me know about this project. Marlyn Norquist, Angela Breedlove and Mike Sullivan have been helpful contacts at U.S. Bank, which administers the Leo Adler Trust. I save special thanks for the trustees; J. Tabor Clarke, Dianne Ellingson, Dr. Chuck Hofmann, Norman Kolb, Gene Rose and Jack Wilson. I applaud any organization that takes time to examine what their founding or core values are and a biography of Leo is a fine way to start. After choosing me to write the biography, they always conveyed confidence in my work and enthusiasm for the story I was telling. This was a great gift because I know Leo lives and breathes in their memories in a very different way than he can live in my research.

Introduction

To many of the early travelers who passed through the area on their way to some other place, the resources of Baker City, Oregon were not readily apparent. For a traveler carrying visions of gold in California or the farmland in the Willamette Valley, the majesty of the area's scenery and its spare beauty did not stir the soul. Or at least not the souls of travelers who had been trudging toward the Willamette Valley for several weeks or months by the time they made their way to Baker. Although few stopped and stayed at that point in their journey, several made a mental note that it would be a place to come back to. And many did come back to Baker after passing it by the first time. The resources that made the area boom after the first phase of Oregon Trail emigration had to be either dug out of the ground, chopped down from the hills, or tended on the open range. Then as now, the resources and the riches of the area are not immediately apparent. But there is beauty and magic in this place.

Once you've found your way to Baker City, one name pops up continually. Driving along Campbell Street, you see a Leo Adler

Field, and a little beyond that a sign announces Leo Adler Memorial Parkway. Taking a left turn onto Main Street you can see a splendidly preserved Victorian home labeled the Adler House Museum, just one house away from its twin on the same block. If you like traveling with an eye ready for local history, you would make your way to the Oregon Trail Regional Museum. On the wall of that museum is a portrait of a rotund, bald man, his round face dominated by black horn-rim glasses. The man himself, Leo Adler. What's all the fuss about? Further historical curiosity could send you up to the Oregon Trail Interpretive Center at the top of Flagstaff Hill. On entering the building you would note the Leo Adler Theatre to your right. Again the name. Who is this guy?

To put it simply, he was a man who loved his home town. That love expressed itself as a boostering spirit and a willingness to put his shoulder to the wheel, start things rolling, and see that they got done. In a city that didn't lack for avid citizens or hard workers, often the main thing that was needed to get things started was someone who would say, "Yes, I'll do that," and then back the commitment up with an important first check or share the contacts that could help to raise the necessary chunk of money. Leo Adler was that man for Baker City. His favorite form of exercise was philanthropy. Always generous throughout his 98 bachelor years, on his death he became, if not a town father, then certainly a favorite great-uncle.

He learned early in his life that giving to others felt good. Although he didn't receive formal instruction in the Jewish religion of his parents, he absorbed the idea of mitzvoth, acts of loving kindness, through the example of his parents and relatives. He also learned it for himself as he became successful in his chosen profession of magazine sales and distribution. He traveled widely throughout the United States and saw the many things this country had to offer a man, just as his father Carl had seen when he emigrated from Germany in the nineteenth century.

Throughout his long life, Leo also saw what giving could do for a community. He learned this in the 1920s when the community was raising money for the Hotel Baker. He saw it played out during the war bond drives of the Second World War and he saw it again in the 1980s when Baker was making plans for the Oregon Trail Interpretive Center. He believed that if a community doesn't pull together, it pulls apart. America in the twentieth century weathered a wide range of incidents that could pull a community apart. Throughout his travels from the First World War through the 1990s, Leo continued to believe that Baker offered the best, and he was always happy to return to what he called "God's country."

His life has been compared to a Horatio Alger story in which a plucky young man moves from rags to riches. It is not an apt comparison, since Leo's life never encompassed the "rags" element of that story; his father Carl's life may have been a better example of that. This is the story of how his family came here, prospered, and sowed the seeds that allowed him to sink his roots deeply into Baker County, and how Leo Adler's work yielded a lifetime of philanthropy.

Coming to America

On February 22, 1871, a few months shy of turning seventeen, Carl Adler stood before a bureaucrat in the city of Mergentheim, Germany, to apply for a one-way passport to immigrate to North America. One of nine children born to Jacob Adler and Therese Gutmann Adler, he was born on May 23, 1854, in Oberdorf, District of Neresheim, Kingdom of Württemberg, a small town that in the years since he immigrated has been enfolded into the larger town of Neresheim. When young Carl applied for his passport, he was a resident of Weitersheim in the Mergentheim district, now Bad Margentheim in Baden-Württemberg, Germany, on the Tauber River. According to the bureaucrat who examined him, Carl was five feet, five inches and of medium stature. He had an oval face; his facial color was good. He had blond hair and gray eyes, his cheeks were "filled in," and his legs were straight. In the formal language of the passport, this document would allow him to leave the kingdom and "reach his destination free and unhindered." The destination was either the port of Bremen or Hamburg. From there he would make his way to America. The back of the document shows the required passport was stamped by the Ministry of the Interior and the Ministry for Foreign Affairs on May 15, 1871, a short three months later and just a few days before his seventeenth birthday. He would be traveling alone.[1]

What was he leaving behind? He was one of the younger sons in a family that had six daughters (Adelaide, Mathilde, Bertha, Recha, Rosalie, and Anna) and three sons (Moritz, Josne, and Carl).[2] Out of economic necessity, the Kingdom of Württemberg, so formally mentioned in Carl's passport, had recently joined the North German Confederation to form a united Germany along with several other southern German states. Fresh from the Austro-Prussian War of 1866, German Chancellor Otto Von Bismarck had encouraged a rift between the powerful North German Confederation and France in the hopes of encouraging the southern states to join the confederation. When war was declared on July 19, 1870, the states of southern Germany responded as Bismarck had intended. The Franco-Prussian War was waged between 1870 and 1871, until Paris fell to Germany in January 1871 after several months of famine. The newly formed German empire was now in the Second Reich phase of its history.

It's unlikely that Carl was mulling over this level of world politics as he stood before the magistrate. But he knew that his future prospects in Germany were not strong. It isn't mentioned anywhere in his passport documents, but Carl Adler was Jewish. During this time, discriminatory taxes were levied on Jews in various German states. In Bavaria, which was east of where Carl lived, an 1813 edict on the status of Jews curtailed the size of Jewish families. It limited the number of families in towns and the occupations that they could pursue. While immigration to America would promise hardships, there would be many opportunities unavailable to young Jewish men in Germany.

In coming to America in the early 1870s, Carl Adler was at the end of what has been referred to as the German Period (1820-1880) of American Jewish history.[3] Jewish men who immigrated to the United States in the early years were generally seeking wider economic opportunities. Because peddling and mercantile work had been one of the main areas Jews were allowed to work in while in Germany, their entrepreneurial skills and abilities to set up systems of trade where none had existed earlier were in demand, especially as America expanded westward. In America, there was also the opportunity for citizenship, which was something denied to the Jews in the villages of their native German states.[4]

So Carl Adler said good-bye to family, friends, and the familiar terrain of his homeland. He set out for a new land and new beginnings. It is likely that he had a network of contacts to draw upon once he got to America. According to family lore, he traveled in steerage.[5] It is likely, but not certain, that his ship landed in New York.

The first surviving document of his life in America is a letter of reference from an L. Froehlich, a wholesale and retail dealer of dry goods, clothing, and notions. He was based at 10 Franklin Street in Clarksville, Tenn., and on August 31, 1872, he wrote the following note in English for Carl Adler, or Charles Adler as he was calling himself at that time: "The bearer, Mr. Chas Adler has been in my employ in the capacity of salesman and [I] recommend him as a faithful and capable young man."[6] Carl's deeper connections to Mr. Froehlich are unknown. He may have known him in Germany, he could have been a friend of the family or he could have been a friend of a friend. What is most important is that Carl had entered the world of work in America and his employer was pleased with him. On a personal level, Carl may have felt that calling himself "Charles" made him sound more American.

In June 1873 "Charles," now in Memphis, Tenn., received a letter from a friend in New York City. The letter is written in English in a beautiful flowing script, but the writer is unknown because of a final flourish on the signature, making the last illegible.

> *Dear Friend Charles,*
>
> *In reply to your last epistle, I would say that it found me enjoying good health and I hope that this will meet you enjoying the same great blessing.*
>
> *In looking over the newspapers the last few days back, I notice telegraphic dispatches from your city reporting quite a number of deaths daily from cholera. This is a very contagious and dangerous disease, and I hope that you will be careful with your person and keep yourself out of harm's way.*
>
> *I received a letter from your parents lately, in which they informed me that they intended to remove from [illegible] to Nordlingen. About May 5, '73. I suppose they feel themselves quite at home in their new quarters by this time*
>
> *Please answer this immediately and let me hear from you at least once a week during the prevalence of the disease in your city.*
>
> *My parents send their best regards and hoping to hear from you.*
>
> *I remain*
Your Friend,
S. B. [last name illegible][7]

Copy of a letter of recommendation from L. Froelich, Carl Adler's first employer in the United States. (Oregon Jewish Museum)

Living through and observing the cholera epidemic in Memphis was an experience the not-yet twenty-year-old Carl would talk about for the rest of his life. He soon left Tennessee and the eastern United States. He went west to see his sisters Adelaide and Mathilde, who had preceded him to the United States and to Oregon, and he may have had extended family beyond that. He traveled by ship and while reports vary as to whether he went around Cape Horn or through the Isthmus of Panama, he soon made his way to Oregon.[8] Carl may have spent some time in San Francisco because his sisters were based there before coming to Oregon.

Adelaide Adler, born in 1842, married Leopold Hirsch of Salem in September 1872. A prominent merchant in the Salem area, Leopold Hirsch was born in Hobach, Württemberg, Germany, in 1823. He came to the United States in 1845, the first of five brothers who made their way from Germany to Oregon. He settled in

Solomon Hirsch, brother of Leopold Hirsch, was involved in Oregon politics and was appointed ambassador to Turkey by President Benjamin Harrison. (Adler House Museum)

Connecticut, living there until 1852, when he came to Oregon by way of the Isthmus of Panama. He spent time in Portland and eventually located in Salem, where he made his home. Reminiscing about Leopold Hirsch to the Salem *Statesman Journal* in 1893, S.A. Clarke mentioned that he had first met Leopold in Portland in 1852. He described him as a trader in Portland on a small scale, who had gradually expanded his business. His brothers J.B. and Mayer came over in 1853, Edward in 1856 and Solomon in 1858, just a year before Oregon became a state. The brothers ran a general merchandise store in Salem. While their work never strayed far from merchandising and sales, their interests soon led them to other areas. Edward Hirsch was Oregon state treasurer for four terms starting in 1878, and in 1890 became a state senator. Solomon became a partner in a wholesale merchandise operation, L. Fleischner and Co., which was based in Portland. He was twice chairman of the Oregon Republican Party and was elected to three terms in the Oregon State Senate. President Benjamin Harrison appointed him ambassador to Turkey in 1889, a position he held for three years before coming back to Portland. Several of Oregon's public officials working on the national stage during that time

Adelaide Adler Hirsch ca. 1870. (Oregon Jewish Museum)

were not known for their high ethical standards, but Solomon Hirsch was widely respected for his.[9]

Leopold Hirsch married his first wife, Miss Alise (Lizzie) Goldman of San Francisco, on May 8, 1858.[10] Alise was born in 1837 in Wurttemberg. How she made her way to the West Coast is not known, but in marrying Leopold Hirsch, she was connecting herself and her family to a prosperous pioneer citizen of Salem. Within five years of their marriage they had had three daughters, Rosa (1859), Sally (1862), and Laura (1864). Alise died of "brain congestion" at age twenty-seven in 1864, leaving her husband and three daughters under the age of five.[11]

Eight years later in San Francisco on September 27, 1872, the thirty year-old Adelaide Adler became Leopold Hirsch's second wife.[12] It is not known when she came to America or if she came over specifically to marry Leopold. They may have had some familial connections back in Germany, or there may have been a larger, extended network of German Jewish friends and relations who helped to bring them together. It appeared to be a first marriage for Adelaide. Entering into this new family, she was to become stepmother to the three Hirsch girls aged thirteen, ten, and eight.

At the time she married, Adelaide's brother Carl was in Tennessee and her sister Mathilde was likely in the United States as well. Just over a year later on November 16, 1873, Mathilde married a prominent Eugene citizen, Sampson (Sam) H. Friendly in the Salem home of her brother-in-law and sister, Leopold and Adelaide Hirsch.[13]

Sam Friendly was born in New York City in 1840; his parents were originally from Bavaria. He migrated to San Francisco in

Mathilde Adler Friendly (left) and her sister, Adelaide Adler Hirsch. Both sisters married well. (Oregon Jewish Museum)

Mathilde Adler Friendly. (Oregon Jewish Museum)

1863, worked there as a clerk for two years, and then came to Eugene to open a general merchandise store and warehouse that handled hops, wool, wheat, and oats. Sam Friendly would go on to become one of the driving forces behind the establishment of the University of Oregon, as well as the mayor of Eugene from 1893 to 1895.[14] A grandson, Ferdinand Friendly Wachenheimer, would change his name to Fred Friendly and revolutionize the scope of television news in the 1940s and 50s.[15] But that is in the future. On the afternoon of November 16, 1873, the Rabbi Mayer May (recently arrived from Bavaria to serve as rabbi for Congregation Beth Israel in Portland) performed the marriage ceremony between Sam Friendly and twenty-one year-old Mathilde Adler.[16] On the day of her wedding she had one sister by her side, a brother who was either in Memphis or making his way west, and very likely the prayers and hopes of her family in Germany.

Two of the Adler daughters had married extremely well. Another sister, Anna, six years younger than Carl, would come to live with Mathilde in the Friendly household in Eugene.[17] Carl eventually reunited with his sisters in Eugene and Salem. Family lore had Carl arriving on a ship in the little town of Flavel, just outside of Astoria, Ore. The ship was said to have docked in Flavel because the port in Astoria couldn't take a boat as large as the one he was on. Carl came to live with the Eugene branch of the family while he was getting his feet on the ground in Oregon. If he didn't already possess the knowledge, his extended Hirsch and Friendly family network would soon initiate him into the "mysteries of clerking and keeping books" that helped to make a successful merchant. Carl became an American citizen on November 6, 1876, his certificate of citizenship filed with the Circuit Court in Lane County.[18]

1876 was a time of transitions for Carl. Earlier in the year, he had received from his family a small note in old-fashioned German script. Preserved in family collections for over one hundred years, a translation follows:

Nördlingen, June 8 1876

We announce (full of pain) to concerned relatives and acquaintances that our dear wife, good mother, sister, mother in-law, grandmother and sister-in law, Therese neé Gutmann, peacefully died last night after two months of intense suffering and 39 years of happy marriage and 60 years old.

In hope of your condolences,
Jacob Adler,
with nine children
and the remaining mourners.[19]

It was clearly a blow to the family in Germany and because of their remove, the American portion of the family must have felt the loss sharply. They were far away from the rituals they would have observed in a time of mourning, but their father Jacob worked

Therese Gutmann Adler, Carl's mother, Leo Adler's paternal grandmother. (Oregon Jewish Museum)

to keep them connected with their religious traditions and their family heritage.

In an almost indecipherable letter written in German, Jacob thanks Carl for his correspondence and support. He particularly reminds Carl of his religious obligations.

Wuerzburg, March 20, 1877
My good son Karl!*

We properly received your dear letters and cash remittance and I give sincere thanks, good son, for your sacrificing filial love. If only you don't do too much for me given your circumstances, dear Karl, although I [can] use it all quite well. Well, God is just and will certainly reward your filial love! I bless you a thousand times, as my remaining dear children, who do so infinitely much for me and pray daily for your dear well being. The heavenly one will bless you and give you strength, so that you can support me as long as God is still granting me my life.

You requested the exact date of your mother's death's anniversary, it is according to the Jewish calendar on [Hebrew not translated] which is according to the German date this year on —May 28th 1877—by the way you need to figure it always according to the Jewish calendar, not the German one, that means it is always the 16th day of the month Sivan. If it is possible for you, dear son, say Kaddish on this day: we will, if God grants us health, be at the grave of the blessed one in Pflaumtal, where a tombstone will be erected, thank you for your and Tillie's [Mathilde's] contribution, which you will let her know.[20]

---

* Germans spell the name both "Karl" and "Carl" although Karl is more common.

The Spark and the Light: The Leo Adler Story

Jacob Adler, father of Carl Adler. Of Jacob's nine children, at least three daughters and one son immigrated to the United States from Germany. His descendants included grandson Leo Adler and great grandson Fred Friendly, who would revolutionize television news. (Oregon Jewish Museum)

As the only male family member in America, Carl would have had the main responsibilities for saying *Kaddish* (prayers for the dead) during the *jahrzeit*, which is a prescribed period of mourning for eleven months following the death of a child or parent. For Carl to formally observe his religious responsibilities, he would need to recite the ancient prayers daily with a *minyin* (at least 10 Jewish men) standing and facing the direction of Jerusalem.[21] Putting together a daily *minyin* for *Kaddish* would have been quite a chore at that time in Eugene or Salem, although they may have said *Kaddish* together as they observed the Sabbath. While Carl grieved the loss of his mother, it is unlikely that he was able to give a great deal of time to the mourning process. The twenty-two year-old Carl was likely working with one of his relatives in Eugene at this point, or he may have been in the initial phases of setting up a new business in Astoria.[22]

His father Jacob went on to respond to requests from his American children for him to join them.

> *Now, regarding my coming to America, I can tell you no different than in my preceding letter of Febr.18, which was confirmed by our dear Bertha [a sister still in Germany] as well. My reasons then are still valid today, and in particular my great rheumatic suffering would have to be fully eliminated. G.L. [gout lumbago] is not dangerous, but very, very burdensome and incapacitating, which you can even see in my poor handwriting. Oh if only the unwed sisters were taken care of — I would gladly bear it all! The bad, damp weather which goes on and on, is also of influence. Let's hope for improvement once the weather clears up! . . . We received good letters from*

the loved ones in Eugene City and Salem, only Josan & Latie [Adelaide] didn't write, and by now Tilli will have safely delivered, the news of which we hope for daily with great expectations. I've performed the usual prayers for her for some length of time. You stay well, I will have to write to the remaining siblings in a moment—continue to write diligently to your faithful father

Jacob Adler

Carl's sister Mathilde (Tilli) gave birth to her second daughter that year. She was named Theresa after her recently departed grandmother, and joined her older sister Carrie, born in 1875. Jacob was concerned with the family religious obligations both in Germany and in Oregon. In a final postscript to Carl, he sends the following information.

P.S. This week I made an ongoing donation for the dear blessed mother at congregation Oberdorf, whereby:
1. *the name of the blessed is entered into*
    a. the donation book
    b. onto the donation plaque that hangs in the synagogue and
    c. into the Memory book which will be read during the date of Jahrzeit during services.
2. *and on each anniversary 17 [crossed out] 16 days in the month of Sivan the Rabbi has to perform a Schema and a Kaddish & light a candle in the synagogue, not all years for eternity.*
3. *on <u>each</u> Yom Kippur the name of the blessed mother with*

Unidentified sister and brother of Carl Adler. (Adler House Museum)

> *that of the other deceased will be read out loud by the Rabbi before the Nita prayer, he then has to say Kaddish and so, to the reassurance of all of us, the name of blessed mother is sanctified and eternalized, as was entrusted to us by the dear one.*
>
> *[Written in Hebrew] Amen.*
>
> *Be so good, dear son, since I can't write much, and inform the loved ones in Eugene City & Salem of this donation in all the detail.*
>
> *Your father, J. Adler*[23]

The Adler family worked at remaining connected to one another. In the surviving letters in the Adler Family Collections at the Oregon Jewish Museum, that connection to family is easy to see. The March 20 letter was six pages front and back with notes from four members of the Adler family, including notes from his sister Bertha and his sister Recha, perhaps the unmarried sisters that Jacob referred to.

Dear Brother Karl!

Since the longest time I wanted to answer your dear additional letter, so full of love, caring & filial sacrifice, but something got always in the way. The dear father read the letter & was surely entitled to read it. I don't know how to answer it and might perhaps respond to it later. Dear Father has his own opinions & wishes & and can't be directed towards anything, also never feels well, which doesn't surprise in this wet and cold winter. You find so much changed in Germany & so different from what one expected, which has cost me all my energy & I no longer want to take on the responsibility of one who persuades, <u>since I don't have any more strength to bear reprimands from all sides</u>. May the Almighty let my journey be a blessed one, since it will be undertaken in the truest, most sacrificing intentions. <u>Only He knows this</u>! Let's courageously hope for the best!

Dear Rosalie is still receiving medical treatment, which, as you can imagine, does not bode well for my well-being – ! It also means a continual sacrifice for my family members, for which I have barely any strength left. Forgive me, good Karl, I did not want to increase your worries, it just entered my quill involuntarily. . . .

Your Loving sister,
Bertha

Good Karl!

I'd love to write much to you today, however the letter needs to be posted & and it is only a few days until Pesach [Passover] & and today is Friday & and so I'm very, very busy. Your heartfelt letters, dear brother, always move us to tears and I regret much that it is not possible today to respond to them in detail, let me just tell you as much, that I will only be happy when I'll be <u>able</u> [doubly underlined] to hurry to my precious siblings.

Heartfelt regards and kisses from your loving sister,
Recha

While still deeply tied to his family in Germany and in America, Carl Adler was on the verge of stepping into a new territory of his own. Now an American citizen of twenty-two, he had crossed the Atlantic Ocean, survived a cholera epidemic, made his way to the West Coast of the United States, reconnected with his growing American family, tackled a new language, and was creating a life as a well-connected young Jewish man in Oregon. With these accomplishments behind him, he would now set out to build a business of his own.

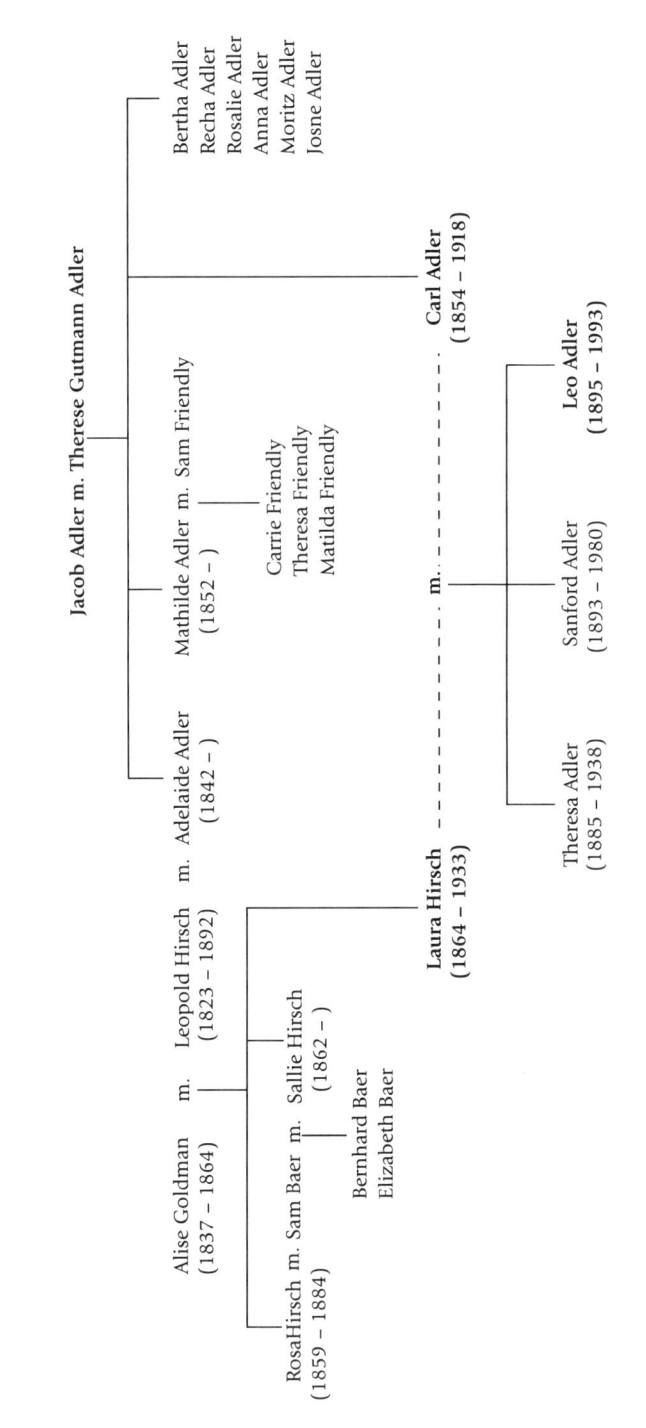

Building the Crystal Palace

Perched at the mouth of the Columbia River, the city of Astoria looms large in Oregon history. Captain Robert Gray sailed his ship the *Columbia Rediviva* over the bar into an uncharted river to claim the land for the United States on May 11, 1792, barely two weeks after the British Capt. George Vancouver passed by it. On April 27, Vancouver noted in his ship's log passing an unusual opening in the shoreline:

> . . . the sea had now changed from its natural, to river coloured water, the probable consequence of some streams falling into the bay. . . . Not considering this opening worthy of more attention, I continued our pursuit to the N.W., being desirous to embrace the advantages of the prevailing breeze.[1]

Explorers and ship captains had been searching for the illusive Northwest Passage for years, and sites along the Oregon and Washington coast such as Deception Bay and Cape Disappointment bear out the named results of those early searches. John Boit, second captain aboard the *Columbia Rediviva*, wrote in his journal on May 11, 1792:

> *This day saw an appearance of a spacious harbor abrest the ship, hauled our wind for itt, observed two sand bars making off, with a passage between them to a fine river.... We directed our course up this noble river in search of a village. The beach was lin'd with natives, who ran along the shore following the ship, soon after, above 20 Canoes came off and brought a good lot of Furs and Salmon, which last they sold two for a board Nail. The furs we likewise bought cheap for Copper and Cloth. . . . Capt. Grays named this river Columbia's. . . . This river, in my opinion would be a fine place for to sett up a Factory.*[2]

Thirteen years after Gray's discovery, Lewis and Clark passed a cold, damp, flea-ridden winter between 1805 and 1806 at nearby Fort Clatsop as they explored the Pacific Northwest reaches of American territories. In 1811, John Jacob Astor's Pacific Fur Company established the first American commercial settlement on the Pacific Coast, validating John Boit's earlier judgment. The site was named Astoria after the German-born Astor. It was renamed Fort George when the British attempted to claim the area for Great Britain between 1813 and 1818, but it went back to its original name of Astoria.[3] The Columbia River and a river pilot's ability to guide a ship across the nausea-inducing Columbia Bar helped import merchandise for Oregon and export the products that early Oregonians had to sell. While the Columbia River was not a true Northwest Passage, it was a finger that could reach farther into the northwestern interior than any other trade route.

Astoria went from a population of 639 in 1870 to 2,803 in 1880. The city experienced this boom for a number of reasons. It had become an important transfer point for the shipment of wheat and salmon. In 1866, 4,000 cases of Columbia River salmon were packed. In 1867, 18,000 cases were packed, and by 1874 salmon packing was a major industry for the town. Between 1874 and 1876, the population of the town nearly doubled. The shippers, canneries, and fishermen were making a great deal of money, with much of it circulating in the town. Because such large amounts of money were changing hands, it was said that small change was seldom used, with the quarter being the smallest coin in general use. This was the period of Astoria's greatest growth. From a small shipping station in the 1860s, it had grown into a town that controlled one of Oregon's most important industries on the lower Columbia. Improvements followed as a matter of course. When Western Union Telegraph Company completed its line between Portland and Astoria in 1876, Astoria had communication and transportation connections to the whole world.[4]

Astoria, Oregon, ca. 1867. (Clatsop County Historical Society, 194-900)

During the summer fishing season of 1877, there were eleven canneries in operation in Astoria and more than a thousand fishing boats in use on the river. Just before sundown, during the fishing season, the river would be covered with white-sailed boats, all moving briskly along their way to their favorite drifts. The city's newspaper, the *Daily Astorian*, spoke of the immense building boom. "It may seem surprising, but nevertheless it is true, work is progressing in all stages upon one hundred and eighty-nine new buildings in the City of Astoria at this moment.... Houses are being erected at an alarming rate. Last Saturday ten new structures were raised—one for every working hour of the day."[5]

Twenty or more steamers, large and small, were engaged during 1878 in making daily trips between Astoria and upper river points as far as Portland. Seven steamers were making regular trips between Portland and San Francisco, with a stop in Astoria that brought many passengers and much freight to the town. The *Astorian* of May 5, 1877, noted that "Last month 2,628 bonafide immigrants landed at Astoria by steamers. About 1,700 proceeded inland in search of homes."[6]

In the summer of 1877 Carl Adler went to Astoria to set up a book and stationery store. It was a chance for him to test his mettle and merchandising skills in a boom town. He likely received solicited and unsolicited counsel from his brothers-in-law and he had a $300 financial stake from Sam Friendly. There may have been more opportunity for him in this new outpost than in Salem, Eugene, or Portland. By 1860, a network of Jewish merchants stretched all along the Pacific slope. This network often consisted of cousins and brothers, with the older ones usually more permanently established in the larger cities and the younger ones trading from general stores in the smaller towns.[7] While this may have been an established pattern of trade, it still would have been a new adventure for twenty-three year-old Carl.

The town of Astoria had a fluid population. Itinerant workers came to Astoria for the fishing season and then returned to California for the winter. The steamship routes between San Francisco and Astoria made this a reasonably easy proposition. During the early years of the salmon industry, Astoria acquired a reputation for vice and crime, with the city supporting forty saloons in 1877. There were a variety of dives and gambling houses that were only too happy to relieve businessmen, cannery workers, and fishermen of some of their hard-earned wages.

Carl Adler formally commenced business on August 1, 1877. On July 25, 1877, the following announcement appeared in the *Daily Astorian*. "Carl Adler, a heavy dealer in stationery, books, etc., will occupy the stand vacated by Gallick & Brash next door to the White House." Soon further advertisements appeared in the *Daily Astorian*:

> *Oh! how delightful! Oh, how enchanting! Is the new and elegant book and Stationery store of Carl Adler's next door to the White House.*
>
> *Give me liberty or give me death: and if you don't want to give me either, give me one of Adler's Medal cigars, right away!*[8]
>
> *All San Francisco and Eastern papers can be had at Carl Adler's book store on Chenamus Street, next door to the white house, to arrive by steamer. Also a fine stock of stationery and books always on hand.*[9]

Carl Adler, second from left, stands in front of his store in Astoria. (Adler House Museum Collections)

Adler understood the importance of advertising at an early point in his career and he understood the value of getting involved with the community. According to the minutes of the August 24, 1877 Alert Hook and Ladder Co. No. 1 meeting, Adler attended the meeting, "came forward, paid the fee, signed the constitution" and was declared a member.[10] It was a wise move for his social and civic life. It introduced him to the men of the community and it involved him in maintaining that community. At that time, fire companies were groups of volunteer men, who, when the fire alarm rang, would gather their equipment and race to the fire. The company that got to the fire first was the company that got paid. Fistfights would occasionally break out among different groups when the question of who got there first was in

A page from Carl Adler's stock and invoice book. It shows his first months of business in 1877. (Oregon Jewish Museum) doubt. Carl was likely more interested in the camaraderie, but extra money was not to be ignored.

Just as he was beginning to find his way in the community, toward the end of his first months in business, Carl received a circulating letter from his father in Germany addressed to all the American siblings.

Wuerzburg, November 12 1877
My dear children
Leopold, Adelhaid, and dear children!
Sam, Mathilde, Ana plus dear little kids!
Karl!

I beg your understanding that, for this one time, we are writing to all of you loved ones together in Oregon, and I request of you, Leopold, to forward this letter soon to Eugene City and ask there that dear Sam forwards it soon to dear Karl. It is, as you can imagine, <u>very difficult</u> to write separately to each of my beloved and start a serenade, so please bear with it at this time, and bear with how little [is written], we are all unfortunately still deeply shaken and I also suffer much from arthritic pain in my limbs.

It has been a long time that we have not written to you, despite the fact that we received your dear letters and pretty photographs of the dear children in Eugene City but how should we, could we and what could we write? You all, my dear children, must have been prepared through our earlier letters for unfortunately not good news, and yet we were unable to bring ourselves up until this moment to relate the message of mourning and to say

The dear Rosalie is no longer, she met her maker after long illness on September 5 this year some days around Roshashona. Peace to her ashes, she, the blessed one, is well after so much suffering!

Comfort yourselves with blessings and allow reason to prevail and bend to the will of the Almighty.

. . . I have to close, be confident all my dear ones, there was nothing spared for the treatment and care of the blessed one and the most renowned Professor of the local University was asked his advice. May God support us with his mercy in the future.

Amen!

Your as of now still deeply grieving father

Jacob Adler[11]

Carl and his sisters may well have felt that their German family was coming apart. And an additional note from their sister Recha likely did not ease their feelings.

My Dear ones!

How much anxiety and worry will you all experience, not having heard from us in such a long time! Who could have predicted such a calamity? How I tremble for you, in the face of this horrible news, when the first serious wound has not yet scarred over. Oh father in heaven protect us & hold us in the future! Our noble, dear Rosalie joined our precious, sweet mother. Cry with us for the blessed ones, but she is well, believe me. Just a day before Erev Roshashona, after 6 months of severe suffering, she departed as gently and quietly as she lived, peace be with her!

Times were horrendous, the last bitter strokes of fate too shocking particularly for our good father. May God preserve his health for a long, long time. Dear Bertha is feeling jittery as well, is so undecided regarding her departure, the season so unfavorable & dear Isi so impatient, he is in Frankfurt for a couple of days now, sending warm regards. These unrequested pictures of sweet Carri and Therese [Friendly] soothed us much. May God preserve their health. . . .

Your Recha[12]

It's difficult to know when Carl may have heard the news of this new loss in the family or what other things in his life he was juggling. A brief and rather odd note appeared in the December 8, 1877 *Daily Astorian*. "Adler returned without a wife, and we immediately sought our informant with 'tears in our phists and eyes doubled up' when he assured us that 'the expected event' would come off after the holidays." If Carl had been in the beginning stages of a courtship, things may have come to a grinding halt while he and his family were observing a period of mourning for their sister.

Although romance wasn't blooming for Carl, his store certainly was doing well. By his own reckoning on January 1, 1878, in his first five months of business he had made a net gain of $569, and a year later he saw a net gain of $1,705. In November 1879 the *Astorian* described his shop as "the handsomest variety store in the city." The paper goes on to describe the store's and Carl's development:

Commencing business in 1877, he has, by selling only the best goods in his line, by close attention to business and by honor-

Theresa, Carrie, and Rosa Friendly, ca. 1886. Pictures of Theresa and Carrie are mentioned in the letter that brought the news of Rosalie Adler's death in 1877. The youngest daughter, Rosa, born in 1879, may have been named in memory of her aunt. (Adler House Museum)

able dealing, so increased the volume of his trade that he found it necessary to establish a branch store. A fitting location was obtained on Main Street and now his premises open upon Chenamus and Main Streets, both forming an "L," as it were from the one to the other."[13]

In the 1880 U.S. Census, Carl Adler is shown as having two employees working for him, Charles Moffett, twenty-six, as his clerk and Henry Butterfield, twenty-two, as a jeweler. His business was growing and his line of merchandise was expanding. In September 1881, he purchased storefront property in Astoria from Nancy Welch for $100.[14] Perhaps now was the time to think about what else he would like to have as a part of his new life in America. Carl's thoughts turned to finding a wife.

In an unusual turn of events, he didn't need to look much farther than the circle of his extended American family. The woman who agreed to marry Carl may have known him from his earliest days in Oregon. She was Laura Hirsch of Salem, the youngest of Leopold Hirsch's daughters and Carl's sister Adelaide Adler Hirsch's stepdaughter. Laura had been eight when Adelaide married Leopold in 1872 and became her stepmother.

Not a great deal is known about Laura's early years. From hints left in a family scrapbook kept by her sister Sallie Hirsch Baer and from information found in a scrapbook she started that was later maintained by the family, it appears that Laura and her sisters were educated at the Academy of the Sacred Heart in Salem.[15] The Academy opened in Salem in 1863 and was run by the Sisters of the Holy Names of Jesus and Mary. The school focused on educating young women and accepted students from all denominations. While the choice of a Catholic education for a young Jewish girl might seem surprising at first glance, Laura's parents followed generations of other parents in providing the best education they could for their children.[16]

At the time of their marriage, Laura was eighteen and Carl was almost twenty-eight. They were engaged in November 1881 and married on February 16, 1882, in Salem.[17] In the Adler family scrapbook, there are telegrams of congratulation and "maseltoff" from Memphis, San Francisco, Eugene, Salem, Walla Walla, and Portland. The Alert Hook and Ladder Co. of Astoria sent their congratulations and thanked Carl for a box of cigars he had sent to them.[18] A nun who had taught Laura and her sisters congratulated her on her wedding.

> *My dear Laura,*
>
> *I received some days ago the announcement of your marriage with Mr. Adler. Many thanks, my dear for your courtesy and kindness in apprising me of the happy event. In return I will ask the Almighty to bless the life you have chosen and make of it a [word unclear] of happiness and joy. If my wishes can contribute to either, please do accept them as the offering of one who loves you and yours sincerely and well. Although not personally acquainted with Mr. Adler, I take the liberty of offering him my congratulations on his success in marrying our gentle and well-loved Laura.*
>
> *With Kind regards to Mr. and Mrs. Hirsch and fond love to Rosa, Sallie, and your dear self, I remain, my dear Laura,*
>
>   *Yours affectionately,*
>   *Sr. M. Patrick*[19]

Laura Hirsch Adler, ca. 1882. (Oregon Jewish Museum)

Pictures of Laura Hirsch show a handsome, dark-eyed woman with dark hair. In many of her portraits there is a pleasing roundness to her face and it does appear that her big, dark eyes do not miss very much. Laura was very close to her sisters, perhaps because they had suffered the loss of their mother at such an early age. A wedding announcement that ran in the Salem paper mentioned that she had many friends who would be happy to attend her wedding.[20] And so Carl and Laura were wed in Salem. Now Laura would be entering an entirely new world. She would be leaving her father's home to set up a new life in Astoria. For Carl, it was a momentous step on a road that had begun eleven years earlier when he applied for his passport in Germany. They were surrounded by family and the good wishes of the many early Jewish families in the Pacific Northwest.

The young couple began their married life in style. They moved into a home in Astoria that appeared in the *West Shore*, a magazine of literature and the arts that promoted the Pacific Northwest.[21] Laura probably did not assist her husband in the store because he already had other employees. Although her father Leopold Hirsch had worked hard to get where he was, it would

Building the Crystal Palace

Carl Adler, ca. 1890, Baker, Oregon. (Oregon Jewish Museum)

The June 1883 West Shore *magazine shows the Astoria home of Carl Adler.* (Oregon Historical Society, OrHi 104746)

have been unlikely that his daughters were raised with the expectation of working outside the home. Keeping house would have been occupation enough. The move to Astoria would have been a big adjustment for Laura since there was no longer family nearby to talk with. In 1882, a comfortable trip from Salem to Astoria entailed a steamship ride on the Willamette River, passing through the ship locks at Willamette Falls and then down the Willamette to Portland. Depending on the timing, there could have been an overnight stay in Portland and the next morning the boat would have continued down the Willamette to the Columbia River and then on to Astoria. As Laura was finding her place in her marriage, she was also finding her place in a new community.

Building the Crystal Palace

On July 2, 1883, almost a year and a half into their marriage, all that Carl and Laura had built was nearly taken away from them. It was described in the Astoria *Daily News*.

The Most Disastrous Fire in the History of Astoria

Yesterday was an exceedingly warm day. The wind blew steadily from the west, but the streets and house walls felt warm. The long continued drought had made the whole city unusually dry and even where a careless passer dropped a careless cigar stump, the smoldering plank showed how little cause was needed to start a dreadful blaze. About six o'clock the breeze had gone down in a measure, the streets were full of people when suddenly the dreadful fire alarm was sounded. A dense volume of black smoke and a column of fire showed that it was not common scare, but that Astoria's worst fears were realized. Quick as it takes to write it the companies were on the group to find the Clatsop mill, formerly Geo. Hume's, in a sheet of flame. The fire swung round from the engine room where it seemed to have originated and up the lumber piles and store house, giving out the most intense heat. No. 2's were stationed by Chief Barry in front of Hume's dock. The efforts of the department were at first to confine the fire to its original limits, but the cursed wind fanned the fiery mass which set the houses across 6th street in a blaze. A large barn standing on Squemoqua street was full of goods and coal oil, this was the point centered on by the department. Streams were put onto it and an opening being made in the building, hundreds of cases of coal oil were carried up Olney street. The goods were thrown into the water, and notwithstanding the intense heat, every case of coal oil was got out.

We have never seen a hotter fire; nor one in which the firemen worked harder. Indeed nothing but the most superhuman exertion saved

THE SPARK AND THE LIGHT: THE LEO ADLER STORY

Lumber mills burning in the July 2, 1883 Astoria fire. Photo by 16-year-old Thad Trullinger. (Clatsop County Historical Society, 9026-930)

that building. Everyone worked. The idea suggested to blow up the building was a good one, and should our unfortunate little city ever be scourged so again the first and ONLY thing to do will be to blow up or pull down all in the way of the fire on the roadway between the saw mill and O'Brien' hotel was doomed. No time was there to save anything. The dry houses were glowing and burst into sheets of flame that instantly spread. Every available force was brought into requisition. Men worked till they dropped and others took their places. They stood in clouds of smoke and kept the fire at bay; Flavel's pump sent a good stream; the one lack was sufficient hose to throw another stream; the old hand engines was brought up from the Hustlers wharf but was of little avail. The fire leaped across the street and beginning at the O.K. Lodging house burned that, Greenburg's store went next and the great column of crimson flame swept down the roadway. Amid the roar of the advancing flames swept on by the breeze, could be heard the crash of falling timbers and the sharp detonations of cartridges. The roadway

BUILDING THE CRYSTAL PALACE

The progress of the fire in Astoria. Photo by Thad Trullinger. (Clatsop County Historical Society, 3-930)

was one solid mass of flame. The houses, the street itself, the sidewalks, everything. The history of that dreadful hour can never be written. There was no frenzy. From Frank Fabre's down past Luigi Serra's and Mrs. Grants, to Ike Foster's and across to Foard & Stokes, and on the other side from Spexarth down past the Centennial, everyone saw that there was not help and that their property was doomed. Nothing left but to seize money and valuables and rush out up the hill. It was awful. It is useless to attempt any description of it. Where everything was built of wood, dry and seasoned, a wind blowing and the great masses of flame advancing with appalling speed, the wonder is that there is no loss of life to report.

. . . By half past seven the fire was at its height; the O.R.& N. dock was one mass of yellow flame; the steamers swung out into the stream, their decks filled with silent spectators; —.With men who ceased throwing water on roofs and walls to gaze on that sublime spectacle. The flames were resistless; a blast took the fire under the roadway to burst

up in a dozen places, and house after house twisted into ruin. At the upper dock it spent itself for want of further material, one of the thickly settled area from the sawmill to O'Brien's hotel, nothing at eight o'clock was left but the mentioned building. On the hillside the saving of the private residences seemed miraculous. Ed Taylor's house was the point of danger. By superhuman exertions it was saved, and with it a large number of buildings that stood in the greatest peril. Everyone in the vicinity had packed up in readiness, and had Mr. Taylor's, Mr. Adler's, the hospital and one or two others caught, the whole of that portion of the city would have been devoured. Through out all, the fire companies did all that men could do; they deserve the highest praise for their efforts, as do the citizens that at the risk of life went into the burning warehouse and carried out case after case of coal oil. To individualize the loss is impossible. Fortunately there was no serious mishap to life or limb.[22]

A later edition of the paper commented, "the houses on the hill were only saved by the most strenuous exertion. At Carl Adler's, Ed Taylor's and other private residences, the ladies worked most faithfully."[23]

The fire devastated the town. It destroyed several blocks of business houses, wharves, and dwellings. The wooden streets, which were built on pilings over the water, were a burning highway that carried the fire from building to building.[24] The Oregon Railroad and Navigation docks, a main transfer point for ships coming into and leaving the Columbia River, were smoldering ruins. But as a reporter for the *Oregonian* noted, "with their customary energy and enterprise the officers of the OR&N had already re-established their office and were engaged in the transaction of their regular business, just as though they had not lost

$100,000 of property within the last twenty-four hours."²⁵

To those that knew Astoria it was a sobering sight. "Passing down the river front of Upper Astoria, it was indeed a sorry sight. The smoldering ruins of the wharves, the charred and useless piles for blocks beyond, were all that remained of a most thriving portion of that industrious and growing city which has in the past so often prided herself upon the right to the title of the 'Venice of the Modern World.'"²⁶

Astoria's correspondent for the *Oregonian*, E.G. Holden, was honest enough to note the terrible beauty of it. "Soon it was evident the fire fiend would have it all his own way. Soon the extensive and capacious warehouses running with the coal bunkers some 900 feet along the river front were aflame. It was a beautiful, even if it was a pitiful, sight."²⁷

The fact that there was no loss of life was quite astounding, particularly given the superhuman effort the various fire departments put in.

> *Blackened, blistered, burned and bruised were the hands and faces of those gallant fire laddies who had already fiercely fought the flames and watched over the unwilling death during sixteen long, weary hours, almost without intermission, but still they stood in their work uncomplainingly. Every man's voice sounded like a death-bed whisper, and the skin seemed ready to fall in flakes from their parched lips. The hands held out to greet their Portland friends were in many instances raw with blisters but in the eyes of each and every one there flashed a light of honest pride at the openly conscious thought of the noble duty they had performed.*²⁸

There was certainly noble behavior but there was also looting. As the fire burned, stores of liquor were removed from saloons in the path of the fire and carried to places of safety. They were then stolen by looters. Riots broke out in the vicinity of the fire and the officers were powerless to stop further looting of goods from shops and houses. Drinking continued through the night. The looters moved to the lower part of town, know as "Swilltown." Thad Trullinger, a sixteen year-old at the time of the fire, recalled seeing more drunks that night than at any other time in his life.[29] Later some of the fishermen threatened to burn the rest of the town in retaliation. An *Oregonian* reporter commented, "If anything of value was saved, it was carried away by thieves unless it was too heavy to be carried. The scenes of vandalism that were enacted during the fire are almost beyond belief to those who did not witness them." The sheriff and the police were unable to maintain order. The businessmen of the city organized a vigilante committee. An order was put out that all stolen property was to be returned to the city hall. When this brought no results, an arresting committee went after "one of the known leaders of the thieving bunch....After a short trial, he was found guilty of having stolen property and given a choice of hanging and a whipping with a cat o' nine tails. He defied the committee." He was escorted to the graveyard and a rope was put over the limb of the tree. With a grave waiting for him, he changed his mind and took the whipping. He was kept under guard the rest of the night and put aboard a morning boat leaving for Portland.[32]

Ten thousand cases of salmon were still smoldering on what remained of the docks. Trullinger recalled that "Salmon burns without much flame but plenty of smoke. Many of the cans exploded and kept up a continuous roar of small explosions all that night and part of the next day."[33] Losses in the fire totaled $250,000, with only $50,000 of that amount insured. Carl Adler lost $1,000 worth of merchandise, but fortunately it was insured. He still had his wife, his home, and his business. The losses from the 1883 fire were very heavy, but the fishing season was at its height and money was plentiful. In a short time new buildings were erected in place of those destroyed by fire.[34] Astoria clearly didn't need time to lick its wounds. There were more salmon to catch and process, and the town needed rebuilding.

Carl Adler didn't waste any time either. On October 20, 1883, barely three months after the fire, an ad ran on the front page of the *Daily Astorian* proclaiming the "Grand Opening of the Crystal Palace, Carl Adler's Magnificent New Store!" He had gone from selling stationery and books at Adlers to a whole new range of merchandise at The Crystal Palace. Advertisements from Astoria

View of Astoria looking northeast, ca. 1884. (Clatsop County Historical Society, 43-900)

Left. Carl and Laura's first child, Theresa, ca. 1885. Theresa and Laura Adler, ca. 1887. (Adler House Museum)

papers show that he continued to sell books and stationery and along with musical instruments. He even had pianos to rent.[35]

With business going well, now was the time to start a family. On January 7, 1885, Carl and Laura Adler had their first child, a daughter. She was named Theresa, after Carl's mother, just as her cousin Theresa Friendly had been named for her in 1877. Pictures from an Astoria photo studio taken of Theresa within a year of her birth show a dark-haired little girl with big, dark eyes. She would have her parents to herself for several years, and judging from pictures that survive, they clearly doted on her.

The Adler family's time in Astoria came to an end in 1887. Carl had been in Astoria for ten years and been married for five years. Having pushed westward as far as he could, he may have felt restless. He may have been looking for a new challenge. On September 23, 1887, a short ad ran in the *Daily Astorian*. "Carl

Adler is clearing out his stock and packing some of it in boxes for his new store in Baker City, to which place he intends removing next month." In the paper the same day, there was an auction notice announcing that "the entire elegant furniture of the Adler residence the corner of Cedar and west 8th streets" would be for sale on September 29.[36] The word elegant appears six times in the extended ad. There was furniture and decorations from the parlor, bedrooms, dining room, and kitchen. The ad ends with the following comment: "the attention of purchasers is respectfully called to this sale as no such opportunity has offered itself in this city to purchase such goods, either at private or public sale." It seems a subtle sales pitch, but it was probably quite true. Carl, Laura, and two year-old Theresa were leaving a very comfortable and well-furnished home in Astoria. What was inducing them to move eastward to Baker City?

Heilner Commercial and Commission Company. (Oregon Historical Society, OrHi 88326)

MAKING A HOME IN BAKER CITY

Although the land around Baker City was unfamiliar to the Adlers, they were moving in the direction of family. Laura Adler had a sister who lived in the town. Her oldest sister, Rosa, married Samuel Baer, a prosperous Jewish merchant, in 1884. Sam Baer came to Baker City in 1874 and established the Baer and Ottenheimer General Store, later named the Baer Mercantile Company. Sigmund Heilner, perhaps the most important merchant in the city, had arrived there shortly before Sam Baer.[1]

Sigmund Heilner was born in Urspringen, Bavaria, in 1834. His father, Aron Heilner, did a variety of work to earn a living for his family and at the same time comply with the restrictive Bavarian laws that governed Jewish life. He worked as a schoolteacher, a farmer, and a moneylender. Sigmund's older half-brother Seligmann immigrated to America in 1845 when he was twenty-two. Seligmann stayed in the east until 1849 when, like so many others of that era, he went looking for gold in California. Unsuccessful with his gold prospecting, he eventually started a dry goods business in Crescent City, Calif.[2]

Sigmund came to America in 1853 and began a correspondence with his family in Germany and in America. The correspondence was saved and later translated by his grandson Sanford Heilner. Sigmund received advice from both his father in Germany and his brother in Crescent City. In a July 1853 letter, Aron reminded Sigmund of a few things.

> *You know my principles: Endure, be patient, and do without if you must, but never despair! Never take refuge in that which does not agree with your conscience. God will not forsake those who remain faithful and do not despair! I, myself have many times been in distress and knew no way out. It did not take long, however, before God showed me the way out. . . . Remain in New York, or, at least, in the area, and seek to build a future. Just do not try to get rich overnight."*[3]

Seligmann was known in America as E. D. Cohen. His advice to his younger brother was of quite a different character, with an August letter telling him which shipping line to take to Nicaragua to get out to San Francisco and passing on information about people Sigmund should stay with when he got to town. Sigmund stayed with family friends in New York, Washington, D.C., and Baltimore. He was waiting for permission from his father to travel westward, but Aron was not pleased with the lack of candor about his oldest son's circumstances and told Seligmann so plainly.

> *You know how I feel about Sigmund coming to you. I will certainly insist that if he does come, it will not be before a considerable length of time. His circumstances must be adequate and*

you must improve yours. You tell me that you could pay your brother $60 a month. Anyone that can pay someone else that much money in one month must be wealthy. In two months, that is more than I make in one year. I would feel much better if you would leave California and go to the states on this side of Panama and, united with your brother, establish a business. We would also feel that the possibility of seeing you once again was more a reality.[4]

Aron Heilner finally relented and allowed Sigmund to go west. He sailed steerage from New York to Panama on December 12, 1854, and arrived in San Francisco on January 6, 1855. Not long after he arrived in Crescent City, Sigmund left for a small gold and copper mining settlement on Althouse Creek called Browntown in southwest Oregon near Jacksonville. He ran a small dry goods store supplying miners for four years, and then briefly went into the money lending business, which was a risky venture. He often felt isolated but he did make friends with the brothers Bernard and Isaac Goldsmith. They owned jewelry/assay stores in Crescent City and Browntown. Bernard Goldsmith would go on to become mayor of Portland from 1869 to 1871.[5]

In 1861, Sigmund returned to Crescent City and went into the freight forwarding business. He had hoped to return to Bavaria with Seligmann to visit his family, but the purchase of their store in Browntown fell through and he was not able to see his family. He was bitterly disappointed that he wasn't able to make the trip. He kept a diary during this time. On June 27, 1861, he wrote of his sadness in not seeing his family, but he also wrote the following:

The Spark and the Light: The Leo Adler Story

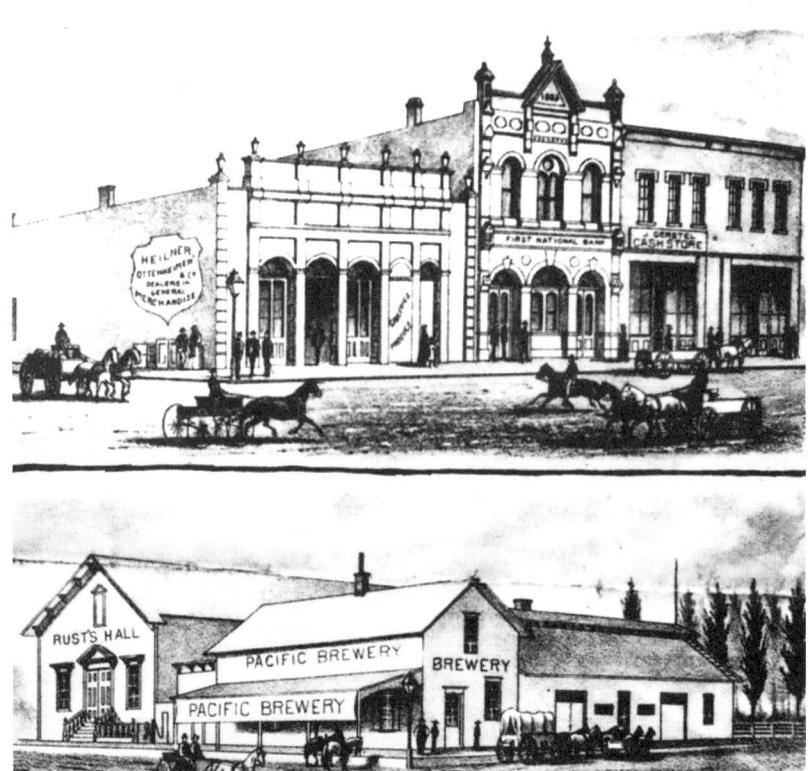

Baker City business blocks as shown in an 1885 West Shore *magazine.* (Oregon Historical Society, OrHi 51975)

Making a Home in Baker City

Let us look toward the future with good courage. Let us not worry so much. Patience, energy and perseverance will accomplish everything, even some things of which we do not think. The sun is shining so brightly. I take that as a good omen. Even butterflies are coming to my window, flying back and forth as if they want to participate in my thoughts and I am enjoying taking a breath of the good mountain air. Every breath inspires me with more courage and perseverance. Should I not think that I am the happiest one to be in good health, to enjoy breathing the fresh and healthful mountain air. Therefore, why worry so much?[6]

Sigmund stayed in the Browntown area until the mines were largely depleted. He moved north to Portland, where he lived for a while with Bernard Goldsmith. He tried packing goods into Montana and he took on some portrait- and landscape-painting work, which he had trained for while in Germany. In 1872 he and Seligmann moved to Sparta in Union County, where there was a mining camp with several hundred Chinese miners, and set up a store. He returned to Portland in 1874 to marry Clara Neuberger and they started a new life in Baker.[7]

Sigmund Heilner established the Heilner Commercial and Commission Company. This eventually became the Neuberger Heilner Banking Company, an early bank in Baker City and a forerunner of the First National Bank of Baker City. The Heilners built a large house that was shown in the *West Shore* magazine along with an illustration of Heilner & Ottenheimer and the First National Bank.[8] The home would become a center for the small Jewish community in Baker. They would use it to hold the High

Holy Day services of Rosh Hashanah (New Year) and Yom Kippur (Day of Atonement).[9] In coming to Baker City in 1887, the well-connected Adler family would be welcomed into the prosperous yet small Jewish community.

At the time the Adlers arrived in Baker City, Baker County was just over twenty-five years old. Henry Griffin struck gold in what was then the eastern part of Wasco County in 1861.[10] Baker County was created out of Wasco County by the state legislature on September 22, 1862. It was named for Edward Dickinson Baker, who was elected to the United States Senate from Oregon in 1860.

Sigmund Heilner residence as shown in West Shore *magazine.* (Oregon Historical Society, OrHi 104745)

He was killed in the Civil War at the battle of Balls Bluff just after he had been appointed a major-general and Oregon named its newest county in his honor.[11] While the city took its name from the same source, the actual name varied between Baker (1911-1989) and Baker City (1866-1910 and 1990 onward).

Carl Adler and his family were coming into another boom town. Between 1870 and 1880 Baker City had grown from 312 to 1,258, and to 2,604 in 1890.[12] In population it was roughly the same size as Astoria. As of August 19, 1884, railway connections had made their way into Baker; now the city could connect its goods with bigger and different markets. The first export out was fifteen cars of barley. In 1884, the Oregon Horse and Land Company branded over 8,000 horses and in 1885, almost 11,000. In June 1885, the same company imported 151 Percheron horses from France at a cost of $1,000 apiece.[13] The presence of so much valuable horseflesh brought a number of thugs and desperadoes to the vicinity. One writer noted, "Not a few of these characters terminated their earthly pilgrimage at the end of a hempen cord" but claims of lynching weren't substantiated.[14]

The area was filled with miners looking to make a big strike, and a range of merchants were there to supply the miners with whatever they might need. In the late 1880s, Baker City had three breweries, twenty-one saloons, and gambling houses that never closed. At that time the streets were not paved or numbered. The sidewalks were wooden and the crosswalks were long planks laid out about four feet wide.[15] It could be a rough and dangerous town. Seligmann Heilner (E D. Cohen) was murdered in front of the Heilner store in 1888. Family lore had it that he got into a quarrel with someone over a mining deal.[16]

The Spark and the Light: The Leo Adler Story

Baker City Railroad Station. Kane's Illustrated West, *Nov. 1886.* (Oregon Historical Society, OrHi 104747)

What brought the Adlers to Baker? A story circulated in the city for many years that had Laura telling Carl "I will marry you, but only if we move out to Baker City so that I can be near my sister." There is truth and untruth in this story. Laura and Carl had had five eventful years in Astoria before they came to Baker City; moving there clearly was not a condition of marriage. It is more likely that after her sister Rosa's untimely death (between 1885 and 1886) and the marriage of her middle sister Sallie to Sam Baer (between 1886 and 1887), Laura wanted to be closer to her remaining sister.

The tug of family feelings as well as a new sphere of opportunity may have come together nicely for the Adlers, and it may have led them to Baker City. There could have been a nudge from the extended family as well. The Adler and Hirsch families had business connections that extended to Portland, Salem, Eugene, Astoria, and San Francisco, and the move to Baker City extended that reach eastward. They likely would have been acquainted with Sigmund Heilner by reputation if they had not already met him through other contacts. Sam Baer was a family member at this point, so the start they were making in this community was different than in 1882 when Carl and his bride had come to Astoria.

Carl quickly set up a new store and named it the Crystal Palace once again. Stationery, notepaper, and envelopes for the business would proudly proclaim, "Crystal Palace, established 1877." Still describing himself as a bookseller and stationer, Carl continued to sell musical instruments, sheet music, and jewelry, and he also did watch repair. He had a range of wares that were of interest to his customers during their leisure hours. While their leisure time may not have been plentiful, they would have enjoyed using it in a productive manner. Various late nineteenth and early twentieth century memoirists comment on the fact that Baker had a store as fancy as the Crystal Palace, so it must have made quite an impression in its day.[17]

The Adlers settled into their new life. Pictures from the period show young Theresa in various costumes, and her mother appears to have been a strong client of Baker City's Hazeltine Photo Studios. A new cousin, Bernhard (Bernie) Baer, was born in 1888 and another, Elizabeth Baer, born in 1891. Professionally, Carl was thriving, but personally the family was going through some difficulties. A black death announcement found in the collections of the Adler House Museum tells of a son, Jerome J. Adler, who died on August 3, 1891. His age at the time of death was not mentioned. A new baby, Sanford, joined the Adlers on May 29, 1892. Carl Adler became a member of Congregation Beth Israel in Portland, on July 6, 1892, about the end of the prescribed pe-

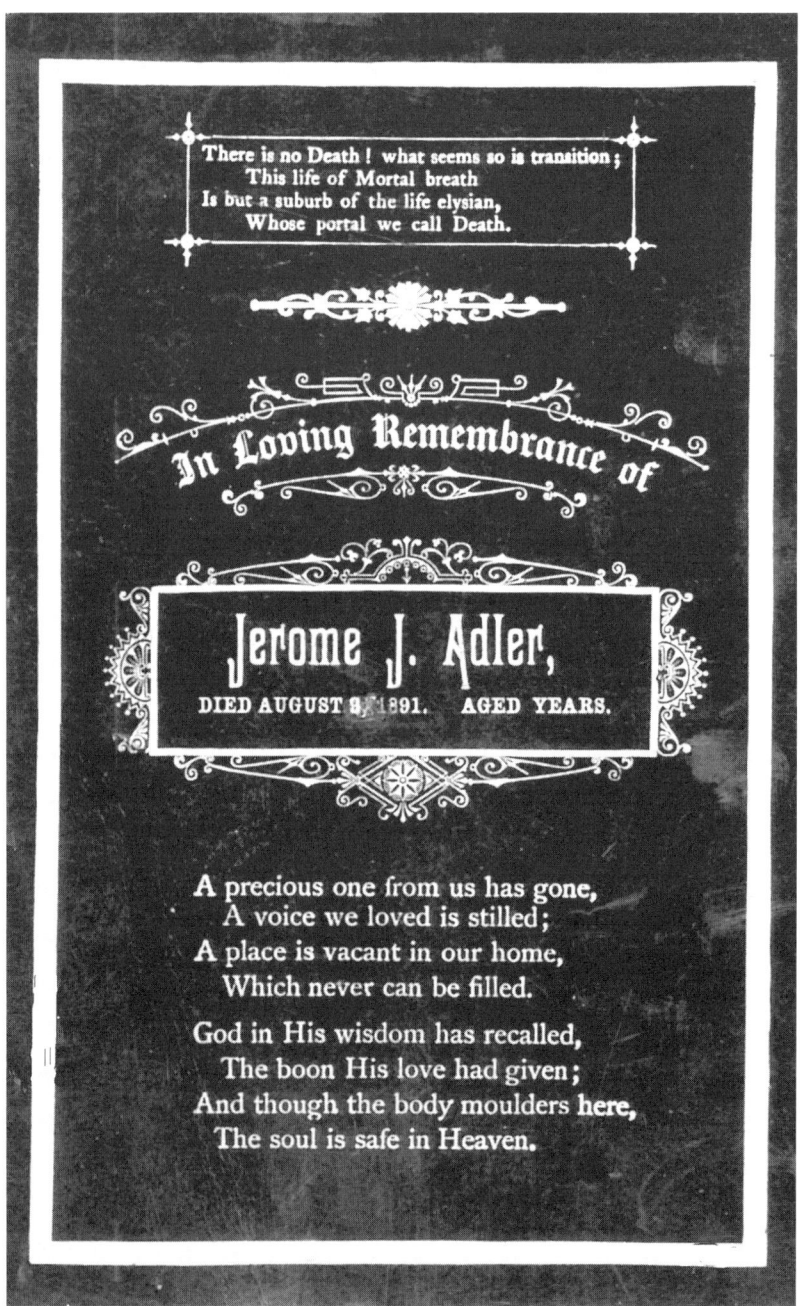

Opposite. The funeral card for Jerome Adler, Carl and Theresa Adler's first son. The child did not live through his first year. (Adler House Museum)
Above. Carl Adler's certificate of membership to Congregation Beth Israel. (Oregon Jewish Museum)

riod of mourning for the baby he and Laura had lost.[18] After such a troubled year, Carl may have been looking for some deeper spiritual connections than what he was able to find with the small Jewish community in Baker. And having a new son may have strengthened his sense of connection with his religion.

There was further sadness ahead for the Adler family. Leopold Hirsch, father of Laura Adler and Sallie Baer passed away on October 17, 1892. A copy of the obituary that ran in the Salem *Capitol Journal* appeared in the Baker *Morning Democrat* on the front page. It stated that he died of paralysis in his home in Salem after two weeks of suffering. It then went on to speak of him in surprisingly tender terms.

> *Of his personal worth as a man and citizen much might be said. He was a good and pure man, the soul of goodness, never doing an ungenerous act knowingly. He was a humane man in every respect and a tender father and husband. His death affects dearly those who knew him, and knew his worth as a man, but most deeply a loving wife whose devotion to him and his children was remarked by all. He was a man who had the singular faculty of attaching the affections of others when anything more than a mere acquaintance was formed. It can truly be said that he was best loved by those who knew him best and especially by those in the closer ties of relationship. His brother Edward Hirsch and wife were constant attendants and share the grief of the widow.*
>
> *While not ostentatiously a religious man, he exercised a liberal charity toward the needy, but in a very quiet way. His life passed as he had lived, very peacefully.*

Making A Home in Baker City

> *He will receive the last rites paid to the dead by Rev. Dr. Block, the Hebrew ritual for the dead, to which faith he remained faithful to the end.*[19]

Leopold Hirsch's death was clearly a loss to his community and to his family. The early years of the 1890s were personally difficult for the Adlers and they may have been professionally difficult as well. In the same newspaper that gave Leopold Hirsch's obituary, there was a small ad that stated the following: "From and after this date, no goods will be sold at the Crystal Palace but to those who are able to settle their accounts inside of thirty days. This decision is made on account of retiring from business. Carl Adler, Baker City, Oct. 18, 1892." What would make Carl decide to pull out of business at this point in his life? He was forty-eight years old with a seven year-old daughter and a son who was just shy of five months. His wife was grieving the death of her father, as well as attending to the needs of an infant. The family had been living in Baker for about five years at that point and perhaps Carl was ready for another change. Another notice ran in the October 23 newspaper. "Having decided to close out business in Baker City, notice is hereby given to all persons owing me that accounts must be settled within ten days from date hereof, or all such accounts will be placed in the hands of an attorney for immediate collection. This is positively the last warning."

Perhaps there were responsibilities or opportunities within the Hirsch family businesses that were of interest to Carl. With the death of Leopold Hirsch and his sister Mathilde now a widow, he may have felt a double family commitment. Was this time of family crisis a chance to take a hard look at what he and his fam-

The Adler and Baer children. Top photo, Bernie Baer is second from left in an elaborate French court dress-up game. Bottom left, Theresa Adler holds her new brother Sanford. Right, Bernie and Elizabeth Baer. (Adler House Museum)

ily were doing in Baker City? Perhaps he was facing his own mortality with Leopold's death and the birth of his son Sanford. How does a man move forward in these circumstances? Carl Adler ultimately decided that the best way to move forward was to stay in the same place. The Crystal Palace did not close down and the Adlers decided to put down their roots deeply into the soil of Baker. Then they had another child.

Leo Adler. (Adler House Museum)

Leopold Adler was born on June 21, 1895. Just as his older sister Theresa had been named for her departed paternal grandmother, Leo was named for his maternal grandfather, Leopold Hirsch. Leo was born into an extended family network that included aunts, uncles, and cousins in Baker, Salem, and Eugene. They would all need photos of the newest family member. Many baby portraits of Leo show him smiling warmly at the camera as though he is ready to strike up a conversation.

The family lived on Sixth Street between Washington and Centre at the time of Leo's birth.[20] He probably received a warm reception from his sister Theresa, who was ten. The response from his brother Sanford, who was just barely three, was probably a bit cooler, since Sanford was now no longer the baby of the family. He certainly would have received a warm welcome from the Jewish community in Baker and likely from the Baker community at

The Spark and the Light: The Leo Adler Story

The unsmiling Adler children on the steps of their new home, ca. 1899. (Oregon Jewish Museum)

large. In 1899, when Leo was four, the family moved into the home that Leo Adler would live in for the rest of his life, an Italianate house that was the twin of the home the Baers lived in at the other end of the block.[21] A family photograph taken at around that time shows the children sitting on the front steps of the house. A very young Leo has long dark hair and wears a light shirt, a flowing Lord Fauntleroy bow, britches, long stockings, and high button shoes. He is scowling or pouting into the camera, and Sanford and Theresa look rather grim as well. Perhaps no one was in the mood for family pictures that day.

The parents and extended family of many of the first-generation German Jewish children in Baker worked hard to give them

Leo, Carl, Laura and Sanford Adler on the steps of their home. (Oregon Jewish Museum)

a sense of who they were and where they had come from. Leo may have learned some German in the home or he may have spoken it with his father. Elizabeth Baer remembered that Carl Adler worked to introduce German language courses into the high school. She would eventually go on to teach German in Baker schools, but she did not recall speaking a great deal of it in the home. When she and her mother went visiting, she recalled having a difficult time understanding the Neubergers.[22]

Leo recalled that the Jewish families in Baker got together on Sunday nights in a lodge hall, with everyone bringing some food. Sanford Heilner, the son of Sigmund Heilner, remembered his family observing the High Holy Days and occasionally observing the Sabbath on Friday nights, with his mother praying from the prayer book and lighting candles. His family would also occasionally go into Portland to worship at Temple Beth Israel, where his father was a member. Elizabeth Baer remembered going occasionally to religion classes taught by a Mrs. Dilsheimer who would teach the children about what it meant to be Jewish, the history of the Jews, and what Judaism was all about. Only Elizabeth Baer mentioned being taunted as a child because she was Jewish. "I can remember when we were quite young, I think we were riding bicycles or something and some youngsters called us some names and I can remember that I didn't know what it meant." When she told her family about it, they discussed it with her. She was surprised to learn that people might think that she was different somehow.[23]

Leo went to Baker public schools and received an education that kept him curious about what was going on and engaged with the world around him for the rest of his life. A copy book that he wrote while in the elementary grades at North Baker School survives in the collections of the Adler House Museum. It contains an essay on the French painter Rose Bonheur (1822-99), who was known for portraits of agricultural scenes. It was a clever choice for a teacher to assign and a surprising one. Where would they have found copies of Bonheur's work? Perhaps at the Crystal Palace? The penmanship in the essay shows that Leo may have had either a new or a tenuous grip on the idea of cursive writing, so it could have been written between 1905 and 1906. Judging from the letters written by his grandfather Jacob Adler in Germany, rough penmanship ran in the family. Leo would be known for his indecipherable penmanship for the rest of his days. When asked by a frustrated teacher what he would do if he ever needed to write a letter, his response was "I'll get my secretary to type it for me."

Business at the Crystal Palace continued to go well. Carl Adler had tried to engage Sanford in taking on some work as a paperboy, but Sanford said no. Leo was interested and it was an interest that would color the rest of his life. Leo began by selling the *Saturday Evening Post* and the *Ladies Home Journal* out of a newspaper sack. He sold them on the street for a nickel. Selling newspapers

> The Oxen Plowing or Rose B onheur.
>
> Rose Bonheur was born in Bordeaux France in 1822 and died in 1899. Her mother died when seven years old and after the death to Paris where her father pasted, when she was a child she used to run around in a wild life. In school she was teased by richer children, but she dared not say anything, she drawed pictures and sketches and was caught at it and too them her father took her out of school and she took care of the other children and acted like housekeeper.
>
> All her pictures were of animals, the names of her pictures are hights and cattle. After the fair, The horse fair, The Lion in the cage and the Oxen Plowing.
>
> The picture of the Oxen Plowing is about 4 o'clock in the afternoon, the picture has eight oxen and 2 plows.

Leo's copy book from North Baker School with his essay on Rosa Bonheur. (Adler House Museum) at that age was not an unusual thing for a boy to do; in fact, Leo had lifelong friends, Francis Leipzig and Norris Poulson, who had also delivered papers in Baker City.[24] Leo likely did not have the turf battles that boys in larger cities struggled with. This is not to say that there were not a few tough characters to deal with. A 1907 article in the Baker *Morning Democrat* decried a new sight on Baker streets. "A very edifying spectacle it is to notice the number of small boys barely into knee trousers who of late are making public exhibition of their newly acquired art of smoking. A youngster certainly not more than 11 years old made his way up Front Street yesterday at the noon hour ensconced behind a monstrous black pipe and leaving a trail of smoke behind that would have done credit to a Sumpter Valley engine on a mountain grade."[25]

Leo was selling newspapers because he liked the challenge of it, not because he needed to bring home money for the family. In larger cities, newsboys would hawk their wares at major intersections during rush hours. The boys fought each other for prime locations, and were often exploited by circulators who distributed the papers on commission and refused to redeem unsold copies. A former Portland newsboy from the same era as Leo recalled, "I was ten years old when I started selling papers. It wasn't very safe to go downtown and sell papers before you could handle yourself on the street. The boys were very jealous of the corners on which they sold and interlopers were made unwelcome . . . . competition was very heavy; it sometimes resulted in fights, black eyes and bloody noses. Each one had to bring money back to his family."[26]

Ladies Home Journal was a perfect magazine for Leo to be selling at that time. It was started in December 1883 when Cyrus H. Curtis decided to transform the women's pages of his *Tribune and*

Farmer into a separate magazine called the *Ladies' Home Journal*. Strong writing and vigorous advertising pushed the circulation of the *Journal* to 200,000 in 1885, 400,000 in 1888, and 600,000 in 1891. While other magazines of the period kept advertising corralled to specific pages at the front and back, the *Journal* displayed advertising handsomely, set in with the articles and stories. It may have been the first magazine to change its cover design with each issue, which combined a monthly novelty with a familiar packaging. It's the same way magazines are sold today, but it was new at the end of the nineteenth century.[27]

The *Journal* was a splendid medium for entertainment. It published Rudyard Kipling's *Just So Stories* as well as the work of Mark Twain. It also published music, everything from John Philip Sousa marches to Strauss waltzes. This was a tie-in that Carl Adler might have found useful, since it would encourage Baker City readers to broaden their music-buying tastes. It also guided its largely female audience in putting together and managing a gracious home. Through its early years, the *Journal* gave its audience practical household advice, moral counsel of the Dear Abby sort, and instruction in how to be respectable. The *Journal's* editorial tone assumed that its audience needed instruction in these areas.[28] The homes of the majority of *Ladies' Home Journal* readers had been won through hard work, not through family connections, inheritance, or education. What magazine could be better in a mining town during its boom times? Families certainly wanted to spend the money they were earning; how to do it in a way that showed they had good taste and intelligence? In 1903, *Ladies' Home Journal* went over the 1,000,000 circulation mark.

The *Saturday Evening Post* was another Curtis Publication.

Curtis had bought the magazine and its 2,000-name subscription list for $1,000 in 1897. George Lorimer became the magazine's editor on St. Patrick's Day 1899. Lorimer wanted to make the *Post* a magazine without class, clique, or sectional interest. He meant to edit it for the whole United States—a truly mass magazine.[30]

Of course, ten-year-old Leo had no inkling of this when he was lugging around magazines in his news sack. He was a young boy, trying something new. To get started, he simply filled out a coupon and was sent ten free copies of the *Post*. It sold for five cents; he earned a cent and a half per sale. He also delivered a variety of newspapers around town: the *Oregonian*, the *Oregon Journal*, the *Spokesman Review*, the *News Telegram*, and the *Boise Statesman*. It turned out that he was very successful at it. He had a bit of assistance from a dog named Prince, whom he would later call his first business associate. The *Oregonian* shipped second-day from Portland, so that Wednesday's paper would arrive on Friday. Leo had to be up at 5:30 every morning to meet the train to get the *Oregonian*; if he tried to sleep in, Prince would whine until he woke Leo up and they were on their way. Leo always claimed his dog knew the route better than he did, and if he tried to fool him and go a different way, the dog knew it and would have none of it.[31]

It's hard to say why Leo connected so strongly with selling newspapers and magazines. It may have been a way for him, as the youngest in the family, to claim some independence. The paper route and delivering magazines were an easy way for him to get out of the house and out on his own. It also gave him money that he could use for what he was interested in. He remembered

Leo advertising Ladies Home Journal *with the help of his dog, Prince.* (Adler House Museum)

buying his first suit with knickerbocker pants (full breeches that were gathered just below the knees) and a coat. It was probably memorable for him not only for the fact that he bought it himself, but also because knickerbockers were the transitional clothes an adolescent boy wore between a boy's short pants and a man's long pants. But there were also hard moments. One year in December, Leo planned to buy something for his mother and father. At that time, the Sunday *Oregonian* was a nickel. "I'll never forget: one Sunday I sold my last paper, and I had to give ninety-five cents change. I put that dollar in my pocket, a silver dollar. I had a hole in my pocket and I lost it. My heart was broken. I can just remember that."[32]

His father Carl must have been quite pleased with his initiative. Leo also may have found that his magazine work gave him a special bond with his father. Carl was probably the person responsible for igniting Leo's lifelong interest in firemen and fire departments, likely with vigorous tales about the great 1883 fire in Astoria. Leo would occasionally travel with his father as well. A 1911 notice in the Astoria *Daily Budget* mentions a visit the two of them made together during Astoria's centennial.

> *During his residence here Mr. Adler took an active part in the civic and commercial development of the city and at one time was president of the famous Alert Hook and Ladder Company in the days of Astoria's gallant volunteer fire department. Thirty years ago Mr. Adler took the liberty to address a letter to John Jacob Astor in the hope that he would erect a memorial in Astoria which would be dedicated to the achievements of his illustrious ancestor. Mr. Adler had hopes for a grand demon-*

stration at that time and he is pleased to note the magnificence of the present centennial celebration. Mr. Adler is accompanied by his son Leo and will remain in the city for a few days renewing many of his former acquaintances.[33]

Leo also may have picked up his civic sensibilities and interest in community involvement from his father.

Working for the Curtis Publishing Company could have given Leo a sense of being part of something big that was outside of Baker. The Curtis Company worked hard to cultivate its newsboys, sub-agents, and agents. The Curtis circulation bureau sent out a special monthly pamphlet called *Our Teams* published "in the interests of the boy agents of the *Saturday Evening Post* and the *Ladies' Home Journal.*" It had information about new sales incentives. "A baseball will be given to you for selling, of the June *Journal*, 20 copies more than you sold of the May *Journal*." There were various sayings to inspire the boys. "Let the tide help you if it's going your way, but don't be afraid to pull against it"; "The only way to prove your ability is to do a thing"; "If customers do not come your way, change the way"; and "There is no advertisement equal to a pleased customer. Have this in mind every time you sell a copy." There was even an ad for a young boy from Georgia who had bought land with his earnings.[34] It painted a rosy view of all the things that were possible for a newsboy. But it was a view that inspired Leo Adler from an early age. At the age of ten or eleven he served as an advertisement for the *Ladies' Home Journal*, with Prince at his side. It mentioned that he sold 250 *Posts* (a weekly) and 110 *Journals* (a monthly). Just on those sales alone, he would have earned over $16 a month. It's hard to know what

Leo Adler's senior portrait from the 1914 Baker High School Rosemary
(Baker County Library)

he was earning during his high school years, but it had probably increased a great deal by that point.

Leo continued with his schooling and he added new customers. He put ads in the Baker High School annual, the *Rosemary*, and the school literary magazine, the *Nugget*, describing himself as "Leo Adler, magazine specialist." A picture of him in the 1914 *Rosemary* shows a young man in a suit and tie with slicked-back hair, protruding ears, and a sober look on his face. He is looking calmly into the camera. For each member of the class there are seven categories. For Leo it says:

Victim—Leo Adler

Alias—"Kipe"

Looks—Modest

Affliction—Acquiring a bank account

Worst Fault—Too coy

Aim in Life—To be president of the German Verein

Current Literature—"Aw-go-on"[36]

While it is hard to guess at what teenage humor was like in 1914, the brief description zeroed in on the specific things that made Leo different from his classmates. Looking at it from an early twenty-first century perspective, "kipe" sounds an awful lot like "kike," a highly offensive reference to Jews. The reference to his wanting to be president of the German Verein (or club) may have been in connection with his father Carl's interest in bringing German language into the high school. In an interview done with Leo in 1977, he was asked the question "Did being Jewish make you feel different from any of the other children?" His response was "No, not a bit and we always were accepted in schools."[37]

Leo was an unusual high school graduate in that he already had a path laid out before him. He was a successful businessman with money in the bank. But there might have been other paths he wanted to follow. His brother Sanford was attending college at the University of Oregon. His cousin Elizabeth Baer had been offered a full scholarship to Whitman College, but had decided to attend the University of Oregon and would transfer to Wellesley College in Massachusetts.[38] She later came back to teach in Baker. Leo's sister Theresa didn't attend college, but she taught at various schools in the area, at Wingville and Unity.[39] Many people around Leo were making their way out into the wider world. They would come back to Baker, but for now they were testing the possibilities elsewhere. He talked with his father about what his future path might be. His father advised him to stick with his magazine business since he was already several years ahead of where his contemporaries would be when they graduated. Carl certainly knew that there was much in life that was uncertain and Leo already had a good business going. But from a man who had seen and done so much by the time he was twenty-five, Carl's advice of "stay put and stick with it" is surprising.

So Leo decided to stay in Baker, continuing his work in magazine distribution. The next question was, how could he expand the business? It wasn't a question most nineteen-year-olds ask themselves, but Leo was certainly ready for the challenge.

A cover from one of the magazines sold during Leo's earliest days as a "magazine specialist." (Oregon Jewish Museum)

Magazine Specialist

Leo Adler turned nineteen on June 21, 1914. One week later, a world away in Sarajevo, Bosnia, Archduke Franz Ferdinand, heir to the Austro-Hungarian empire, was assassinated. In less than two months, Germany and Austria had become allies, and Germany had declared war on Russia and France and had invaded neutral Belgium. On August 4, Great Britain declared war on Germany; on the same day, President Woodrow Wilson reaffirmed a policy of neutrality for the United States.

These events probably had no immediate impact on Leo's life in 1914. "Leo Adler, Magazine Specialist" now had office space in the Crystal Palace. His brother Sanford was back in town after graduating from the University of Oregon; he had some hopes of becoming a doctor and had applied to the medical school at Columbia University in New York City.[1] Sanford was working with his father in promoting the wares of Adler's Book and Music Store. Trying out some new advertising techniques to bring folks into the store, Sanford may have been behind the luridly worded ad that proclaimed "Slaughter in Pianos." A $300 piano could be had for $125 because, to put it bluntly, "We need the Money—You need the Pianos."² It's hard to know if this actually helped to sell pianos, but it does show a certain promotional zeal.

Sanford and Leo would often go on trips to sell musical instruments and magazines to the various mining establishments throughout Baker County and beyond. In 1915, they took a memorable trip up to the Cornucopia Mine. They were near the mining company dining hall when the car they were in stalled, skidded off the road, and fell over on its side. Gasoline poured from the underseat tank. Sanford stopped the flow of gasoline and told Leo to run to the dining hall for help. Leo came back fifteen minutes later with no help; as he told Sanford, the men were eating and he didn't want to bother them. The air turned blue with Sanford's response. Sanford then went for help, and a crew of miners righted the car and got it back on the road.

Since the car was in a more delicate state than they might have liked, he and Sanford were offered horses to navigate the terrain that separated the Cornucopia from the Last Chance Mine. This was Leo's first time on a horse. Sanford was more of an outdoorsman than Leo, so it likely was not his first horse. Leo's only question about his horse was "Is he tame?" and off he and Sanford went. Leo won $150 at poker and he sold several magazine subscriptions to the miners.³ Even if Leo had been a little slow in assisting with the car, the trip was clearly a beneficial one. It shows Leo pushing out into new territory and developing markets that others had overlooked. He was twenty years old and busy developing his magazine business. His clients were hungry for the news he could provide them. In 1915, he won fifth place in the Curtis Publishing Company's December contest for sales, and in December 1916 he won fourth place and a check for $125 that came with it. The *Morning Democrat* stated, "Baker's subscription specialist is a hustler and if he keeps on moving up in the annual contest as he has started, he'll land first money in three years more."[4]

With his growing reputation for magazine sales, Leo's picture appeared in numerous publications describing him as the "Magazine Specialist." Because of the promotions he had been doing since he was a young boy, he received a sad letter from a Mrs. B. Klevansky of Reading, Pennsylvania. Mrs. Klevansky saw a picture of the young Leo published in a weekly magazine for which

Slaughter in Pianos

OUR ENTIRE STOCK OF PIANOS TO BE SACRIFICED TO MAKE ROOM FOR AN IMMENSE STOCK OF HOLIDAY GOODS NOW ARRIVING.

We Must Have Floor Room

$125.00 Cash Down will buy a $300 Piano
$187.50 Spot Cash will buy a $400 Decker Bros.
$225 buys an elegant $450 Radle.
$375 buys a celebrated $500 Lyon & Healy.

All Must be Sold at Once

We Need the Money---You Need the Pianos.

AT THE PRICES OFFERED POSITIVELY YOU GET A PIANO AT HALF PRICE. FIRST COME FIRST SERVED

ADLER'S Book & Music Store

Searching for new ways to bring in customers, Sanford Adler tried this approach. Baker Morning Democrat, *Nov. 10, 1914.* (Oregon Historical Society OrHi 104807)

he was a local agent. She was convinced that he was her son, who had run away to join the Army in 1912. She traced him down through the magazine and wrote him a letter, begging him to answer her, even if she was mistaken. He wrote her back immediately, expressing his regret that she had not been able to find her son.[5]

Throughout 1914 and 1915, the Baker *Morning Democrat* reported almost daily on what was happening with the war in Europe on various fronts, but it wasn't until the Cunard cruise ship *Lusitania* was torpedoed by a German U-boat while sailing from New York to London on May 7, 1915, that the war became more personal to Americans. Early reports showed that 1,364 were lost on the sunken ship. Of the 133 U.S. citizens on board, 73 survived.[6] New York City was stunned by the loss of a ship so recently in its harbor.

It is hard to know what effect these events might have had on Leo personally. In his high school yearbook he had been teased about wanting to become the president of the German Verein, a local German culture club that was active in Baker and occasionally gave music recitals.[7] Leo had German ancestry on both sides of his family. More than 8 million German-Americans lived in the United States at the outbreak of the Great War, and many were sympathetic to the cause of their homeland. Anti-German feeling was strong among the upper classes on the east coast, and was particularly intense among those with social and business connections to Britain or France. Most Americans, however, did not feel strongly connected to the European conflict and were not interested in waging war overseas.[8] Almost as if to prove the country's ambivalence about war, on Feb. 25–27, 1917, the movie

Magazine Specialist

The Carl Adler family. Front row, Laura and Carl. Back row. Sanford, Theresa and Leo. (Oregon Jewish Museum)

"The Battle Cry of Peace: A Call to Arms Against War" played at the Baker Theatre. In mid-March Ewald Nobach, president of the Baker German Verein, circulated an anti-war petition to be sent to Congress that protested "The manufactured war sentiment and all actions that would lead warward." Other German-Americans in Baker were indignant that he would circulate such a petition.[9]

Less than three weeks later, on April 3, 1917, the Baker *Morning Democrat* ran banner headlines that shouted, "WILSON ASKS WAR: ISSUE UP TO CONGRESS." A smaller headline read, "Against government of Germany, not the people." President Woodrow Wilson concluded his request for war with the following.

> *We are, let me say again, the sincere friends of the German people.... We have borne with their present government through all these bitter months because of that friendship, exercising a patience and forbearance which would otherwise have been impossible. We shall, happily, still have an opportunity to prove that friendship in our daily attitude and actions toward the millions of men and women of German birth and native sympathy who live among us and share our life, and we shall be proud to prove it towards all who are in fact loyal to their neighbors and to the government in the hour of test.[10]*

The United States Senate voted to declare war on Germany with only six senators opposed, including Oregon's Senator Harry Lane. As the country prepared for war, the country at large became more suspicious of German-Americans and any display of German language or culture. The German language classes that Carl Adler had worked to have included in the high school curriculum ceased as fourteen states banned speaking German in public schools.[11] Dachshunds were renamed "liberty dogs" and German measles were renamed "liberty measles." The City University of New York reduced by one credit every course in German.[12] In Portland, streets with German names were changed. Frankfurt became Lafayette after the American Revolutionary War

Young Baker City recruits to the Great War stand at attention. Sanford Adler is in the first row, far left. (Oregon Jewish Museum)

general. Frederick became Pershing after Gen. John J. Pershing, who was leading the U.S. forces in France.[13] The military adversary was thousands of miles away, but German-Americans provided convenient local scapegoats.

The first U.S troops arrived in France on June 26, 1917. The German troops, who had previously been known as Germans or Teutons in the press, now became "Huns." Boys from Baker enlisted and did their part. On November 19, 1917 a death notice was published on Harry Miller "The first Baker boy to give his life in the service of his country."[14]

This must have been an extremely difficult period for many of the German families in Baker. Although Carl Adler's father Jacob had passed away in 1886, Carl likely still had relatives in Germany. He had been an American citizen since 1876, but he valued and was nurtured by his German culture, the sound of the language, the music, the taste of the food. Leo spoke warmly of his mother cooking knockwurst, sauerkraut, and dumplings for his father.[15] The country was moving into a period when that heritage was devalued. Germans in Baker were asked to register with the chief of police; many responded so quickly that the chief was unable to register them because the proper forms had not been received. According to Chief Jackson, the Germans all seemed anxious to comply with the regulations, and it was believed that few if any German "slackers" would be found in the community. All people of German birth who had not been granted their final naturalization papers were compelled to register.[16] American-born Sanford Adler enlisted in the military. Leo was in the process of selling his business so that he could enlist, but then the Armistice was declared.

Baker's contributions to the war effort came in surprising ways. On January 27, 1918, the following headline ran on page two of the *Morning Democrat*: "All Honor to Jew Peddler: Accused by many, Louis Reens a better patriot than they."

> *Reens was known as a "Jew Peddler," but if all of his race were like him, give us more. He patronized a local restaurant and was often the subject of attack by others in the place, for his pessimistic views of the war and the laxity of the people in taking it serious. He had hard times often to keep from personal encounter, but with the telling of the truth, he has shown himself a real patriot and a better American than many of his accusers.*
>
> *When he applied for enlistment to Corporal Oxley, it developed that he had served through the Spanish War and as a volunteer was also one of those who gave their service in the*

Philippine insurrection. At the age of 45 years he is offering himself once more to the country of his adoption and has gone to sacrifice himself if needs be on the altar of liberty and democracy.[17]

After an illness of many months, Carl Adler died on July 28, 1918, of "dilation of the heart."[18] He was sixty-four years old. Carl's wife Laura, Theresa, and Leo were with him. Sanford was a sergeant in the ordinance department of the Army, stationed at Camp Logan in Houston, Texas, and could not be at his death bed. Leo had been assisting his father with the store for the past few months. In his obituary, Carl was described as one of the most prominent and best-known businessmen of Baker County. He had been a member of the city council and was also a member of the Knights of Pythias and the Elks Lodge. His body would be shipped to Portland and the funeral would be held the following day. Carl Adler was buried in the Congregation Beth Israel graveyard in Portland, joining the infant son who had gone before him. The family would have gone down to Portland for the funeral. Perhaps Leo would have said Kaddish with the other Jewish men of Baker when they gathered for services. With Sanford away in the war, the baby of the family was at this moment the man of the family.

In his last will and testament, dated July 22, 1918, Carl Adler left one dollar to each of his children and $100 to his niece Theresa Eisenberg, the daughter of Carl's younger sister Anna; the remainder of his estate went to Laura Adler.[19] The property and capital that he left behind were surely important to his family. But perhaps the most important legacy that Carl left behind was his values and beliefs. There is no written document to confirm what those were, but the example of his life makes many of those values clear: Work hard. Deal honestly. Love your family. Honor your religion. Get involved with your community. Give your talents, give your time, and give your money.

Embodied in the life that he lived, these were the values that Carl Adler passed on to his children. Now it was time for them to see how they could transmit these values into the world around them.

The Great War ended when Armistice was declared on November 11, 1918, almost four and a half years after it had started. Leo was twenty-three. He made it through the war years with his business intact. There were still thousands of small towns that didn't have access to all the things that his magazines could offer. And the time seemed ripe to set about changing that.

OPENING NEW TERRITORY

With Carl Adler's death, there were adjustments to make within the Adler family. In 1918, 33-year-old Theresa, 25-year-old Sanford, and 22-year-old Leo all continued to live in the family home. As a widow, Laura Adler probably faced the most complex adjustment. She and Carl had been married thirty-six years when he passed away. Laura's main occupation had been making a comfortable and elegant home for the family. While she had never been an integral part of Carl's business, Leo remembered her going down to the store to spend time there two or three times a week.[1]

Theresa continued to teach in the area. A photo album belonging to her in the collections of the Oregon Jewish Museum shows that she had a lively group of friends and that she enjoyed traveling. She had not married. She continued to take teaching assignments around Baker County when she could find them, and she looked for teaching work in California. Sanford had graduated from the University of Oregon, and before joining the Army he had worked with his father in the store. He hadn't pursued his aspirations to go to medical school, perhaps because of changes in the world and in his family. At some point the store became known around town as "Adler's," although the old-timers still probably called it the Crystal Palace. The store continued to sell a range of products, from silverware to pianos to phonographs. Sanford was concentrating more on musical instruments and sheet music.

Leo had a running start in the business that he would remain in for the rest of his life. He was already supplying booksellers and other merchants with various lines of popular magazines from a variety of publishers. He was serving as the middleman between publishers and merchants. For the publishers he was representing, he would go into a store and set the merchant up with a line of weekly and monthly magazines, a specified number for each title. At the end of the month, the merchant would then tear off the covers of the magazines that hadn't sold and send them in to Leo. Leo would credit those magazines to the merchant's account, and then would pass the information on to the publishers. Leo also handled individual subscriptions. He must have learned efficient record-keeping at quite a young age, because there could be no expansion of a business like his if the records and the bookkeeping were in a snarl.

Leo continued to handle magazines by the Curtis Publishing Company and slowly added other publishers' lines. In 1919, a number of publishers sent him to Tacoma, but he stayed there only a few months before refocusing his energies on Baker as his base of operation.[2] He was already servicing the eastern Oregon towns of Haines, Sumpter, North Powder, and Ontario. He took on more territory. He focused his sights on Utah in the early 1920s,

Theresa and Sanford Adler enjoy a picnic in the hills around Baker City. Sanford is in a dark bow-tie and glasses in the back row. Theresa smiles in the second row, next to a gentleman with a child in his lap. (Oregon Jewish Museum)

because there were very few magazine dealers in the state. Provo, Salt Lake City, and Ogden were the only places where there were newsstands. Utah had been ignored, perhaps due to an assumption that its largely Mormon population was not interested in secular reading material. Leo did not make this assumption. He went into small towns all over Utah, often staying in private homes when there was no hotel in town. By the time he left Utah, he had 150 new dealers in drugstores, hotels, and grocery stores.[3]

With so much new business, Leo needed office help. In 1921, he hired his first employee, Zella Smurthwaite.[4] Born in 1901 and a 1919 graduate of Baker High School, Zella worked first for Sanford as a sheet music player at Adler's Book and Music Store. Just as people listen to samples of recorded music before they make a purchase today, buyers in the early twentieth century

Some schoolchildren taught by Theresa Adler. (Oregon Jewish Museum)

wanted to listen to sheet music before purchasing it. It was a smart sales tool to have a good musician playing the music rather than forcing a potential customer to plunk it out in public. One of seven children, Zella also played piano for silent movies and was part of a dance band. The Smurthwaites had originally come from Utah to work in the David Eccles sawmill.[5] Eccles was president of the Oregon Lumber Company, which came to Baker in 1890 because of the strong prospects for a lumber business.[6]

Zella quickly became the answer person in the office for those who had questions about their accounts. This allowed Leo to travel and develop more accounts. In the beginning, she may have worked part-time for Leo and continued with some of her work for Sanford, since the offices of "Leo Adler, Magazine Specialist" were on the mezzanine level of Adler's store. She was bright and efficient, and she kept things moving forward. Nedra Roske, who was also an early employee, handled subscriptions.

There was an elegant simplicity to the idea behind the work that Leo was doing, although the bookkeeping and record-keeping was probably frightening. A sample 1927 contract from the Pictorial Review Company survives in the collections of the Adler House Museum. To put it simply: For each yearly subscription

Leo sells to the various Pictorial Review publications, he will receive 80 cents. If there are three Pictorial Review titles and Leo sells ten copies of each to a dealer (30 subscriptions), he receives $24. If he sells the same number of titles and copies to 150 dealers, he receives $3,600, a nice amount of income from one publisher's titles. This, of course, ignores the fact that it was seldom this simply and easily calculated; but Leo was very quick with figures, and as the business expanded, he hired more people to do the record-keeping.

So the business grew. Leo was out in the field and Zella was back at the office. More staff members were added. The 1920s were a period of growth and Leo was working hard, winning sales incentive prizes, and taking magazines and paperback books into areas that had either had none or were poorly served. He continued to go into new markets. He was selling information and entertainment in weekly and monthly doses, and people were hungry for it.

Sanford was continuing to work in the family store, but not making quite the splash that his brother was. He joined local fraternal organizations, the Masons and the Elks. With what seems like great abruptness, at the age of 36, he traveled to New York and married Mary Louise Weiden on June 12, 1929.[7] When they married she was working at the New York Public Library, but she had previously worked for three years at the library in Baker. During her work in Baker, she had developed a friendship with Sanford. When he was in New York on business, he would make a point of visiting her. Leo and his family learned about the marriage in a telegram that Sanford sent. It seems surprising that Sanford would not have talked about such a momentous step with his brother, but the element of surprise may have been necessary. A letter from a family friend of Mary Louise's seems to confirm this: She says that she remembered Mary Louise's mother saying that she would have to be married suddenly, because if she waited overnight she would change her mind. Sanford recalled years later that he'd had no intention of getting married when he went to New York, but something made him alter his plans.[8] The couple went to Europe for their honeymoon and visited England, the Netherlands, Germany, Austria, and France.

Although Leo was busy expanding the lines of magazines he was offering and was opening up a lot of new territory, at some point in the late 1920s and early 1930s his thoughts may well have turned toward starting a family. His business was doing well, and he wasn't getting any younger. His thoughts settled on a woman he already had a close working relationship with, Zella Smurthwaite.

Zella was dark-haired, smart, and well-organized, and she seemed quite able to keep up with Leo and what he had planned for the business. Leo would describe her to other Smurthwaite family members as "a good-lookin' woman." She had received marriage proposals from three other men and eventually had the diamonds from those engagement rings combined into one diamond ring. Leo's mother Laura was said to like Zella a great deal. This would have been a plus, since Leo and his mother and sister were all living in the same home. Although Leo was Jewish and Zella was Mormon, it doesn't appear that their different religious backgrounds kept them apart. However, Zella liked her independence and had grown accustomed to it. So she decided to hold on to it. Although she had refused Leo's proposal of marriage, she continued to work as his office manager for the next fifty years.[9]

Opening New Terriorty

Leo increased his involvement with civic activities in the 1920s. He was an up-and-coming young man with energy, intelligence, and money. He liked being part of what was going on, and the local fraternal organizations were a good way to meet new people and keep informed about what was happening in the community. He was a member of the Knights of Pythias, the Elks, the Masons, Scottish Rite, and Shriners. He belonged to the Baker County Chamber of Commerce, the Kiwanis Club, and the Optimist Club.[10] Leo was interested in access to the people who could get things done and he was also was interested in access within the state of Oregon. He was born into an extended family for whom community activities were a high priority. Leo's interest in what was going on in Baker and what was going on in the state worked right in with those priorities.

Leo was an early supporter of the Hotel Baker (locally known as the Baker Hotel) which opened to the public on August 25, 1929. The idea of a new hotel for the community had been bandied about for years, but it always hinged on some outside investor supplying the money. In May or June 1928, Eric Hauser, Jr., paid a visit to Baker. His father was the founder of the Multnomah Hotels Corporation, and had bought the resplendent Multnomah Hotel in Portland fifteen years earlier. The Multnomah Hotels Corporation operated four hotels in Oregon and Washington in 1928. In Oregon, there was the Multnomah in Portland and the Lithia Springs in Ashland, and in Washington, the Evergreen in Vancouver and the Washington Hotel in Pullman. The Washington hotels opened in January and March 1928.[11]

Baker had some splendid hotels, built in the 1880s and 1890s during the boom years of the mines. They had not really been created to take advantage of conventions or tourists, and were also on the small side and aging. The Geiser Grand was built by local merchants the Warshauer Brothers in 1889; it was sold several years later to Al Geiser, who remodeled the building in the 1890s. At that time it was the finest hotel in the inland empire.

It's not known with which of the town fathers Eric Hauser had his initial discussion about the hotel, but after the chat, Hauser became discouraged and assumed it couldn't be done. Fortunately, the man he talked to was forward-thinking and asked him to stay over long enough to talk with several other Baker men who were interested in a hotel. The group included Fred Soll, W.H. Browning, Walter and Charles Palmer, J.W. Stuchell, and several others in the town.

Fred Soll was very enthusiastic about the project. Born in Germany in 1863, he came to the United States as a young man and located in Grand Island, Neb., where he lived for many years. In 1912 he joined the J.C. Penney Company and soon afterward went to Pendleton, where he was employed by the company for a year. After leaving Pendleton he opened a Penney's store in Athena and stayed there a year before moving to Baker to manage the local store. He retired from active service in 1925. Fred Soll was acknowledged as one of the wealthiest men in town. The J.C. Penney Company had been founded in 1902 by James Cash Penney in Kemmerer, Wyo., and Penney was an early innovator in the idea of employee profit-sharing.

Once the initial, interested group was gathered, Louis D. Barr came into the picture in mid-June 1928. It was his task to come up with a successful campaign to raise the money. He was an acknowledged expert in raising money for public institutions and

OPENING NEW TERRIORTY

Rendering of the Hotel Baker by the architectural firm of Tourtellotte and Hummel. (Oregon Historical Society. *Oregon Journal* photo. OrHi 51045)

a member of the Hockenberry hotel financing organization. He realized that the hotel idea was a tough sell, but he thought it could be done. An executive committee to promote the campaign was organized and on June 20 and 21, 1928 a four-column announcement about the project ran in the Baker *Democrat* and in the Baker *Herald*.[12] The committee planned to finance the campaign with the sale of $150,000 in preferred stock and $125,000 in bonds. Thirty-four year-old Leo Adler was a member of the executive committee. As of July 3, advertisements started appearing in the Baker *Democrat* and the Baker *Herald*, touting the seven percent preferred stock offering. The idea of a new hotel was sold as "Baker's Modern Hotel" and "Baker's Fireproof Hotel." Full-page ads touted the idea of a community-owned chain hotel. The ads ended with the phrase "a Conservative Business Men's Investment and a Civic Duty. Do Your Part...Work For Baker." Further newspaper articles went on to explain that the Multnomah Hotel Chain would not take profits from the operation of the hotel until the expenses of operation, taxes, insurance, building depreciation, interest on the mortgage, and the seven percent preferred stock dividends had been met. The net profits after that would be divided fifty-fifty between the Multnomah Hotel Chain and the holders of the common stock.[13]

Many of the wealthier men in town bought several thousand dollars worth of stock in the hotel, with Fred Soll acknowledged as the largest investor of all. The campaign met its goal on August 8, 1928. Baker was going to have a modern hotel! Sadly, Fred Soll was not alive to see the finished hotel that he worked so hard for. He passed away on November 7, 1928. He was remembered in the Baker *Democrat-Herald*:

Opening New Terriorty

> *Mr. Soll was probably the wealthiest resident of Baker during the latter part of his life. He is remembered for his kindly, friendly ways and for his many private benevolences, many of which did not become known until after his death. He was a member of the board of directors of the Chamber of Commerce, a member of the Kiwanis club and a large contributor to most of the welfare agencies of the city.*[14]

It's not known if Leo had a particular friendship with Fred Soll, but they shared a range of interests. They had their German heritage in common, they were involved in growing businesses that ranged throughout the west, and they were committed to giving something back to their community. Leo had lost his father ten years earlier and a man like Fred Soll could have been a very knowledgeable and pleasant friend to talk with.

Baker was bursting with pride over its major new hotel. The Hotel Baker looked very sleek and modern. Designed by the Portland architectural firm of Tourtellotte and Hummel, the ten-story building had eighty guest rooms, a coffee shop, a dining room, three club rooms, a barber shop, and a beauty parlor. The Chamber of Commerce planned to move its new offices there. The *Oregon Journal* took note of the Hotel Baker's opening.

> *Not only are the people of Baker proud of the new hotel but the residents in the neighboring communities are likewise interested. The hostelry is interpreted as a mark of progress for this section of Eastern Oregon and is heralded as such by the people in the entire trade territory. . . . As one of the most progressive cities in Eastern Oregon, Baker is certain to become a con-*

spicuous trade center and she is already on her way.[15]

A local editorial also had comments about the hotel.

We think the greatest benefit the hotel will confer upon the city will be in the prestige it will add to the name of Baker. Everyone who passes through the town on the highway, whether he stops or not must say to himself that this must be a real city or it would not have such an institution. Those who stop will be certain of it. The fact that the people themselves built the hotel makes it their own achievement. Had it been built by outside capital it would be our good luck. Built by ourselves, it is our very great community accomplishment.

. . . To be known as the city with the great hotel will be our good fortune. Perhaps most significant of all is the effect of this upon ourselves. Every one of us thinks more of Baker today than we did 13 months ago. We have more faith in the city and have more faith in ourselves. If we can put over a project like this we can, by cooperation, put over others that may arise in the future. We have demonstrated that we have a real community spirit, and we will be reminded of it every time we look at the big structure that dominates the skyline of the city. The hotel is here because the people put up the money and built it. It is the greatest civic achievement in the history of Baker.[16]

It was a good thing that the community investment in the Hotel Baker was a source of such immense pride, because it was an investment with difficult timing. Scarcely two months after the Hotel Baker opened, the stock market crashed on October 24,

1929, a day that would be known as Black Thursday. The country slowly spiraled downward. In the United States, at the depths of the Depression (1932–33), there were 16 million unemployed, about one-third of the available labor force. But hard times didn't appear to cramp Leo's enthusiasm for the possibilities of Baker City. As a newly elected president of the Chamber of Commerce for 1932, he put together a string of speakers that displayed his access to the decision-makers in the rest of the state. The Chamber luncheon speakers (all appearing at the Hotel Baker) included Governor Julius Meier, Secretary of State Hale E. Hoss, and Ted Cramer, secretary of the Oregon Bankers Association and an officer of the Union Pacific System.[17]

The March 11, 1932 edition of the Baker *Democrat-Herald* speaks in measured tones to the range of anxieties Baker and the country at large faced. The lead article covered a riot at a Ford plant in Dearborn, Mich., that killed three. According to the article, several hundred unemployed Communists attacked the Ford plant. It was an early phase of union organization. The investigation about the Lindbergh baby, who had been kidnapped on March 4, was continuing. The New Hampshire primary had just taken place and Franklin D. Roosevelt's star was on the rise. Baker County was eligible for free wheat to go to starving cattle and free flour for needy people. There was a hay famine in the Rock Creek-Muddy Creek area. The city of La Grande had just survived a run on the town's two banks less than a week ago and the *Democrat-Herald* ran this article from the La Grande *Observer*.

> *The recent reorganization of La Grande's banking facilities has been a lesson to our citizens in several ways. In the first place,*

> it was demonstrated that this community has much greater resources—both in money and in human character, than even the optimists would have believed.
>
> In the flood of rumors which overspread the city Saturday night many people were led to believe that both banks had failed and that depositors would lose all they had; but surprisingly few were those who became panicky, and surprisingly numerous were those who took the jolt philosophically, realizing that there is much more to life than money.
>
> And when depositors of the United States National Bank were asked to sign waivers on thirty or fifty per cent of their deposits in order to take care of the charged off assets until they are collected, some men with large accounts voluntarily waived the entire amounts.[18]

There was a run on the banks nationwide. Leo Adler and the Chamber of Commerce were not cowed by these tough circumstances. The Chamber of Commerce decided to pursue new summer tourist business with a brochure distributed with the Ryder Brothers Oregon Trail guide that touted "Baker's pure water and splendid summer climate."[19] Leo worked hard to spread the word about the good things that Baker had to offer even in the midst of such hard times. He was working hard to keep that new hotel as full as he could.

While it would be a stretch to say that Leo was a glamorous figure, his money and his business contacts gave him access to a world that many others in Baker could barely imagine. Private airplanes were a rarity in Oregon at the time and as of 1941 there were only 210 licensed aircraft in the state.[20] In October 1932,

Leo and another Baker resident, Dr. C. J. Bartlett, attempted to fly to Corvallis to watch Baker High School graduate Harold Joslin play football with the Oregon State College Beavers against Washington State. Their plane was grounded in The Dalles because of fog, so they took a train the rest of the way to see the game. Leo reported that Joslin played a great game for the Beavers and got the biggest round of applause from the crowd when he left the game.[21]

Laura Adler, 1864–1933
(Adler House Museum)

Changes were afoot for other members of the Adler family. Through his connections and long-time friendship with former Oregon governor and then Congressman Walter Pierce, Sanford Adler was appointed postmaster for Baker in 1932.[22] It was a helpful place for Leo to have a family member, what with his dependence on an efficient postal system for the shipment of his magazines. Not long after that, Congress decided that postmasters in first-, second-, and third-class offices could hold their jobs for life.[23] Sanford now had a government job for as long as he wanted it.

The Adler family made it through 1932 well enough, but 1933 began with a great sadness to the family. Leo's mother, Laura Adler, died of a stroke on January 28, 1933. She was sixty-nine at the time of her death and still shared the family home with Leo and Theresa. Her body was sent to Portland for burial at Temple Beth

Israel Cemetery, where she would join her husband. An undated newspaper article in the family scrapbook at the Oregon Jewish Museum mentions that the procession to take her body to the train station was fifty cars long. There were seventy-two condolence cards pasted into the same scrapbook. Sanford and Leo were appointed executors of the estate. After going through probate, the net value of the estate was $18,755.67* which was to be divided equally among Theresa, Sanford, and Leo.[24]

Condolence notes that Leo received from his professional contacts were also included in the family scrapbook. He received a sympathy note from a friend who worked for Midwest Distributors out of Minneapolis. While the note was certainly thoughtful, the stationery it was written on holds more interest to a viewer seventy years later. The stationery says:

> *Sell these Magazines for big Profit—Screenplay, Hollywood, Screen Book, Modern Mechanics and Inventions, True Confessions, Startling Detective Adventures, Battle Stories, Triple X Westerns, Hooey, Mechanical Package Magazine, the Amateur Golfer and Sportsman, How to Build It, Flying and Glider Manual, Shortcuts to Par Golf and others including Whiz Bang, Smokehouse Monthly, Winter Annual and Smokehouse Poetry Classics.*[25]

The majority of these titles came from the Fawcett Publishing Company, but they show the range of magazines available to readers in 1933. They also show the range of entertainment (and distraction from one's troubles) that these magazines could supply.

* In 2004 dollars, that amount would equal roughly $273,000.

The majority of them were ten or fifteen cents at a time when a loaf of bread was five cents, potatoes were two cents a pound, and a quart of milk was a dime. A console radio sold for $49.95, which was about $7.50 less than the price of a used 1929 Ford car.[26] If someone had the money to spend during the thirties, a magazine was a small indulgence to buy without feeling as though it would break the bank.

Because, in 1933, the banks were broken. On the morning of March 4, 1933, the day of Franklin Delano Roosevelt's inauguration, every bank in the nation had to close its doors in what was later called a "bank holiday." Leo Adler was on the board of directors of the First National Bank of Baker, and it cannot have been an easy time for him or his fellow directors, especially since they had so recently seen the run on the banks in La Grande. President Roosevelt called an emergency session of Congress; the next day his emergency banking bill went through the House unchanged in thirty-eight minutes. When the banks reopened on March 9, deposits exceeded withdrawals. On March 3, 1933, in his first radio broadcast to the country as president, Roosevelt said "Confidence and courage are the essentials in our plan. You must have faith; you must not be stampeded by rumors. We have provided the machinery to restore our financial system; it is up to you to support and make it work. Together we cannot fail."[27]

Although he was a quiet man, Leo certainly had confidence and courage. He continued to keep Baker connected with business opportunities throughout the state. He looked at what benefits there were to be derived from government public works programs, and he traveled to Spokane to take a look at a Northwest Mining convention that was held there, likely hoping to recruit

A view of Baker City in the 1930s. The Hotel Baker rises proudly at the center of the photo. Photo by Wesley Andrews. (Oregon Historical Society, OrHi 13967)

them for a future convention at the Hotel Baker.[28] Leo's mind was percolating with a variety of ways to help Baker move forward. He continued to travel and increase his business. In February 1934, he gave one of the principal addresses at a San Francisco convention of magazine wholesalers from eleven western states. His speech was titled "The Value of Personal Contact."[29]

Leo continued to work hard throughout 1934. He worked, and perhaps overworked, to make his business successful. He was profiled in a 1935 distributors' newsletter that said the following:

> *We believe there does not exist a distributor in the country who is more respected not alone by the publishers, but by dealers themselves than Leo Adler. Leo's business code is summed up in one word—service. It has been truthfully said that he stands at all times ready to bend over backwards for those with whom he*

does business. In this way he is constantly building good will among his dealers by frequent personal contacts and is not hesitant about constantly adding service and favors which cost so little and mean so much in the magazine business in which he has been so successful.[30]

In early 1935, he contracted rheumatic fever and went to the Mayo Clinic in Rochester, Minn., for treatment. Rheumatic fever can arise if a strep throat infection is left untreated. It is much less common today because is widely treated with penicillin, which had not yet been developed when Leo contracted the illness. At that time, his territory was advertised as extending from The Dalles, Ore., to Grand Island, Neb., so it seems likely that he contracted the disease while traveling.

The common treatment for rheumatic fever at that time was complete bed rest, flat on your back, for three months. Leo convalesced at the Mayo Clinic for two months, probably the longest period of rest he had experienced since he was a boy. In his long return to Baker, he spent twenty hours traveling across Nebraska in a dust storm. Lights were burning on the train and cars had their lights on because of the extreme darkness.[31] The Plains states were plagued with dust storms that spring, with an especially dramatic one occurring on April 14, 1935, known as Black Sunday; it's quite possible that this was the storm through which Leo traveled. During the Black Sunday storm, a black cloud of dust swept over everything at sixty miles per hour. In an article for the *New Republic*, the writer Avis D. Carlson described the storm as "a shovelful of fine sand flung against the face. . . . We live with the dust, eat it, sleep with it, watch it strip us of possessions and the hope of possessions. It is becoming Real. The poetic uplift of spring fades into a phantom of the storied past. The nightmare is becoming life."[32]

Upon arriving in Baker, which he described as "God's country." Leo did not see anything like the nightmare world he had just passed through. With his usual optimism, Leo commented that although business was not strong in the Midwest, they were all looking forward to better times. And then Leo set about trying to bring some of those better times to Baker.

Becoming Mr. Baker

Leo's return to Baker City led to a whirl of new activities. In no time at all he was announcing that the 1935 annual convention of the Pacific Coast Magazine Wholesalers Association would be held in Baker, June 20–22. Magazine publishers from New York, Chicago, San Francisco, and Denver were expected. Wholesalers from Canada, California, Washington, Oregon, Idaho, Utah, Wyoming, Colorado, Nevada, and Arizona planned to attend and with circulation men included, it was expected that approximately seventy people would be in Baker for the meeting. This was quite an accomplishment in Depression-era eastern Oregon. The conventioneers were shown a very lively time with a Mining Jubilee Dance, a Chamber of Commerce luncheon, and a trip to the Balm Creek Mine.[1]

Judging from the way his business grew, Leo's bout with rheumatic fever didn't slow him down at all. In January 1936, he added Montana and northern Idaho to his territory list for magazine distribution by four publishing companies. He was doing distribution for the Curtis Publishing Company, the Kable News Company, Butterick Publications, and Fawcett Publications. This new territory added 400 accounts to Adler's business. He was now servicing 2,000 accounts, with an office of eighteen to handle the work.[2]

By the mid-thirties Leo had a three-decade relationship with Curtis Publishing, but his connections with Kable News Company, Butterick Publications, and Fawcett Publications all point to his shrewd business skills. Although the country was still in the midst of the Depression, Leo had allied himself with three publishers whose businesses would go rocketing forward in the thirties and forties.

Butterick was founded by Ebeneezer Butterick, a tailor in Stirling, Massachusetts, during the Civil War in 1863. He had revolutionized home sewing when he created graded sewing patterns. Prior to his innovations, patterns were designed to serve as a rough idea. They were available in only one size and the seamstress had

A sunny shot of the growing staff of "Leo Adler, Magazine Specialist". (Adler House Museum)

to estimate how to adjust the pattern to the size needed. It was easy to make mistakes and waste cloth—a potentially costly matter.

In 1867, the Butterick Company began publishing its first magazine, *Ladies Quarterly of Broadway Fashions*, and in 1868, it added a monthly bulletin, *Metropolitan*. These publications showcased Butterick patterns along with the latest fashion news. They helped women all over the world buy the latest Butterick patterns. By 1876, E. Butterick & Co. had 100 branch offices and 1,000 agencies throughout the United States and Canada. Butterick was one of the largest manufacturing concerns in the world and the largest private publishing company in America. In the early 1920s the company began providing an improved instruction sheet with its patterns. Butterick patterns were designed to be clearer and easier to understand and use. The changes were well received, and sales increased.

As the country went through the Depression, pattern sales increased even more. Many women began or resumed making the family clothes, and Butterick was the main company they turned to. Pattern sales increased, setting new records, and Butterick opened more U.S. sales offices.[3] Leo Adler was there to provide the infrastructure to assist those sales in his expanding territory.

Established by Harry Kable in 1932, Kable News Company of Mount Morris, Illinois, was organized to handle the newsstand distribution of magazines.[4] One of Leo's successful early innovations had been to think of newsstands not just as stand-alone operations but as a magazine rack in a drugstore, grocery store, or hotel gift shop, so the Kable News Company newsstand connections were of special appeal to Leo.

The Spark and the Light: The Leo Adler Story

Fawcett Publications had its start in Minneapolis, Minn., in 1919. Wilford H. Fawcett—Captain Billy, as he was known to friends—started collecting and writing jokes while he was serving in the First World War. After the war, he began to put out a bulletin of humor that was intended to cheer up disabled ex-soldiers in veterans hospitals. Wilford's brother, Roscoe Fawcett, who spent over a year in army hospitals recuperating from his war injuries when his plane crashed near the cliffs of Dover, England, may have been the inspiration for the work. That bulletin evolved into a pocket-sized magazine of jokes that sold for twenty-five cents. Dedicated to the armed forces, it was called *Whiz Bang* after a well known artillery shell from the war. The magazine became

This full newsstand and thousands of accounts between The Dalles and Grand Island, Neb. are what powered Leo's business. Photo by John Vachon. (Library of Congress LC USF34-008939-D DLC)

Becoming Mr. Baker

Leo Adler, left, watches as Roscoe Fawcett signs an important contract. (Adler House Museum)

known as Captain *Billy's Whiz Bang* and within a few years it was selling more than 500,000 copies a month. Roscoe later joined his brother in the business, but not before he spent a brief stint as the sports editor for the *Oregonian*. Both brothers were great outdoorsmen and athletes. Roscoe competed in international balloon races and Wilford enjoyed big game hunting. Fawcett Publications went on to develop a line of magazines that were of a more popular and sensational nature, including movie, detective, love-story, and mechanical magazines (several Fawcett titles were listed on page 100). A photograph from the collections of the Adler House Museum (above), likely taken in the early thirties, shows a suited and boutonniered Leo sitting next to Roscoe Fawcett, who is signing a contract with a pen in one hand and a cigarette in the other. Roscoe Fawcett died in 1936, at the age of forty-nine, and Wilford followed him in 1940 at the age of fifty-five.[5] The family continued to run the business, and in 1939, staffers Bill Parker and Charles Clarence Beck produced an anthology to launch the Fawcett foray into comic books. The book was called *Whiz Comics*, and its lead feature, Captain Marvel, proved a sensational hit. Captain Marvel was described as the only truly successful rival to DC Comics' Superman character.[6] And Leo Adler was fortunate enough to usher Captain Marvel into the interior Northwest.

By the end of 1936, Leo was increasing his staff and looking for new business quarters. Zella Smurthwaite continued as office manager. He added even more territory by purchasing the Calkins News Company of Spokane, which was going out of business. He and his staff were now servicing 2,300 dealers.[7] One of Leo's new employees in 1937 was a woman named Johannah Fleetwood. She had been living in an apartment with a friend in Baker, working in the kitchen of the local hospital earning $20 a month and not enjoying it at all. The apartment was in a house owned by Jessie Hoskins, who worked for Leo. Jessie invited Leo and Zella Smurthwaite over for dinner one night and introduced them to Johannah and her friend Ann. They chatted for a while and within a week, Johannah and her friend were both offered jobs. Johannah said, "It was during the Depression. Times were tough and I thought I'd died and gone to heaven when I got a job with Leo." Soon she was earning $50 a month, over twice what she had earned at the hospital.

Johannah initially worked in the returns department, pulling the covers off returned magazines, counting the covers, sorting

A formal portrait of the Leo Adler staff, ca. 1937. (Adler House Museum)

them by publisher, and then sending them back for credit. Almost everyone who worked in Leo's office started in returns and moved on from there. She would later work in the credit department and within two years she was working in the billing department.

Remembering those days, Johannah recalled:

You really earned your money. But I was very glad to get a job like that in those days.

They were kind of on your back a lot. There was a lot of work to do. There were all those statements that had to be out by the first of the month. And we had to do all this posting and

> at that time, the publishers sent galleys. They were the charges. The publishers sent everything direct to the dealers and then they sent Leo the charges and the staff had to post them on a statement. Every magazine was listed on a long statement. It had to be done towards the end of the month so that all the statements would be out by the first of the month. It was quite a job to get all that posting done.
>
> They posted everything in a big book and the dealers received a copy. Then when they returned the covers they got credit for those, so then they would post it in this big book. When Zella would make out the charges, if they ordered five magazines and they only sold two, well, just give them three next time. They would adjust their count.
>
> It was a continual readjustment. They were dealing with monthlies and weeklies. It seems easy but just to think about it, it's a lot of work.

1937 was a year of many new exploits and undertakings for Leo. He was re-elected Director of the Baker Chamber of Commerce in February, and in March he invited the public to view the new quarters for Leo Adler, Magazine Specialist. His new offices were in the First National Bank Building on Main Street. He also hosted the officers of the Pacific Coast Magazine Wholesalers Association.[9] Along with several other gentlemen in the town, he filed the articles of incorporation for Baker Flood-Lighting Corporation so that eventually Baker might have some well-lit evening activities. This is discussed more fully in chapter 10.

Leo's travels would often receive coverage in the newspapers, which continuously describe him either as "Mr. Baker" or as "one of Baker's most optimistic citizens."¹⁰ Professionally, he was at the top of his game, and in September 1937 he was elected president of the Pacific Coast Magazine Wholesalers Association in Del Monte, California, at a convention attended by more than 150.¹¹

Leo continued his involvement in a range of activities that would bring attention, tourism, and dollars to the Baker area. In 1938, he became a member of the Anthony Lakes Playground Association, an early effort to look at and develop the recreational possibilities of the Anthony Lakes area.¹²

Theresa Adler, 1885–1938. (Oregon Jewish Museum)

In November 1938, Leo's sister Theresa died suddenly of an acute bronchial condition at the age of 53. She had traveled extensively throughout the United States and had been a tireless worker for the Civic Music Association. Her obituary mentioned that she had taught kindergarten until 1933 and that she had been a first reader in the Christian Scientist Church.¹³ She was buried in Portland near her parents in the Temple Beth Israel Cemetery. Ten years separated Theresa and Leo. The sudden loss of his sister was likely quite a blow to Leo. His remaining family in Baker was dwindling, with only his brother Sanford and his cousins, Bernie and Elizabeth Baer, to connect him with his family ties.

At a time when many might turn inward, Leo continued to look to the wider world around him. As chairman of the program committee for the Chamber of Commerce, he helped to bring Dr. William Landeen to town for a February 1939 address titled "Hitler over Europe." The presentation by Dr. Landeen, who was described as a noted traveler and lecturer, may have had special resonance for various members of the audience. The Neubergers and the Heilners of Baker were likely already aware of what was happening to the Jews in Germany. In 1933, a young Oregon journalist named Richard (Dick) Neuberger (who, in 1954 would go on to become a U.S. Senator from Oregon) wrote one of the earliest nationally published articles that talked about what was happen-

A view of the interior of the Neuberger-Heilner store. (Adler House Museum)

ing in Germany to the Jewish population. Born in Portland, Dick Neuberger was a cousin of the Baker Neubergers who ran the Neuberger-Heilner store. In 1933, between his sophomore and junior years at the University of Oregon, he traveled to Germany with his uncle Julius Neuberger, who was a Navy physician. What he saw in Germany during Hitler's first year in power left a powerful impression on him. His article, "The New Germany," was published in *The Nation* on October 4, 1933, and the magazine's editor, Ernest Gruening, said "It was the first realistic firsthand revelation in any American magazine of what was taking place in Nazi Germany. It was an epoch-making article."[14] The Portland and Baker Neubergers still had family in Germany in 1933, and it is likely that Dick Neuberger made contact with the family on that visit. When Hitler invaded Poland on September 1, 1939, the February lecture from Dr. Landeen would look like great foresight as world events began to unfold. But it would be some time before those events would touch Baker.

In 1939, Leo was chairman of the Mining Jubilee and Rodeo. This year, the Pasadena Tournament of Roses Band would be stopping in Baker for a three-day appearance July 2–4. The band was on its way to New York for an appearance at the 1939–40 World's Fair, and Baker was a good stopping point. The band had previously played in Baker in 1937 and 1938 on its way to appearances at the Portland Rose Festival. The *Record-Courier* reported the upcoming event with relish.

> *Be-costumed exponents of pep music, comic acts and novelties as well as band music, the big band will first appear Sunday afternoon in their show at the city ball park. That evening they*

provide music at the Colburn-Sorenson rodeo. . . .Tuesday night they appear under the $7000 floodlights of the Baker Ball Park.[15]

That brief paragraph shows several different levels of Leo's planning and relationships coming together. The Pasadena Rose Band was making its third appearance in Baker since Leo had become director of the Chamber of Commerce; this was also a second trip for the Colburn-Sorenson Rodeo after its 1938 visit. This year the visitors would be appearing under new floodlights that the members of the Baker Flood-Lighting Corporation had planned for two years earlier. Leo and the citizens of Baker City

From left: Supreme Court Justice William O. Douglas, Stanley Jewett and Francis Lambert at Hart Mountain in 1948. (Oregon Historical Society, OrHi 57171)

were making sure that the city had some of the infrastructure elements that would be needed to help the city grow. Perhaps the example of the Hotel Baker had helped them realize what the city could do for itself.

The 1939 Jubilee also had a dash of celebrity. Phil Harris and His Orchestra were there. Born in 1905, Phil Harris was a drummer, a bandleader, and an actor. He had played in and led bands since 1924, and in 1933 he started a film career. Known in the thirties as a bandleader and the husband of the singer Alice Faye, Harris would be known to the baby boomer generation as the voice of Balou the Bear from Walt Disney's animated movie *Jungle Book*, along with many other Disney movies. Leo recalled that after finishing his set at 3:30 a.m. at the Covered Wagon, a mile north of Baker on Hwy. 30, Harris wanted Leo to give him a call so that he could help rope off the parade route. The newest member of the Supreme Court, William O. Douglas, also joined them in setting up the parade route. Douglas had a vacation home in the Wallowas and had come over to Baker for the festivities.[16] The mind reels at the notion of this trio of a Supreme Court justice, a bandleader, and "Mr. Baker" loping none too steadily through the streets of Baker as they gave the parade route their special care.

After an extremely successful Jubilee, Leo's business and civic interests seemed to just keep rolling along. A February 1940 article described Leo's activities at that point.

> *Mr. Adler has expanded his business to the extent that he employs 28 persons who take care of the needs of 2150 dealers.*
>
> *He has been president of the Baker County Chamber of Commerce 3 years and is at present a director of the organiza-*

Leo Adler's staff on the front steps of their office building. Leo in in the back row with his office manager Zella Smurthwaite (top row, center) and Nedra Roske stands to the left of Zella. Barbara Sturgill has her hands on the shoulders of an office mate. Johannah Fleetwood stands in the second row, second from the left. The photo was likely taken to promote the business in a trade publication for magazine and newspaper distributors. (Adler House Museum)

> tion. He is also president of the Baker Flood Lighting Corporation, vice president of the Baker Hotel, chairman of the Baker county re-employment service, director of the First National Bank, director of the Eastern Oregon finance company and director for the Anthony Lakes playground association.[17]

At forty-five years of age, Leo was deeply embedded in the financial and civic institutions of Baker. He was nationally known and respected within his industry. His business and his base of employees continued to grow.

Barbara Sturgill was one of the young women who joined the Leo Adler work force in early 1940. After working in the Baker office of Montgomery Wards in 1939, she found out that Leo Adler paid more money for fewer hours. Hearing about a job opening, she went for an interview with him and he hired her. She started in the returns department, as had many others. One of the bonuses of working in returns was that when whole magazines were returned, if the women in the office wanted one they would tear off the cover and take it home, with Leo's approval.

Barbara would give her counting tally to Helma Fossum, who was in charge of the galleys, huge books with the names of the customers in them. Helma sat up on a tall stool and could whip through the book, which was the master inventory, with amazing speed. The office was one huge open room, with a small glass-enclosed cubicle up front that served as Leo's office. Zella Smurthwaite, the office manager, sat up front, where she could see everything at all times. In the office, Barbara remembered Leo as being:

> *Gentle, quiet, I never heard him challenge anything. I don't know as I've ever heard him bawl anybody out. I heard Zella bawl him out. . . . Oh, she'd keep him on top of it, let me tell you. Because Leo was gone a lot, he traveled a lot. To New York and Chicago. . . . She was just in total command. She had everything in good hands when he was gone. When he was gone he would always send home a big, big box of cookies, cakes from the delicatessens wherever he was.[18]*

Barbara was working for Leo when she contracted polio in

The Spark and the Light: The Leo Adler Story

October 1940. A vaccine had not been developed at that time, and no one really knew how the disease was transmitted. Barbara mentioned that Leo feared that it had come in on a magazine somehow. She went to Portland for physical therapy as well as to other hospitals in the region. When she eventually returned to Baker and had recovered her strength, she went back to work with Leo.[19] Because his offices were on the second floor, he encouraged her to use his office for her breaks rather than going downstairs. It was a kindness she remembered over fifty years after it had happened.

While the country seemed to be slowly crawling out of the worst of its hard times, there were still new difficulties to master. The war that was raging in Europe was not directly knocking at the country's door, but it was walking up the sidewalk. Stepping out of his plane on November 23, 1940, Lord Lothian, the British ambassador to the United States, announced to waiting reporters at New York's La Guardia Airport, "Well, boys, Britain's broke. It's your money we want." The recently re-elected Roosevelt felt that "The best immediate defense of the United States is the success of Great Britain in defending herself." He went on to describe it with the following parable. If a neighbor's house was on fire and he needed your hose to put it out, you wouldn't haggle about the price; you would lend him the hose, and he would return it when the fire was out. Roosevelt was proposing that the United States lend Britain whatever supplies were needed with the understanding that the United States would later be repaid in kind. The program became known as Lend-Lease. The president announced on January 6, 1941, that he was sending the Lend-Lease bill to the Congress, and ended the speech saying that his policies were ultimately aimed at securing the "four essential human freedoms": freedom of speech and religion, and freedom from want and fear.[20]

The acceptance of the Lend-Lease bill in March 1941 edged the country one step closer to the edge of war. If America did involve itself, the country was going to need money and munitions to become "The great arsenal of democracy." The rising tide of military spending helped to put unemployment below 10 percent for the first time in over a decade.[21] America was about to learn a whole new way of pulling together, and Leo Adler and Baker all would have their part to play.

The War Years

In September 1941, Leo Adler served as vice-chairman for the Baker County Defense Bond Group. Twenty-seven men and one woman gathered at the Baker Hotel to spearhead the city's role in this national program. Launched in May 1941, the Defense Savings Bond and Stamp program was the brainchild of Secretary of the Treasury (1934-1945) Henry Morgenthau. In 1940, Treasury officials began to plan for greater defense spending, estimating that a global war in the 1940s could cost the United States hundreds of billions of dollars. The sale of defense bonds would not only help finance a possible war, it would also drain off purchasing power at a time when there would be fewer goods to buy. Along with price and wage freezes, the Treasury wanted to immobilize consumer spending power, all in an effort to keep down inflation. With the sale of defense bonds, the government could fund a possible war by taking money out of the consumer's hands and putting it into its own.[1]

In 1940, ninety-eight percent of Americans had incomes of $5,000 or less. If taxation was the main vehicle for funding the

THE SPARK AND THE LIGHT:

Poster board on truck promoting the sale of war bonds and stamps in Portland. (Oregon Historical Society, OrHi 72688)

war effort, it would draw from the higher income groups, whereas borrowing with bonds could provide money from all income groups. From a general point of view, it was felt that being taxed made one feel poorer, whereas "investing" in bonds made one feel richer. Gaining the support of the average citizen would be easier if Americans felt they were not only contributing to a national cause but also gaining from it financially. Henry Morgenthau felt strongly that voluntary contribution was an integral part of the American way, and was more effective on a psychological level than was the idea of compulsory savings. Morgenthau felt that while the nation mobilized for defense, the government would "use bonds to sell the war, rather than vice-versa." Bonds would act as a physical reminder of the owner's stake in the European war and serve as a symbol of unity to potential enemies; and if America did enter the conflict, the bonds

The War Years

could be the foundation for postwar prosperity.² Available in denominations of $25, $50, 100, $500, and $1,000, the bonds were purchased at seventy-five percent of their face value, returned a 2.9 percent interest rate, and matured in ten years. A bond purchased for $18.75 in 1941 would be worth $25 in 1951. So that children and those with less money could participate, stamps at 10 cents, 25 cents, 50 cents, $1, and $5 helped them start saving for a bigger bond purchase.³ On April 30, 1941, President Roosevelt, Secretary Morgenthau, and the postmaster general announced the new bond program on the radio. President Roosevelt asked Americans to "join in one great partnership." Morgenthau described defense bonds this way.

> *Defense Savings Bonds and Stamps are not for the few; they are for the many. They are for the great mass of people—for the laboring man, the skilled mechanic, the office worker, the employer, the housewife, the retired businessman—even children can save their pennies to buy the stamps. . . .The Defense Savings Bonds and Stamps are presented as an opportunity…for each citizen to buy a share in America.*⁴

Given Leo Adler's enthusiasm and interest in civic involvement and the range of projects he was involved with, the Defense Savings Bond program brought together several of his interests in one neat package. It looked for deeper community involvement, and it did not look to one particular group to shoulder the responsibility for making things happen. Combining this with his earlier experience of what the community could do when it worked together on the Hotel Baker, these were the seeds of Leo's philanthropic vision. On top of the important work he had done in the 1930s organizing the Miner's Jubilee and funding lights for the Baker baseball field, the Defense and later War Bond program helped Leo add a new dimension to his work as "Mr. Baker" and as a philanthropist.

With the bombing of Pearl Harbor on December 7, 1941, defense bonds turned into war bonds, and the citizens of Baker stepped up to do their part in a variety of ways. Henry Levinger, owner of Levinger Drugstore, enlisted in the army at the age of thirty-four. Henry grew up in Baker and eventually went into business with his father Louis Levinger.

The youngest of thirteen children in a German Jewish family that lived near Augsburg, Louis Levinger came to America at the age of thirteen in 1877. He was ten years younger than Leo's father Carl. As a young boy, he took special courses in English to rid himself of his German accent. After opening drugstores in Oregon City and Portland, Louis came to Baker City in 1898, ten years after the Adlers came to town. According to family stories, on coming to town, Louis saw Sanford Heilner, the fourteen-year-old son of the town's prominent merchant Sigmund Heilner, sitting on the corner, and asked him if he liked this town. Sanford said that he did. After surveying the town and noting that the mines were all operating, Louis decided to open up another drugstore.[5]

Louis met his future wife, Lyle Lawrence, in Baker. A graduate of Oregon State College in Corvallis, Lyle taught first and second grade in Baker. They were married in 1901 by Rabbi Stephen Wise in Portland. Lyle converted to marry Louis, but the family was not observant. In 1977, Henry Levinger recalled that even though they liked Louis, his grandparents had been upset that their daughter was marrying a Jew. The Jewish community in Baker was upset that Louis was marrying outside the faith. Henry said that his parents had been dropped socially and that he was not raised in a religious home.

Born in 1907, Henry got most of his schooling in Baker. He graduated from Stanford magna cum laude with a degree in economics in 1928. A man of many interests, Henry was part of the same dance band as Zella Smurthwaite; he played clarinet and she played piano. He and Leo Adler were long-time friends and had a brotherly fondness for one another without the weight of a shared family history. Watching Henry go off to Stanford and his pursuit of further education, Leo may have looked on some of his younger friend's experiences as "the road not taken."

After a brief stint with National Cash Register, Henry took a two-year pharmacy course at Oregon State University and joined his father's business in 1933.[6] Henry's mother died in 1935 and his father in 1940. A single man and thirty-four when the war broke out, Henry enlisted, hoping for a commission that might take him overseas. In a 1977 oral history, he remembered receiving a telegram that told First Lieutenant Levinger to report to the San Francisco Port of Embarkation:

> *So I thought, "here I am going over to the Pacific," which was great. Everybody was fired up and wanted to get into the action so I went down to San Francisco to Fort Mason and an old crow of a doctor, a full colonel, he said "Do you know anything about running a warehouse?" and I said "Not a thing in the world," but he said, "we're going to open one up in the Presidio."*

> . . . . We handled all the vaccines and narcotics that went to Pacific. . . . it was the most interesting time of my life and during this time we talked to the Surgeon General every morning on a direct line. I said "get me out of here, I want to get out there where the fighting is."[7]

Henry Levinger didn't make it overseas, but he did make it back to Baker to run Levinger's Drugstore after the war.

Bob Young, former Baker fire chief and a long-time friend of Leo's, got to know him during the war when he started work in 1943 with the fire department. Although his father Carl Adler had always had a great interest in the fire department, Leo hadn't shown a great deal of interest in the fire department prior to the war. Otto Karg was the fire chief and brought Leo on as a civilian fireman. As a civilian fireman, Leo had a particular set of tasks to perform during blackout exercises.[8]

Leo was also a member of the state War Production Board. Nationally, the War Production Board was created in January 1942 and headed by a former Sears, Roebuck executive, Donald Nelson. Nelson liked to brag to reporters that in his previous work, he had edited the largest-circulation publication in America—the Sears, Roebuck catalogue.[9] Any public official talking about circulation was likely to pique Leo's interest. Leo involved himself in the many ways Baker was finding to mobilize for the war effort. In April 1942, Baker War Industries Inc. was organized, and Leo was one of the five-member board. He received information from the state War Production Board and used that information to Baker's advantage when possible. The purpose of the newly formed corporation was to secure contracts on war work for vari-

The War Years

A summer banquet to commemorate the 100th anniversary of the Oregon Trail in July 1943. The banquet is at the home of Louise and Sanford Adler. Sanford stands in the back row with glasses and mustache. Louise stands behind the seated guests in a white blouse and dark necklace. Leo stands to the right of Louise. (Oregon Historical Society, OrHi 105025)

ous industrial concerns in Baker. Members of the local procurement committee had been advised by representatives of the War Production Board that to secure war contracts, a corporation pool must be formed. The capital stock of the corporation was $10,000 and seven local concerns subscribed for one-half of the stock within two hours. Once the stock had been fully subscribed, the board of directors and officers planned to tender their resignations so that those subscribing to stock in the new corporation could select directors and officers of their choice.

The board issued the following statement:

We are very hopeful that through this organization we will be able to secure employment for local people, and at the same

129

time have this community doing its part in the war effort. All those who have subscribed for stock have been advised that the amount for which they subscribed should be treated by them as a donation. We do not promise any profit or a return of the money invested. This corporation was not organized for the purpose of making profits, but is being formed primarily for the purpose of getting the people here to work on articles that are essential to the armed forces.[10]

Baker War Industries' first contract, for wooden portions of army truck cargo bodies, was approved on July 6, 1942.[11]

While recruitment proceeded for war-based industry, Leo continued with his tourism and history contacts. He was part of the Old Oregon Trail Centennial commission, which planned the commemoration of the Oregon Trail that originally led pioneers into and through the Baker area in the 1840s. Plans had initially been afoot to have commemorative license plates, but because of steel shortages, no new license plates would be issued in 1943. It was decided that commemorative stickers would be used instead. Leo was also involved on the state level with the war bond and stamp committee and kept the citizens of Baker informed about new developments.[12]

The Baker Chamber of Commerce and Kiwanis were active throughout the war years. In reviewing the 1942 activities of the Chamber, President James T. Donald noted the following:

During the past year, the Chamber of Commerce has had as its main purpose the throwing of the whole power and energy of our community into winning the war. . . . In the midst of this war effort we have not lost sight of our duty to strengthen and prepare our community to meet the problems of a victorious peace.

Several local businessmen had worked hard to secure placement of soldiers and officers in Baker. At the Baker Airport three runways had been completed in 1942 and a flying school came to Baker that year as well. Baker citizens were not only working on the war effort, they were also working on giving Baker the infrastructure it would need to grow in the future.[13]

Aside from his many civic activities, the early forties were an even busier time for Leo's business. To ward off inflation, wages and prices had been frozen across the United States. There weren't a lot of new things to buy, but it was a great time to sell magazines, which still cost between 10 and 15 cents on the news stand. It was a time of long train and bus trips for many Americans, and what better way to while away the hours than with a magazine or a paperback book? Leo had roughly 2,000 dealers that he and the office were servicing at this point, and he was handling between 100 and 150 magazines. Johannah Fleetwood, who worked in the billing department during the war, remembers it as a busy time.

There were a lot of dealers. Girls were always quitting to go see their boyfriends or husbands, especially in the billing department. Zella could really get on your tail sometimes, and she probably had to, to get that work done. If you didn't get your work done you were in trouble. They never paid overtime, you just had to get your work done in the time allowed. . . . during the war wages were frozen, so he couldn't raise us very much.

> But he used to give us maybe at Christmastime a little bonus, things like that. He would also send goodies while he was traveling.[14]

Barbara Sturgill, who also worked with Leo in the forties, remembers: "He paid as much as anyone did, during the war when they froze wages. . . . he felt bad about that, so he would appoint two girls every month, to put on a dinner party for the whole office, so we had a party every month."[15] There are a number of pictures that show Leo's staff all sitting down in party clothes to enjoy a meal together. Sometimes the parties would be held at his home; sometimes a dinner was a bigger event, a banquet at the Baker Hotel. Although most of the contact with the staff went through Zella, Leo tried to show his appreciation for the work that they were doing in the ways he could.

Leo arranged for the Old Oregon Trail Centennial Commission to meet in Baker over July 4 and 5. With the coming of war, the Miner's Jubilee had been discontinued, but Leo was still working to keep Baker or connections with Baker in the public eye. In October 1943, Leo went to the launching of the Liberty ship *Oregon Trail* at the Kaiser Shipyards in Portland, and he brought along Jane Fernald from Baker to act as a "maid of honor" at the launching.[16]

In 1944, Leo joined the board of the Baker Community Chest. The Community Chest was a cooperative organization of citizens and social welfare agencies in a city. The idea of cooperative collecting for charitable purposes originated in Liverpool, England, in 1873 and had its American start in Denver in 1887.[17] Also known as a united fund, the Community Chest had two purposes:

THE WAR YEARS

Planning for the Old Oregon Trail centennial were (from lower left) Philip Parrish, Charles Reynolds, Leo Adler, Francis Lambert and Walter Meacham. (Oregon Historical Society, OrHi 105023)

to raise funds through an annual campaign for its member agencies and to budget the funds raised. In Baker, the beneficiaries of the Chest fund at that time were the Boy Scouts, the Girl Scouts, and the Young Men's Christian Association (YMCA). When Leo joined the board, it was for a combination community chest and war bond drive. Never short on optimism, Leo said "I am confident that Baker County can and will raise its quota of $26,500 for the community war chest fund in one day."[18] Leo had started the campaign with special gifts totaling $8,000 and his goal was set at $10,000. It was one of many community-based fund-raising campaigns he would be a part of throughout his lifetime.

Leo was also involved in the politics of Oregon, but not in a public, obvious way. He supported candidates rather than any particular political party, although he was probably more inclined toward the Democrats. His brother Sanford and his wife Mary Louise were strong Democratic supporters. It was likely through the 1944 Oregon elections for the U.S. Senate that Leo Adler first came into contact with Wayne Morse and became a firm Morse supporter.

Wayne Morse started his political career as a Republican, became a Democrat, and then wound up his career as an Independent. Born in Wisconsin in 1900, Wayne Lyman Morse came to Oregon in 1929 to teach law in Eugene at the University of Oregon. An ambitious young man, he was made Dean of the Law School in 1930. In 1939 he was named Pacific Coast Arbitrator of all disputes between the ILWU (International Longshoremen's and Warehousemen's Union) and WEA (Waterfront Employer's Association) by Secretary of Labor Frances Perkins. In 1942 Morse was

A handbill that shows Leo's early interest in touting the "Old Oregon Trail." (Adler House Museum)

appointed to the twelve-person War Labor Board (WLB), and in 1944 he decided to run for the Senate.[19] Leo likely knew of Morse through his WLB work.

In January 1944, Morse announced that he was going to run as a Republican against incumbent Republican Senator Rufus C. Holman. Before deciding he was going to run as a Republican, Morse hadn't claimed any strong party affiliation. In 1938, he wrote to a former University of Wisconsin speech student of his, governor-elect Harold Stassen of Minnesota:

Senator Wayne Morse. (Oregon Historical Society, OrHi 90702)

> *I have always retained my membership in the Republican party because it has been impossible for me to swallow a good deal of the New Deal. At the same time, I have been unable to take to bed with me Hoover republicanism, with the result that I voted for Roosevelt in 1932 and again in 1936, and I shall vote for a Democrat again. . . .*[20]

It should be noted that this letter was written before he had been appointed Pacific Coast Arbitrator and to other positions of increasing responsibility by Democratic administrations.

Morse's decision to run as a Republican was a shrewd move.

In the early 1940s, the Oregon Democratic party was going in several different directions after tearing itself apart over the issue of public power in Oregon during the 1930s. Voting patterns from the thirties and forties showed that the Democratic Party could not pull itself together to support its party candidate. The state voted for Roosevelt, but continued to send Republican representatives to Congress.[21] If Morse could win the Republican primary, he had a good shot at becoming the next senator from Oregon.

Morse's opponent in the primary was Rufus Holman, a conservative Republican who was an isolationist. Isolationism was a popular stand in the 1930s, but a very unpopular one in the 1940s. Although he was ridiculed in the press as "Rattling," "Rampant," and "Raving" Rufus, he had a large following and had never lost an election.[22] Forward-looking Republicans wanted a new candidate, and so did Oregon's small but well-connected Jewish community. Holman had been an officer in the Ku Klux Klan during the 1920s, when it was very strong in Oregon, and was also thought to be anti-Semitic. While in the Senate he had voted against the liberalization of immigration laws that would make it easier for persecuted Europeans (many of whom would likely have been Jewish at that time) to come to America. Holman was also not the brightest bulb in the chandelier. When he was accused of being anti-Semitic, his response was "Anti-Semitic? Now why should I be anti-Semitic? My own father was an Englishman. I have relatives in England." The remark was quoted in the British magazine *The Economist*, likely with some glee.[23]

Morse won the Republican primary and then went on to trounce his Democratic opponent in the 1944 elections. He won every county in Oregon and he took Washington, D.C. by storm.

The War Years

Leo Adler's office staff, Feb. 1945. (Adler House Museum)

Senator Wayne Morse was an intelligent, articulate, and ambitious man who did not mind ruffling feathers; in fact, he rather enjoyed it. Leo Adler would call on him in Washington as a friend and supporter for many years to come, and Morse would visit Leo when he was in Baker.

On January 20, 1945, President Franklin Roosevelt delivered his fourth inaugural address. At 573 words, it was the shortest in the country's history. "We have learned that we must live as men and not as ostriches," he said. "We can gain no lasting peace if we approach it with suspicion and mistrust...or with fear."[24]

A photo taken of Leo Adler's staff in February 1945 shows a handsome group of twenty women and three men looking steadily into the camera. The smiles are small, the faces are strong. Most of them look as though they have just had a good laugh. Zella Smurthwaite stands in the back row, the second from the left. Barbara Sturgill, who had recovered from polio and come back to

137

work for Leo, stands tall in the back row with both hands on the chair in front of her (sixth from the right). Johannah Fleetwood, who was so happy to get a job with Leo in 1937, sits in the front row, second from the right. Leo sits solidly at the far left of the photo, with the blind office dog Nifty at his feet. To call it a portrait of Leo's working family is not too far off the mark. With this group of women and men, Leo kept his business going and growing through the war. They could likely get through whatever might be coming next.

Of course, no one could guess that what was coming next would be the death of the man who had led the country since 1933. On April 12, 1945, Franklin Delano Roosevelt died of a cerebral hemorrhage. Almost a year earlier, his health had been described by his cardiologist as "God-awful." Less than four hours after Roosevelt died, Harry Truman took the presidential oath.[25]

On April 20, 1945, just over a week after Roosevelt's death, a policy memorandum was prepared by the Research Institute Staff for executive members of the War Production Board on the topic of Victory in Europe (V-E) Day. A copy of the memorandum can be found in the collections of the Adler House Museum. The memo, written prior to V-E Day on May 8, 1945, looks at the prospects of demobilizing the war effort. The memo came with a letter that requested Leo's assistance on a tin and paper salvage drive to be held in September of that year.

The memo was put together so that business and industry throughout the country could plan for changes in business practices in the next several years. It provides an interesting look at the thinking of the time, especially under the section "When will Japan be defeated?"

> *Military and procurement plans are based on conservative estimates of at least a year following Germany's defeat. Privately, there is talk of planning for two or three years of Pacific war. But several recent developments, including denunciation of the Russo-Japanese Pact, have led to increasing questions whether Japan may not prefer unconditional surrender to unconditional destruction. The German object lesson may be persuasive.*
>
> *In your planning, assume at least a year between V-E and V-J Days; but keep in a corner of your mind the consequences of sudden Japanese surrender. Much of America's hope for stability rests on an extended period of half-war, half-peace. There is the certainty of severe business shock and deep unemployment if Japan gives up a lost cause in 1945.*[26]

After the bombing of Hiroshima and Nagasaki on August 6 and 9 respectively, the Japanese surrendered on August 15, 1945. So much for the year between V-E and V-J days. The war had ended, and the troops were coming home. On August 16, the War Production Board revoked many of its controls on industry. Gasoline rationing came to an abrupt end, and soon magazines were trumpeting reports of all sorts of consumer goods that had been hard to come by during the war.

As for the tin and paper drive, Leo supported it with an ad in the September 5, 1945, *Record-Courier* that stated "Leo Adler Magazine Specialist urges the fullest cooperation from everybody in this final paper and tin salvage drive." The war may have been won, but there were still chances for Baker citizens to come together and work for a good cause, and Leo always enjoyed finding a good rallying point for the community. Because they were now moving into a brand new era.

Finding the New Normal

While the United States was very happy to have the war completed and the troops coming home, no one knew quite what to expect next. For the past sixteen years, the country had been digging itself out of the Depression and then marshalling available energies for the war effort. Now that the war was over, things could go back to normal. But what was normal when you'd just been through the Depression and the Second World War?

Men and women came home from the war and from war work. Henry Levinger came home from San Francisco and brought his young bride Mary with him. They met in San Francisco at a cocktail party while she was working as a secretary for the head of Gallen Kamp Shoes and were married in 1944. Born in Imboden, Ark., Mary moved to California after a family mercantile business burned down in 1930. When Henry told Mary about winters in Baker, she couldn't imagine how people could live where it was so cold. But she grew to love the area as she became accustomed to it. Henry resumed control of Levinger Drug Company, which had been run by a druggist from Salt Lake City during the war.[1]

THE SPARK AND THE LIGHT:

Lois Cavallo arrived in Baker in December 1945. She was working at Columbia Aircraft in Portland when she enlisted in the Army in the spring of 1943 as a member of the Women's Army Corps (WACs). She worked as a sheet metal mechanic in Pratt, Kan., during the war and worked on the B-29s, which were the heaviest bombers.[2] Her mother was living in Baker at the time and Lois was waiting to see her brother who had not yet come home from overseas. She applied for work with Leo Adler; when he found out that she had been in the service, he was ready to hire her almost on the spot. Lois remembered him as very gung-ho and very patriotic. While Leo was undoubtedly patriotic, he may have also recalled reading a certain section from a War Production Board that mentioned seniority for women who had been involved with industrial war work:

> *Both management and unions (the latter less bluntly) will press for separate seniority systems for women—object, to push them out of industry. Unions which insisted on equal pay for equal work do not feel the same way about seniority. Women will be urged to give up jobs to returning veterans; as husbands return, some will be glad to.*[3]

Women who worked for Leo Adler were fortunate in that they did not need to fear being pushed out of their work by returning veterans. Less traditional jobs for that time may have paid more, but Leo's staff definitely had job security. Lois started work with Leo in January 1946.

In 1946, former Gov. Charles Sprague was serving as president of the Oregon War Chest and appointed Leo to a state advi-

From left: Leo Adler, Dr. Howard R. Driggs, Philip Parrish and Walter Meacham at a "story spot" along the Old Oregon Trail. (Oregon Historical Society OrHi 105024)

sory committee that would decide on the final disposition of the Oregon Chest.[4] Leo was also reappointed as a regional vice president of the Old Oregon Trail Association for Baker County. Already a life member of the association, as a regional vice president he would help in the marking of "story spots" from the area's history that could be used to attract tourist travelers from within the state and from the greater United States.[5] He recognized early that Baker's history was one of its strongest assets. In a manner that was more connected with commerce than politics, Leo was continuing his work as a voice of Baker on the state scene and increasing the bonds of good will people felt for him throughout the state.

In October 1947, Leo chaired two conventions that were held at Sun Valley, Idaho. The Bureau of Independent Publishers and

The Spark and the Light: The Leo Adler Story

Distributors attracted more than 400 of its members, and the Pacific Coast Independent Wholesalers Association also met there. They discussed a variety of issues, including the plans by various publishing houses to discontinue twenty-one magazines and the critical paper shortages that were expected to plague the industry for at least another year. Ron Savitt, a son of newspaper and magazine distributors who worked in Reno, Nev. from the 1930s to the 1970s, noted that "conventions are about commiseration." They were an opportunity to get away from the daily grind of the business. Savitt's parents enjoyed Leo very much and Savitt recalled "Leo had a reputation for giving a great party. I remember because I wasn't allowed to go."[6]

Leo was an excellent and a very engaged host, as an undated, unidentified magazine (likely an industry newsletter) showed in a photo spread of the convention. A spread of six photos shows Leo at various stages as a host and convention participant. One photo shows him sitting in a full bathtub in his underwear and hat with a caption that says "one too many visits to the taproom prompts Leo to decide to freshen up a bit. He forgot just a few details before submerging, as you will notice, but what's a hat and undershirt at a convention! While dousing on the soap he's making good resolutions a mile a minute. Everything strictly business from now—except, of course, for an occasional drink just to be sociable."[7]

The article makes various jokes about Leo's drinking; while the photographs may have been staged as a convention prank, what they were showing was not untrue. People who knew Leo at that time describe him as having a drinking problem or "liking to party," while others say that he didn't drink any more than anybody else did during that period in America, or that he didn't have a problem with alcohol—he simply couldn't hold his liquor.⁸

Former Baker Fire Chief Bob Young gained his first contact with Leo when he was a young man working in the fire department in the early 1940s. Kept out of the war by a knee injury, Young had many vivid memories of pulling Leo out of bars after closing time.

> *He might go into the Elks Lodge, or he might be at the Baker Hotel where they were having functions and he'd get carried away, and he was a friend of the firemen, and the firemen were his friends. Nobody fought with Leo. If he got out of hand, they'd call the Fire Department and we'd send somebody to get him. Take care of him.*⁹

Leo Adler serving as a congenial host. (Oregon Jewish Museum)

Leo's arrangement with the fire department must have been fairly well known among his colleagues in the magazine world, because in the photo spread that showed Leo composing himself after his dip in the bathtub, the caption reads, "A new man! Well, pretty new. If Leo met a fire engine on the street now he'd look the other way."[10]

At the time of the Sun Valley convention, Leo was fifty-two years old, single, the most successful businessman in Baker, and a well-respected citizen who had shouldered a larger portion of civic duty than many others in the town. There were very few bartenders or people in town who would have said no to Leo when he asked for a shot of Old Granddad whiskey, his preferred drink.[11] Just after the war and throughout most of the remaining century, a drink or two or three was often part of sealing a business deal or agreement. If Leo Adler wanted a drink, he could clearly make that choice for himself. And if he drank too much, there were folks in town that were willing to see that he made it home all right. Sometimes his brother Sanford would take on that chore, and sometimes he would let the fire department handle it. As Leo looked out for Baker, Baker and particularly the fire department looked out for Leo. Bob Young also had fond memories of the fire department receiving well-lubricated phone calls from Leo when he was on the road. Leo would call up and chat with whoever was on duty, and often would order up a steak dinner from the Baker Hotel for the crew and pay for it on his return.[12]

There were rumors that Leo's father Carl had had drinking problems and that Leo's drinking was a factor in Zella Smurthwaite's saying no to his proposal of marriage back in the 1920s.[13] Different women who worked with Leo in the office commented that they never saw Leo have any trouble with alcohol during the work day. If Leo did have difficulties with alcohol, he managed them in a way that didn't tarnish his business or his personal relations.

Leo's involvement with a variety of philanthropic causes continued to grow. In 1948, he was part of the board of directors for the Baker Community Chest and also headed up a special group for the sale of Christmas Seals, which supported the work of the tuberculosis association.

As the country slowly got back on its feet, Leo and his staff continued providing the service that his customers expected. After a three-week trip to three different conventions (wholesalers in Los Angeles, journal publishers in Colorado Springs, and druggists in Richfield, Utah) Leo mentioned that publishers were optimistic for the first time in several years with advertising sales looking up. Now the main worry was the rising cost of production.[15]

Leo did his part to help the industry keep costs in line by lobbying Senator Wayne Morse. In early 1949 a bill came before the House of Representatives suggesting an increase in the rate for second-class mail. In April 1949, Leo met with Senator Morse to discuss the possible increase. In correspondence found in the Wayne Morse Papers in the Special Collections and University Archives of the University of Oregon, there is a statement that Walter D. Fuller, president of the Curtis Publishing Company, made before the House Post Office and Civil Service Committee on March 16, 1949. According to Fuller's statement, section 2 of HR 2945 would triple mailing costs for second-class mail items. The correspondence between Leo and Senator Morse is an interesting window on Leo's lobbying skills.

Much of the correspondence was taken up with details such as "we'll meet at this place at this time," yet Leo slipped in carbon copies of information (such as Fuller's testimony) regarding what was happening with the postal increase bill. In an April 9, 1949, note written to Senator Morse on Baker County Chamber of Commerce stationery, Leo mentioned:

> *This is just to confirm that when Congress is out, and you know you are coming this way and can arrange to speak in Baker before the Chamber of Commerce and service clubs, you will get in touch with me so that I can arrange a suitable date.*
>
> *Too, if you can arrange to spend a day or two "out in the country" I would like to arrange that also.*[16]

Senator Morse responded on April 16:
I have the Fuller statement in my files for reference should the postal revenue bill come before the Senate. It doesn't appear too likely that the committee will report the bill during the present session, but, if it does, I am satisfied it will be in a greatly modified form.[17]

Leo continued to send Senator Morse updates throughout the year about the impact the second-class postal increase would have on the magazine business based on information he received from the National Association of Magazine Publishers. Morse responded politely but without a great deal of enthusiasm. In December 1949, Morse thanked Leo for a visit he had arranged.

This is just a short note to tell you how much I appreciate the wonderful meeting you had for me in Baker. I enjoyed meeting the people very much and hope that I may have another opportunity very soon.

I am leaving for Washington this afternoon, but hope to get back several times before the primary. If you ever get back to Washington, be sure to let me know you are coming.

Morse's response to Leo seems to warm up a great deal after he returns from his visit in Baker. It's hard to know if the change in tone was because of the charms of Baker or if it was because Morse was getting closer to the primaries for his Senate re-election campaign. The postal increase bill was now before the Senate as S 1103.

Leo continued his easy yet firm lobbying, and in early January 1950, the Executive Vice President of Pocket Books, Inc., Freeman Lewis, added his voice to the discussion.

Dear Senator Morse,
Leo Adler of Baker, Oregon has sent me a copy of your letter to him of January 2nd in reference to the postal rate bill. For whatever it may be worth I thought I would drop you a note, if only to convey a delayed "thank you" for the wonderful speech you gave at the booksellers convention several years ago.[18]

The soft touch appears to have had some effect because it brought Senator Morse out to Baker in the middle of winter. In a February 18, 1950, letter to Leo he mentioned, "You certainly did a swell job on the arrangements for my visit in Baker the other day. I thoroughly enjoyed the whole experience, and particularly the opportunity to have some time with you. Thanks a lot for all your kindnesses."

Leo responded with a note on February 24, 1950, and a seven-page letter that he may have sent out to his clients in an effort to raise their awareness of S 1103. The letter is typed on *Leo Adler, Magazine Specialist* stationery. Leo may have composed it himself, or it may have been composed by an industry trade group such as the National Association of Magazine Publishers. In the letter, he says that "Senate Bill S 1103 which is to come up for debate very shortly, threatens, I believe to revolutionize basic policy of this country. I think it is necessary for me to point the dangers that will arise if such a bill is finally passed." Leo states that the low second-class rate for postage was developed so that through their publications, publishers could disseminate information, news, and educational material to people throughout the country at a price the public could afford and at a cost to the publishers that would allow large distribution of their periodicals and still leave them a reasonable profit. Leo then points to the work of the War Advertising Council and the publicity publishers gave to it for the sale of war bonds, all of which were heavily oversubscribed. He mentions the many other drives that publishers supported such as rationing and conservation of food and paper, saying that they met with great success because of the publicity given to these causes by the publishers.

On page two of the letter, one paragraph shows that the country was moving into a new phase in its postwar development.

With many subversive attacks on our way of life from the outside and the growing problems of every day living for our people, problems of government, national safety, business, health and economic security becoming more complex day by day, the dissemination of information and news on all these subjects is more necessary now than ever before.

That the magazine publishers are performing the public service of disseminating this information can be clearly seen in the pages of almost any national periodical.[19]

In the phrase "subversive attacks on our way of life" Leo quickly alludes to what had been going on nationally. Since 1947, the House Committee on Un-American Activities had been holding hearings on Communist activity in Hollywood. This led to the blacklisting of various writers, directors and actors. Soon the hunt for Communists made its way to Washington, D.C., with Senator Joseph McCarthy leading the charge. As he said in his note, Leo felt that the best way to guard against "subversive attacks" was through the "dissemination of information and news." The bill to raise second-class postage was sent to committee, where it was tabled and never voted on. Leo went to Washington, D.C. in early May to act as Baker's representative to the national Chamber of Commerce Annual meeting. The theme of the annual meeting was "Perform Something Worthy to be Remembered."[20] In May 1950, Wayne Morse once again won the Republican primary in Oregon and it appears he had strengthened his friendship with Leo. In a June 2 letter, he says:

Before returning to Washington within the next few days, I want to let you know how much I appreciate your support of my candidacy during the recent primary election.

> *It was certainly wonderful of you to give me so much financial assistance, as well as so much of your time during the primary campaign. You never will know how much I appreciate all you have done for me.*
>
> *This has been a very dirty campaign and the way my friends rallied around to support me has meant a great deal to me. Thanks again, Leo, for your loyalty.*[21]

Leo responded with a warm letter of his own, and also mentioned that on his last visit to Washington, "I talked to several regarding Truman's visit to Baker and they gave me a number of ideas."[22] While in the West for the opening of the Grand Coulee Dam, the train carrying President Harry Truman stopped in Baker on May 11. In his speech to the crowds at Baker, President Truman mentioned that he hoped to return in the near future, so Leo may have been angling for that next visit.[23] Any hopes of a future visit were quashed when North Korea invaded South Korea on June 25, 1950, and President Truman became occupied with the Korean "police action," as he initially described it. Polls taken at the time showed that almost three-quarters of the American public supported involvement in the Korean War.[24]

Proving that promoting Baker was always uppermost in his thoughts, Leo served later that year as an advisor to the planning committee for the Oregon State Federation of Young Republicans convention, which was held in Baker in early September. It brought 250 conventioneers to Baker, including the chairman of the Republican National Committee, Guy Gabrielson.[25] In the November elections, Senator Morse easily won re-election.

In September that year a new bishop took over the diocese of

Baker, a diocese that went from Oregon's eastern border to The Dalles and south to the southern boundaries of the state, an area of 68,000 square miles. Bishop Francis P. Leipzig was not a complete newcomer to the community of Baker. Born on June 29, 1895, just eight days after Leo, his family moved to Baker in 1911 so that his father could start work as a brewmaster for a local brewery. Enrolled in the St. Francis Academy of Milwaukee, Wisconsin, Francis spent the summer of 1911 as a working visit in Baker where he assisted with serving daily Mass at St. Francis Cathedral before he enrolled in the Mount Angel Seminary at Mount Angel, Ore., in 1913. Whether he and Leo knew each other during that time is uncertain, but they may have met in later years either when Father Leipzig was elected chaplain of the Fire Chiefs of Oregon (a position he held for the rest of his life) or through his interest in school athletics throughout the state. Father Leipzig advocated the separation of large high schools and smaller ones into two separated leagues in order to equalize competition. In 1934 a "B" basketball tournament was developed for schools with enrollments of 150 or less. By the time he came to Baker, he was considered the father of "B" basketball. Father Leipzig also had an abiding interest in history and in 1939, the same year that Leo was in charge of the Miner's Jubilee in Baker, Father Leipzig was in charge of the centennial celebration of the coming of the first priests to the Northwest. Bishop Leipzig's installation as Bishop was described as follows:

> *Thus for the third time in 47 years a successor to the apostles was endowed with supreme authority to rule, guide and care for the flock scattered over the monotonous plains of Eastern*

The Spark and the Light: The Leo Adler Story

Oregon grey with sagebrush and brown with sun-burned grass. It was a day of rejoicing for both clergy and laity for once more they had a chief shepherd of souls in their midst.[26]

While it is doubtful that Leo would have been at the installation of Bishop Leipzig, he would have been well aware that a new bishop was coming to Baker, since the St. Francis Cathedral was about two blocks from his home. Leo and the bishop wasted no time in rekindling a friendship. Mary Ann Davis, who served as secretary to Bishop Leipzig from 1951 to 1971, remembers that when they were both in town, Leo, the bishop, and other Baker citizens would meet every day at the coffee shop in the Baker Hotel. It was a simple, low-key way to find out what was going on around town.[27] In March 1951, both Leo and Bishop Leipzig attended the Oregon State Community Chest meeting in Salem, where Bishop Leipzig delivered the main address. They would continue to share civic interests for many years.

Leo was also involved with new concerns. After Carl Adler's death in 1918, contact with the German branch of the family appears to have stopped. While the connection with the German Adlers may have stopped before World War II, it is hard to imagine that those German relatives didn't enter Leo and Sanford's thoughts occasionally. Baker residents such as the Neuberger brothers, Bert, Hans, and Gerson (Gert), as well as Herman David, had all escaped from Germany before the war. The knowledge of what happened to so many Jews during the Second World War would strongly affect Leo's interests and philanthropy in years to come.

On May 14, 1948, Israel proclaimed itself a state and the

United States immediately recognized the new nation. In late 1947, some polls said that over 80 percent of the American people were in favor of the creation of such a homeland.[28]

The newly recognized State of Israel was economically exhausted. Holocaust survivors and displaced persons flooded there by the tens of thousands. Its treasury was empty, its economy was in danger of collapse, and its already meager resources were drained. The government of Israel needed to find a way to raise capital for its continued survival and decided to bring the idea of Israel Bonds to the American public. In October 1950, Israel's future prime minister Golda Meir met with American Jewish leaders in Washington, D.C. to lay plans for launching Israel's first bond issue in the United States. In 1951, the Development Corporation for Israel was created to offer the securities in the United States. That May, Prime Minister David Ben-Gurion launched the Israel Bond sales drive in the United States. He arrived in New York on the third anniversary of Israel's statehood and officially launched the Israel Bond Organization at a rally in Madison Square Garden. A coast-to-coast tour followed and $52.6 million in bond sales was generated for Israel in that first offering.[29] Leo was an early and avid investor in Israel Bonds. While he had many other investments in various stocks and bonds at this point in his life, he had a strong sense of connection with this particular investment. In much the same way that war bonds had allowed Americans to find their way to connect with the war effort, Israel bonds allowed a Jewish gentleman from Baker to be part of building the state of Israel. This was not a handout; it was an investment in the country's future, and those were the type of investments Leo believed in.

Leo's Jewish heritage was important to him. Although he'd had no religious education, he maintained his Jewish connections on a statewide level, collecting for the United Jewish Appeal and encouraging others to invest in Israel Bonds. Herschel Tanzer, who worked for the Anti-Defamation League of Oregon for many years, remembers meeting Leo regularly when he would travel through eastern Oregon. Leo would find out what news Tanzer had to share and Tanzer would find out what Leo knew. Leo kept track of what was happening with the Oregon and Idaho Jewish communities.[30]

Leo also maintained an active connection with his heritage as an Oregonian, and most specifically with his heritage as an eastern Oregonian. He understood the importance of history to Baker when he was chairman of the Baker Miner's Jubilee in 1939 and 1940, and he constantly touted Baker's history as only one of its many charms when he was traveling around the country and the state. In 1943 he was elected vice president of the Oregon Council of American Pioneer Trails Association. In 1952, Baker served as the final stop for the 100th Anniversary of the Covered Wagons of 1852, and Leo Adler was chairman for the Baker event. On July 14, Dr. Howard Driggs of New York, president of the American Pioneer Trails Association, led an automobile caravan from St. Joseph, Mo., which arrived in Baker on Sunday, August 3. There were speeches and historical presentations, and the next day guests visited the extensive antique collection at Langrell's Trading Post in Haines; later, six monuments erected to commemorate pioneer travel through Baker were visited and rededicated. On Tuesday, at a luncheon given at the Hotel Baker for one hundred guests, Dr. Driggs presented an oil painting of Col. Edward Dickinson

Baker, for whom Baker County was named.³¹ Leo was also a longtime supporter of the Oregon Historical Society and in 1955 became a member of its board of directors. He would become a lifetime member and was always very proud of his connection with the organization.

Leo's civic and business interests coincided easily when he attended a Salem luncheon in 1953 that was sponsored by the national travel magazine *Holiday*. The occasion for the lunch was the magazine's feature on Oregon in its June 1953 issue, written by H.L. Davis, author of the classic Oregon novel *Honey in the Horn*. Governor Paul L. Patterson, Secretary of State Earl Newbry, and Treasurer Sig Unander were all in attendance, as were state highway officials and chamber of commerce and magazine representatives. Describing Oregon as a bridge state—meaning it was a place people traveled through to get to California, Washington, or British Columbia—Governor Patterson said, "the average tourist spends $35 a day, and if we do our selling job, the tourists will spend an extra day or two in Oregon. That would mean a tremendous increase in our tourist business, which already is the third largest industry in the state."

As Governor Patterson raved about beautiful photos of Hells Canyon that were part of the magazine's photo spread, Leo took the opportunity to find out exactly when the Governor would next be traveling to Baker. While it is unlikely that Leo thought of Oregon as a place to go through to get somewhere else, he said that he expected 3 million people to read the article.³² For the good work that he did in carrying the "Baker County Tourist message through out the state and nation," the Baker Motel Association honored him in 1954, saying, "He demonstrates enthusiasm, bounce and ability in spreading the good will of Baker."[33]

Leo also continued to display enthusiasm and bounce about his industry. At the September 1954 Central States Distributors Association convention in Glenwood Springs, Colo., he was among eighteen men and two women who were honored as people who had "come of age" in the magazine and newspaper distribution business. It was fitting that a representative of the Curtis Publishing Company, Joseph Mitchell, served as master of ceremonies for the event. Leo was honored as the first wholesaler in the United States to galley pre-date newspapers, which meant that he would write up advance orders from the dealers for certain newspapers and then send the order to the publisher. This was the galley. The publisher would then send the newspaper directly to the dealer so he would receive the paper in the quickest manner. Leo did galley pre-dating for the *Chicago Tribune*, the *San Francisco Examiner*, and the *Denver Post*, and his innovation put him out ahead of other wholesalers. The fact that he started a galley business with many of the small towns around the Baker area was also cited as an important step forward for his thriving business.[34]

In November 1954, Leo saw a long-time acquaintance join Wayne Morse in the Oregon Senate delegation. Richard Neuberger, a freelance journalist by trade, writing for a wide range of the magazines that Leo sold (*Holiday, American Heritage* and the *Saturday Evening Post*), and a recent member of the Oregon State Senate, became Oregon's newest senator. Leo's low-key yet firm political influence would continue to do good work for Baker.

The year 1955 marked Leo's fiftieth year in magazine distribution. The Curtis Publishing Company sent him an award to commemorate their golden anniversary of working together. The award included a pencil portrait of Leo and the following inscription in calligraphy: "Congratulations on your Golden anniversary 1905–1955. Fastest in history of independent distribution. Newsboy 1904, Wholesale distributor 1905. Several years later, friend Leo discovered that records were not phonograph records and has maintained an efficient operation."[35] At fifty years in business, Leo commanded a level of respect in his industry that might have astounded his fellow Bakerites. When asked to describe what it was like working with Leo, employee Lois Cavallo said,

> *He was honest. He treated people fair. He never gave one girl a raise without giving everyone a raise. And the raise was always the same amount. And those are the two things that I appreciated most. He was just very honest and fair. He was a good employer. Well, he was probably the most honest man I've ever met.*

Leo was known for his integrity. On the occasion of another award, a colleague in the business, Norman Bay, sent him a telegram saying, "My finest compliment to Leo comes from my father. 'You won't need a written contract, Leo's word is good.'" Of course, there were always new magazines to sell, such as *Mad* magazine in 1952, *Playboy* and *TV Guide* in 1953, and *Sports Illustrated* in 1954. He and his staff provided excellent service. He was an honest and fair businessman to his clients and staff. After fifty years in the business, he might have been forgiven for taking it for granted, but he never did. Service was always his first priority.

The award given to Leo Adler to commemorate fifty years in magazine distribution. (Adler House Museum)

Airplanes, Fire, and an Ambulance

On his fiftieth anniversary in the magazine distribution business, Leo Adler was a tremendously successful businessman. A congenial and open man, he was a quiet person and physically he didn't cut a very imposing figure. He was square in stature, solidly built, and quite bald. He favored horn-rimmed glasses. His face had a gentle demeanor, yet his eyes didn't appear to miss much. He didn't lavish money on his personal appearance or on his home, a fact that people around town commented on. Norma and Ralph Giles recalled his appearance:

> *You wouldn't believe the way he dressed. To have the money he had, he could have had a fine wardrobe. . . . Sanford had a little more style. Sanford was tall and slender.*
>
> *Leo went into Levingers one day in one of these tacky suits and was talking to Henry. There happened to be a salesman in there who had come in to take an order for something, and he was watching Henry talk to Leo and after Leo left, he went up to Henry and said, "Was that guy putting the touch on you for*

some money?" and Henry looked at him and said, "No, that happens to be the wealthiest man in town. He could buy and sell me." The salesman couldn't believe it and said, "Well, he looks like a bum."[1]

When Leo got a little too absent-minded about his apparel or appearance, his office manager Zella Smurthwaite would let him know that it was really time to take that tie or that shirt to the cleaner.[2] One of his few indulgences was going to the barber every day for a shave.

He continued to live in the family home his father bought in 1899 on 2305 Main Street. Although it was a splendid two-story Italianate home, Leo lived only on the first floor, primarily in the back rooms where the kitchen, his office, and his bedroom were located. One friend laughingly referred to Leo's home as his "one-room shack."[3] It was said that after his mother's death in 1933, he never went up to the second floor again. Electricity was never run to that floor, which may be one reason why he didn't go there, but he certainly could have run electricity there if he was interested. Leo's father Carl passed away in 1918 and his mother Laura followed in 1933; it seems that the intervening years of her life (and the lives of the others in the house) might have been made more comfortable by electricity on the upper floor. Perhaps the family was reluctant to take on that expense during the thirties, although they could have easily shouldered the cost. Throughout his life, it's hard to know if Leo was suspicious of technological changes or if he was just extremely careful with his money.

Many of the members of Leo's staff recall going over to his home for potlucks and opening the sliding, pocket doors to the dining room and living room, or front parlor. Leo would occasionally bring in publishers' representatives or road men for a nightcap, but he preferred to do most of his entertaining in the restaurants and clubs of Baker or Haines. He was especially fond of the Baker Hotel, and during the fifties he enjoyed playing the slot machines in the lobby.[4] The Haines Steakhouse was also popular, and he enjoyed showing out-of-town visitors Baker County's hospitality. He was part of a lively group of friends: Elizabeth Baer, Sanford and Marian Heilner, Henry and Mary Levinger, and his brother Sanford and his wife Louise. Zella Smurthwaite was often his dinner companion. Several people who knew Leo commented that he truly appreciated the company of women and that he never met a woman he didn't think was good-looking.[5] If Leo had relations with other women in Baker or outside the community, he was discreet about it, as were the women involved and the other members of the community.

Leo considered himself a great judge of people. Ralph Giles worked for Leo in a variety of capacities, often acting as a driver so that Leo could visit dealers in the area, since Leo was by several accounts not an attentive driver. Once, while the two of them were in Sun Valley having supper at the Challenger Inn, Leo saw an exceptionally handsome man across the room. Leo nudged Ralph and said "See that man over there, I bet he's a movie star."

Ralph acknowledged that he was a very good-looking man but didn't think he was a movie star.

Leo said, "Yeah, he's a movie star."

Ralph said, "No, I don't think so."

"Well, I bet you he is." said Leo. He sauntered over to the man and bought him a drink. After a while he came back to join Ralph and said, "You should have bet me. You'd have won. He's a Cream of Wheat salesman."[6]

Leo enjoyed his life and the things his business had secured for him, even though he was famously stingy with himself. He was an investor in the stock market, but he was by no means a speculative investor. Leo once said to one of the bankers he worked with in later life, "I never understood the stock market so I've never sold anything."[7] If he bought a stock, he held onto it. The stock investments that he made tended to cluster around his knowledge of the magazine industry or his knowledge of local Northwest industries. It would be a misstatement to say that he was an emotional investor, but his heart definitely informed what his head did with regard to his investment choices. With the exception of the Israel Bonds, which served a different interest for him, he believed in keeping his investments local and supporting Oregon and the Northwest to the extent that was possible.

During the fifties, the northwest retailing legend Fred Meyer asked Leo to run the magazine sections of the various Fred Meyer stores, a large chain of stores throughout Oregon and later the northwest that became known for "one-stop shopping."[8] Fred Meyer's wife, the former Eva Chatfield, had spent her youth in Baker, where her family ran a local laundry. Born in Muskegon, Mich., in 1882, she made her way to Baker with her family, and she came to Portland in 1911. There were rumors that Leo introduced her to her future husband, although newspaper accounts of her life say that they met in a delicatessen in Portland. Her marriage to Fred Meyer, a second marriage for her, occurred in 1920; she worked right alongside him as he set up his first Fred Meyer store in 1922, eventually becoming secretary-treasurer of the Fred Meyer Corporation. Fred Meyer was credited with opening the first self-service drugstore in 1929. At that time, a customer walked into a drugstore and was waited on by a clerk, who would retrieve the desired aspirin or cough syrup and then often try to sell the customer additional goods. The whole process irked Fred Meyer. Watching patrons find and check out the books they wanted at the public library, he wondered why the same concept of self-service couldn't work in a grocery store or a drug store. It worked quite well, and by 1949 his one store and one-stop shopping had grown to fifteen stores in Oregon.[9]

Running the magazine and book sections of the Fred Meyer stores would have been a huge step in Leo's business, but it would have meant relocation to Portland. Leo thought about the offer, but decided that if he stayed in Baker, he might be able to attract other businesses to the area. Just as his father had discovered almost sixty years earlier, Leo decided that the best way for him to move forward was to stay in the same place. He had a solid reputation among his customers and he was providing employment for about twenty. If Leo was a restless soul, the amount of traveling he did for his work probably fed that part of him, and while he was by no means a homebody, he knew that he was deeply rooted in and deeply connected to the community. He drew a great deal of strength from Baker. And at the age of sixty he understood that very well.

Leo never seemed to rest on his laurels. He was actively involved with the Chamber of Commerce's program and convention committee, organizing goodwill trips for the Chamber to various smaller towns in Baker County such as Halfway and Brownlee. He continued his interest in keeping the communities of Baker County connected. He helped arrange a meeting of magazine wholesalers in Baker that brought 250 publishers and wholesalers to town in 1955, perhaps to commemorate his fifty years in the business.[10] In 1956, he became a member of the Council for Independent Distribution, a new association for independent wholesalers who delivered a wide range of periodicals. Its mission was to represent the interests of 825 distributors. And Leo Adler, with fifty years of experience, had become a charter member of the organization.[11]

His travels for business continued, and he shared what he saw and heard with the members of the community. In early January 1958, Leo returned from a national magazine convention in Little Rock, Ark., where he had heard Governor Wayne Faubus address the convention. In September 1957, Governor Faubus had ordered National Guard troops to surround Central High School in Little Rock, to, as he put it, maintain law and order at the school. In reality the troops were there to keep the nine black students from entering. By entering the school, those children would be desegregating the school in accordance with the 1954 Supreme Court ruling on *Brown v. The Board of Education of Topeka*. President Eisenhower eventually sent 1,100 troops into Little Rock and federalized the Arkansas National Guard, which removed it from the command of Governor Faubus. Television cameras and print media sent images around the globe of an angry white mob taunting the children and their escorts.[12] After hearing Governor Faubus speak during the January convention, the *Record-Courier* described Leo as expressing the feeling that "there is a sharp difference in support which the governor apparently has within his own state and the unfavorable impression he makes on outsiders because of his policies." Leo indicated that Faubus's speech was not well received by the journalists and publishers at the convention. While he was in Little Rock, Leo took time to visit with Captain and Mrs. Cam Vermillion, former Bakerites who were now stationed at the Little Rock Army base.[13] Leo always made a point of connecting with former Baker citizens whenever he could in his travels.

On a trip to Washington, D.C., in May of that year, Leo attended the national U.S. Chamber of Commerce convention to pick up a third-place fire safety award for Baker. Ever the diligent advocate for his industry and his city, Leo also took time during that visit to talk with Senator Wayne Morse about the new postal rate bill.[14] Although the outline of Leo's business continued as it had for the past fifty years, some details were changing. A postal rate hike was going into effect on January 1, 1959, and publishers and distributors were looking for ways of getting their product to consumers other than through the mail. It would be a prime topic of discussion at the Chicago publishing industry conventions Leo would be attending in late September 1958. This time rates clearly seemed to be heading upward. Leo could see that the world was changing

A newspaper clipping of Leo Adler commending his civic service. (Oregon Jewish Museum)

around him, but his immediate world would change much more by the end of the year.

Fresh from receiving the award for fire safety, the Chamber of Commerce budget committee recommended to the city budget committee that two additional full-time firemen be added to the fire department. The Civil Service Board, which included Leo as one of its three members, had also made this suggestion.[15] The budget committee took it under advisement, but took no real action on the recommendation.

On December 2, 1958, Baker was preparing itself for the holiday season. Leo's business was on the upper floor of the First National Bank building on Main Street. The building was adjacent to Levinger's Drugs, which was located in the middle of the Main Street block between Washington and Broadway. Henry Levinger remembered the day.

> We were just ready for Christmas. We had all our displays up and I had just gone home for dinner. It was about 6:30 or 7:00 and the fire whistle blew and we never did know what started it. We had an incinerator in the basement. They thought that might have been it, but by the time I got up there, twenty minutes later, the building was just gone. It was the biggest fire Baker ever had. You could see it for thirty miles away with all the alcoholic products and the inflammable material. . . . It just blew the roof off.[16]

Ralph Giles remembered the fire with special clarity. He had just started work with Henry Levinger two weeks earlier. He remembered watching the fire burn. "Brand new job and the business burned up. I'd just moved from working with Leo. The new one burned down, now where am I going? Henry didn't miss a beat. He had the business going the next day. He had a temporary building and we were taking in freight like mad."[17]

The losses from the fire were estimated at $500,000. Over 50 firemen and six fire trucks kept the blaze from destroying the bank building. Henry Levinger lost $200,000 worth of stock, but he sprang into action. He sent wires to the drug companies Squibb, Lilly, and Parke-Davis and told them to send open stock. He then phoned McKeeson & Robbins and Northwest Drug in Portland and asked them to send open stock. There was a vacant building on First Street. Henry Levinger and his employees soon had sheets of plywood up on sawhorses, and within three days, prescriptions were being filled. Ultimately, they did almost as much business in December 1958 as in December 1957, an astounding accomplishment. A contractor, Harvey Witham, was immediately engaged to rebuild and expand the building on its former site. Henry asked if he could have it built by April. Witham said he could do it if it was a mild winter. Fortunately, it was one of the mildest on record.[18]

Leo's work world was turned upside-down by the fire. While his offices were not burned down as Henry Levinger's were, they were so smoke-damaged that he and his staff could not return to them. It must have been a shattering event for him, particularly if his mind was wandering back to the stories his father must have told him about the great Astoria fire. By the time Leo found out about the fire, there was nothing he could do. A friend of Zella Smurthwaite's who lived nearby took him in and tried to help him steady his nerves with a drink, and soon Leo was in no shape to help sort things out. Zella was furious with her friend for giving Leo a drink in the first place, and she was furious with Leo for not staying sober at such a critical time and taking charge of things. She set the wheels in motion toward finding another building for the staff.[19]

The vacant Knights of Pythias building (or K-P building, as many of the staff called it) became the company's new home. Leo had been a member of the non-sectarian Knights of Pythias Lodge longer than any other of his fraternal organizations. In an oral history, Leo remembered that although the fire was still burning at eight the next morning, his new office in the K-P building was operating at nine o'clock. By five o'clock in the evening, the phones were reconnected and they were back in business. Leo received calls from all over the Northwest. The office staff came into work the next morning ready to dive into the process of cleanup.[20]

Norma Giles, a niece of Zella Smurthwaite's who worked in the office, remembered cleaning up after the fire:

> *Most of Leo's files were okay except a lot of the stuff was wet. In those days, you sent a stack of magazines out to a dealer and when you got the new issue, you tore the cover off the old ones and sent it into Leo and Leo credited him and Leo sent it into the publisher and he got credit. Well, a lot of those covers got wet and the gal [Elizabeth Yeakley] that was in charge of that took them home. They had an empty garage and she laid them out all over the garage so that they could dry, and then she counted them and sent them in for credit.[20]*

Airplanes, Fire, and an Ambulance

The whole staff worked hard to keep things running smoothly, and aside from the immense initial shock of the fire, the business continued as it had before. Henry Levinger rebuilt and expanded his drugstore in the same location. While buying a building would seem like a reasonable investment at that time, Leo wasn't interested in buying property. He was happy to let someone else deal with maintenance and upkeep, and "Leo Adler, Magazine Wholesaler" stayed happily at the K-P building for the rest of its existence. This is not to say that Leo didn't make some changes in his business. In August 1959, his shipping department began working out of new quarters in the former Empire Theatre building. With six men working in the shipping department, the new space provided room to receive a wide range of books and magazines. A conveyor arrangement helped speed the fulfillment of orders, and there were facilities for bundling, weighing, and invoicing for the thousands of dealer packages that went out daily to towns throughout the intermountain west.[22]

The 1960 edition of *Who's Who in Magazine Distribution* described the challenges to independent wholesalers, who now

> *. . . staggered under the sheer physical weight of handling more magazines and books than their warehouses had ever held before. Employees were hired, trucks were added and new systems developed, until the last physical challenge was successfully met. . . . Today at the start of a new decade, Independent Distribution faces a set of problems of an entirely different nature. Shifting populations, new patterns of retail selling, subscriptions, censorship, rising costs, the special problems of retailing paperbound books—all of these remain.*

The same *Who's Who* gave a snapshot of Leo's business accounts. The business was listed as Baker News Agency at that time; the article shows that Leo was working with 1,142 dealers ranging through Colorado, Idaho, Montana, Nebraska, Eastern Oregon, Utah, and Wyoming. There were twenty-five full-time and three part-time employees, and two trucks. His range of accounts broke down this way.

> Drugstore chain.................20
> Tobacco/Confectionery...............10
> Independent Drugstores 600
> Sports/Hobby.................3
> Stationery Stores.................15
> Bus Terminals 2
> Supermarket...................35
> Military.....................1
> Independent Grocery Stores..... 99
> Others.......................317
> Hotel /Motel..................13
> City (not reshipped)........... 28

The entry also shows the range of organizations he was affiliated with, which included Oregon United Appeal, Fire Civil Service Commission, the Salvation Army, Boy Scouts, Baker County Chamber of Commerce, American Pioneers Association, United Jewish Appeal, Anti-Defamation League, Israel Bonds, and Kiwanis.

While Leo was keeping up with his industry in his new facilities, he was also working to see that Baker maintained its connections with the state and the rest of the region. Reliable air service was a key component in maintaining that connection. As early as April 1951, Leo took time to get his picture taken with other city

Leo Adler worked hard to maintain air service to Baker. He stands at the foot of the stairs with this group of Baker businessmen, ready to promote travel between Baker and Boise. Baker Democrat Herald *photo, April 2, 1962.* (Oregon Historical Society, OrHi 104906)

luminaries as they gathered to commemorate a twenty-fifth anniversary of air mail.[24] Leo worked hard to bring reliable air service to Baker because it was necessary to the efficient running of his business and also made conducting his civic interests easier. It was a struggle he would put his shoulder to for the next several decades.

In April 1959, Leo represented Baker at a meeting of Civil Aeronautics Board (CAB) officials in Washington, D.C. West Coast Airlines and Frontier Airlines were both looking to extend their service to Salt Lake City. As a member of the Chamber of Commerce's Aviation committee, he thought the extension of service would aid Baker in retaining its air service when a CAB hearing was held in the future.[25] He was trying to keep all the possibilities open for Baker.

Leo was still interested in bringing a range of visitors to town. As chairman of the state "B" Basketball tournament committee, he helped bring a crowd into Baker during the late winter months, not usually a time when people were thinking about traveling to eastern Oregon. In 1960, with the aid of Baker High School Athletic Director Leo Compton and Oden Hawes, secretary for the Oregon school activities association that was the sponsoring organization, Leo helped bring the tournament to Baker March 10–12. There were six games over a three-day period with season tickets going for $5 for adults and $2.50 for students.[26] Plans were also afoot to honor Bishop Francis Leipzig as one of the original members of the state board that had started the tournament twenty-five years earlier. The tournament in Baker would mark the tournament's silver jubilee.[27]

Not surprisingly, there were occasions when "Mr. Baker" did get fed up with the way things were going in the town. There was a clear example of it just two weeks after the announcement about bringing the "B" Basketball tournament to Baker. In early February 1960, Leo and Bishop Francis Leipzig, two of the three-member Civil Service Commission, resigned from it. Leo was not in the habit of resigning from anything, and as a chairman of the commission, it was a bold move for him. On February 8, the city council moved that the three-member Civil Service Commission should expand to a five-member commission. When asked why they should expand the commission, one of the council members replied that with five men instead of three, one man couldn't buttonhole the other two members into a decision. In a statement about his resignation, Leo said that for the past several years, the Civil Service Commission felt its work was handicapped by a lack of cooperation from some members of the City Council. For example, the commission had recommended the addition of two more firemen for several years in a row, but no action had been taken. Leo had been a long-time friend of the fire department, but the fire that had affected him so recently likely solidified his already strong feelings of support for the department. In what may have been an end run around the Civil Service Commission, the City Council did not discuss the addition of two more members with the current members. It was likely this perceived insult that tipped the balance for Leo to resign. He finished his statement by saying, "I hope with my resignation some of the city councilmen will forget their personal grudges against the fire department."[28]

While the decisions of the City Council irritated Leo at that time, he didn't appear to dwell on them. He had other things to think about with potential changes in air service to Baker. In March 1960, Leo called together the members of the Chamber of Commerce aviation committee to inform them that there would be a pre-hearing conference in Washington, D.C., on March 31 regarding West Coast Airlines service for Baker. As he had predicted back in 1958, West Coast Airlines was looking to make changes in its service agreements in Baker, La Grande, and Ontario. Hearings were scheduled before the Civil Aeronautics Board. As chairman of the Aviation Committee and as one of the Baker's citizens most strongly affected by reliable air transportation, Leo wanted to make sure that Baker retained what air service it had. It was a slow process that would drag into the following year.

In April 1961, the Baker County Chamber of Commerce prepared a resolution that opposed the federal government's involvement in education. The chamber wanted Leo, who was at that time a member of the U.S. Chamber of Commerce Policy Committee, to present this resolution to the committee and to the Oregon congressional delegation when he went to Washington, D.C. for the Chamber's annual convention in May. The resolution stated:

> *The federal government must not dictate standards or goals of education and thus usurp the functions of the state. Neither should it give direct financial aid to state educational programs, for to give such aid inevitably causes the individual to shirk his responsibility.*

The Baker Chamber believed that the federal government's role should be to:

> *Awaken every citizen in every community to the fact that support of schools is a local and state function based on the individual's responsibility, to inform every citizen of the nationwide set of goals fixed by local groups and continuously to urge every citizen to meet that responsibility.*[29]

Such a statement coming from any American Chamber of Commerce in 1961 was a reference to the desegregation laws that the federal government was wrestling with at that time. It is not known what Leo's feelings were about the resolution, but he would have been presenting it to the Chamber of Congress and the Oregon Congressional delegation just before the first Freedom Rides were leaving from Washington, D.C., on May 4, 1961. On May 14, one Freedom Ride bus was fire-bombed in Anniston, Ala., and the other was met by Klansmen with lead pipes, baseball bats, and bicycle chains in Birmingham.

On May 12, the *Democrat-Herald* ran an article in which Leo reported that during his visit to Washington, D.C. he found people in high places worried about the gravity of the world situation, and that there was talk that "anything could happen."[30] The newspaper article didn't report the reaction of the Congressional delegations or the Chamber of Commerce's response to the resolution that Leo had brought to them. Leo did mention that there was "complete harmony" in the Oregon congressional delegation.

In late May, Leo went to a Civil Aeronautics Board hearing in Seattle with Bard Johnson, a representative of the city, and Dr. Don Campbell of the airport commission. Leo left for the hearing early. Because the West Coast Airlines schedule would have kept them away from Baker for three days, the other two decided to fly by local charter plane, which got them to Seattle and back on the same day.[31] One hearing proceeded to another, this time in Baker in late July. Leo enlisted the assistance of a young attorney he had come to know through his work on the Chamber of Commerce. Idaho-born and a graduate of the University of Oregon Law School, Gene Rose came to Baker in 1953 to practice law with the Grant and Fuchs law firm. The firm represented Leo, but Rose knew him primarily from Chamber of Commerce work.

In the sixties, the codes of ethics of various professions did not allow their members to advertise their services except in a very limited and dignified way. Many doctors, lawyers, accountants, and engineers throughout the United States made community contacts through their activities in organizations such as the Chamber of Commerce, Kiwanis, or Rotary Club. Businessmen and professionals got to know each other and also had the opportunity to work together on a variety of projects that were of benefit to the greater community. It was one of the reasons Leo Adler had joined so many organizations as a young man and also why he stayed active. It gave those involved a more focused view of what was important to the business and professional community.

In 1961, Rose was a board member of the Chamber, and when a Civil Aeronautics Board hearing was set in Baker, Leo asked Rose to legally represent Baker at the hearing—pro bono, or for the public good, of course. Both West Coast Air and United Airlines would be there, and the federal government sent out Thomas Wrenn, a trial examiner employed by the CAB. The CAB sent examiners into the areas affected by changes in air service for the purpose of holding evidentiary hearings.

Remembering back over forty years, Rose described the 1961 hearings as a combination fact-finding mission and political sideshow.[32] Leo wanted Rose to prepare and present the case for Baker before the CAB as a concerned citizen of Baker. He impressed on Rose that it was his civic responsibility. Rose agreed to do it. Both United and West Coast analysts, witnesses, and attorneys were there. As a young attorney working in Baker, Rose knew virtually nothing about CAB law. The purpose of the hearing was to answer the question "Is continued air service to Baker economically feasible?" Representatives of Baker claimed that the service was not currently designed to attract patrons. Because of multiple stops and inconvenient departure and arrival times, patrons could drive to Portland, the nearest large connecting hub, almost as quickly and more conveniently than they could fly there. The airlines claimed that to be feasible, service in Baker needed to attract five passengers a day. At that time, the airline service that came to Baker was funded primarily through an airmail subsidy.

The evening before the hearing got under way, Leo invited all the out-of-towners up to Boulder Park in the Eagle Cap Wilderness area. The group included Thomas Wrenn, all of the CAB staff and attorneys, and the United Airlines and West Coast Airlines attorneys and witnesses. The visitors were stunned by the beauty of the scenery as well as the hospitality Leo and the community of Baker extended to them. During the course of the evening, Rose found himself sitting next to the attorney from United Airlines. Although United Airlines didn't have any flights coming into Baker, if West Coast Air pulled out, there would be tighter competition in markets that United was already involved in. Whether he was inspired by the beauty of the scenery, the warmth of the hospitality, or the quality of the food and beverages is hard to say, but during the course of his conversation with Rose, the United Airlines attorney suggested areas of questioning that Rose might pursue for the next day. This knowledge was a major windfall for Rose.

Along with the other evidence presented the next day, Rose's questions provided the basis for the argument that West Coast should not be able to pull out of its service agreement. Examiner Wrenn so held; this now led to an automatic appeal before the full Civil Aeronautics Board, which would be held in Washington, D.C. Wrenn strongly urged the city of Baker to not only file a brief to support his favorable decision but also to send Rose to argue the case before the entire board.

The airline work that had started as a pro bono project continued as pro bono work for Rose. In an effort to keep it from interfering with his other work, Rose worked weeks from 4 a.m. to 8 a.m. to write the brief, with coaching in phone calls from Wrenn, who by this time not only was interested in seeing his decision sustained by the full board, but had also become quite enamored of the Baker area. Rose and the Baker city attorney Bard Johnson went back to Washington, D.C., to argue the case. They arrived on Dec. 9, 1961. It snowed fourteen inches that day. Thomas Wrenn took them out to dinner; at the restaurant they saw the head of the FBI, J. Edgar Hoover. Wrenn showed them the magical sight of Washington covered in snow.

Wrenn, who was a friend of Speaker of the House Sam Rayburn and then-Vice President Lyndon Baines Johnson, strongly emphasized the importance of letting the CAB know that Senator Wayne Morse supported what they were doing, which was not difficult since Leo and Senator Morse had continued their friendship over the years. Usually, the Senator would have been there to introduce Gene Rose and Bard Johnson to the board. Unfortunately, Morse was unable to be with them because he was at the United Nations that day, so his administrative assistant, Bill Berg came in his place. Berg had a phenomenal grasp of the issues involved in the case. His introduction gave Rose and Johnson the right launching pad to make their argument. They argued for continued air service and won. Leo was as happy as if Rose had won a case for him personally—and in a sense he had, since Leo was more affected by the continuation of reliable air service in Baker than the majority of Baker's citizens.

Rose credited Leo with tipping over the first domino by sponsoring the party up at Boulder Park. He also covered the expenses for Rose and Johnson to go argue the case. In later years, Rose remembered that in working with Leo on Baker matters, "You had better bring your 'A' game. He wanted nothing less."

After receiving word that air service would continue, to show that they didn't take the service for granted, fifteen Baker businessmen organized a plane trip to Boise to encourage air travel between the two cities and to boost Baker. During their night and day stay in Boise, they appeared on television and received a guided tour of the city. Both Leo and Gene Rose were part of the traveling group. Leo also continued his efforts to find new ways to market Baker by becoming an officer (second vice president) of the Baker Industry and Resources Corporation. Under federal redevelopment guidelines, the corporation would be eligible to borrow up to $250,000 from the Small Business Administration.[33]

Leo made a three-week visit east to New York, Philadelphia, Washington, and Chicago in April and May 1962 to talk with eastern publishers and attend the annual Chamber of Commerce National Convention. It had been an exciting year so far. In February, astronaut John Glenn had become the first American to orbit the globe (three times), temporarily easing anxieties about the United States' ability to compete with the Soviets in the space race. The Seattle World's Fair opened on April 21, 1962, complete with the Space Needle. While Leo was in the east, Gherman S. Titov, a twenty-six year-old Soviet cosmonaut who had completed seventeen orbits around the earth, was visiting the United States. Titov and John Glenn had an opportunity to discuss their experiences in space.[34] Leo didn't see the two of them together, but he did see five of the seven Mercury astronauts while he was at a Chamber of Commerce dinner in Washington. On his return to Baker, in a conversation with the *Record-Courier*, Leo mentioned that the magazine and newspaper industry was in serious trouble economically. While in Washington, he met with Sen. Wayne Morse and Rep. Al Ullman, and he twice saw the Senate presided over by Sen. Maurine Neuberger, who was filling her husband Richard Neuberger's Senate seat after he died of cancer in 1960. He also spoke with Civil Aeronautics Board officials and felt optimistic about the continuation of air service to Baker. He was impressed with the air service he had experienced. He left Chicago at 11 a.m. Central time, "enjoyed luncheon in Denver," and arrived in Baker at 2 p.m.[35]

That summer, Leo hosted the visiting Dr. Howard Driggs, president of the American Pioneer Trails Association. The eighty-nine-year-old professor emeritus from New York University was traveling with his wife from Astoria, Long Island (in New York), to Astoria, Oregon, to promote interest in the preservation of the Oregon Trail. Driggs reminded his audience that Ezra Meeker, a former president of the Pioneer Trails Association, had made a similar journey along the trail and had stopped in Baker in 1906. Leo remembered that he and the other children of Baker had responded well "to the man with the long grey beard" and had contributed nickels to help raise a monument.[36]

Leo was sixty-seven in the summer of 1962. After twenty-seven years as the Baker postmaster, his brother Sanford retired. While Leo was only three years younger than Sanford, he seemed to have no thought of retirement, even if he was reaching an age where he was having many honors heaped on him. In August, *Reader's Digest* announced that Leo Adler had qualified for a solid gold honor emblem. In commemoration of its forty-first anniversary, the *Digest* awarded the emblem to men and women who had ac-

Leo Adler (right) presents Mayor Doug Benton with the keys to a new ambulance Baker Democrat Herald, *Jan. 17, 1962.* (Oregon Historical Society OrHi 104906)

tively sold the magazine for forty years or more. Out of 1,000 *Digest* representatives worldwide, Leo was one of ten to receive the honor.[37]

In 1963, Leo made the first of several growing financial gifts to Baker. Although he had resigned from the Civil Service Commission in February 1961, feeling that the City Council was not mindful of commission recommendations to hire additional positions for the fire department, he still cared deeply about the department's viability. In early July 1963, he offered the city $12,500, the largest gift he had ever given, for the purchase of a new ambulance. It was a well-thought-out gift. Leo gave a specific dollar amount, for the purchase of a specific item, and he wanted to see that the money would support the fire department and the larger community of Baker. In a letter tendering the offer, Leo wrote, "Mindful of the fact that this city and its people have been very good to me during the years that I have resided in Baker, I wish to in some small way reciprocate for the many fine things that have been done for me."[38]

The city took delivery of a new $14,000 (Leo upped his gift a bit) Cadillac ambulance in January 1964. Leo presented Mayor Doug Benton with the key to the ambulance; within minutes of being put into service, the ambulance received its first call.[39] Leo had long given his time, energy, talent, and money to Baker. He was now moving into a new era of giving larger gifts to specific projects that he wanted to support. It is hard to know what inspired this increased giving. He had always been a generous man, but the fact that he was aging may have caused him to give more deeply. Or it may have resulted from a deeper realization of how quickly the world around him was changing. His good friend Bishop Leipzig had returned to Baker from Rome after the first session of Vatican II in December 1962. The United States and the Soviet Union continued to pursue the space race with great zeal. In November 1963, President John F. Kennedy was assassinated. Kennedy's inaugural challenge, "Ask not what your country can do for you, but what you can do for your country," could have been ringing in his ear. Whatever it was that motivated him, Leo Adler had decided to give more deeply to the country of his heart, Baker, Oregon.

Leo and Baseball: An Enduring Love

Leo Adler was born in 1895, the same year as Babe Ruth. While he relished football and basketball, he had a particular fondness for baseball at all levels, from local town games in the early twentieth century to Little League games and on through to the World Series. It's little wonder that Leo Adler loved baseball; given the almost century-long span of his life, it would have been surprising if he didn't have some feelings about the game. He lived during the era when the game became the national pastime, when the country embraced the sport and took it through a range of technological changes from newspaper reports to telegraph to radio to television. And being involved in the sale of newspapers and magazines as Leo was, he was part of an industry that fed the national appetite for the sport. He lived in an age and worked in an industry that was besotted with baseball.

Nationally and locally, baseball was an important part of American culture. In 1905, the same year that Leo began selling newspapers, the New York Giants won the World Series. Christy Mathewson, the pitcher for the New York Giants, was tall, blond, and handsome, and when he agreed to become a professional baseball player, he had promised his mother that he would never play on Sunday. He was nicknamed "the Christian gentleman" by sportswriters of the day. During the 1905 World Series between the New York Giants and the Philadelphia Athletics, he pitched three shutouts in six days. He was worshipped by young boys because he seemed to be the human embodiment of the fictional baseball characters from popular nickel and dime novels of the time.[1]

Residents of Baker also thought it was a grand game. During the baseball months from April to October, Baker residents could follow the scores of the National League, the American League, and the Pacific Coast League (which covered West Coast teams) in their local newspapers. There were also smaller groups such as the Western Tri-State League, of which Baker was a member. Men and boys of the time simply loved to play and watch the game. Below is a taste of the coverage that baseball received in 1907 in the Baker *Morning Democrat*:

> *June 16, 1907*—*Tom Gray from Sumpter came to town last evening and is booming the hill town ball team. Watch the Kommodores take to tall timber when the Baker team wins.*
>
> *June 20, 1907*—*June 19 games: Tacoma—Tacoma 1, Vancouver 0; Spokane—Aberdeen 4, Spokane 5; San Francisco—Los Angeles 1, San Francisco 0; Butte—Butte 10, Seattle 2*
>
> *June 22, 1907*—*Eagles defeat Minstrels in a game of baseball. There was an imitation of the national past time on the Valley Ave. Grounds yesterday. The local Eagles 9 and a troupe of colored gentry from a minstrel show that is passing*

through the city were the perpetrators of the cruel joke which was played on the sport-loving public.

Sunday, June 23, 1907—Baseball on Sumpter Diamond this afternoon. *The local boys have only been together on paper and therefore have no idea of what their strength will be in the field. Added to this the fact that the Sumpter fans in the transport of enthusiasm have strengthened their line-up by the addition of a classy twirler, the Baker team is not sanguine of success.*

The Baker team with their friends will leave on the regular 8:30 train tomorrow morning, leaving Sumpter on the return trip at 3 o'clock. The game will be played about noon as time cuts no figure with the baseball appetite of the fans of the upper camp.

June 29, 1907—*June 28 games: Los Angeles—LA 0, San Francisco 7; Butte—Butte 7, Aberdeen 2; New York— Harvard 7, Yale 2; Spokane—Seattle 9, Spokane 5.*

July 2, 1907—Baker Goes Down Before Sumpter by Close Score. *Excellent support was tendered the Baker players. Nearly a hundred went from here on the special and held their own with the rabid rooters of the hill town on the bleachers. The game was nip and tuck and full of thrills and frills. Considerable excitement was worked up over the outcome of the game and several hundred dollars extra was in circulation in Sumpter Sunday evening which had been passing the week in the pockets of the Bakerites.*

July 27, 1907—Big crowd is assured for Sunday ball game. *The [Valley Ave.] grounds will be materially improved today when scrapers and a gang of men will be put to work to condition them. New lines will be run and the whole field will*

> be leveled and filled.
>
> Aug. 1, 1907—Baker Beats Weiser 11-5. 500 people gathered at Valley grounds yesterday afternoon. It was a great day for baseball and the large crowd vented their pleasure by vociferous rooting.
>
> The home team appeared in their spanking new blue uniforms and christened them by noble work.

It was a splendid summer for baseball, and enthusiasm for the sport in Baker only grew. In 1912, play-by-play reporting of the World Series between the Boston Red Sox and the New York Giants was broadcast by telegraph. It was the most immediate contact people could have with the game without actually being in the stands. All across the United States, towns would post the progress of the ball games.

In 1913, the future Oregon coaching great Wade Williams came to coach athletics at Baker High School. One of eleven children in a family from Neola, Iowa, Wade Williams was an outstanding athlete at Iowa State University, and his work with Baker was his first coaching job.

In March of the same year, twenty-eight stockholders of the Baker Baseball Association met at the Geiser Grand for an enthusiastic baseball booster luncheon. They took up a collection of funds subscribed by the city baseball fans and set about planning their season. Within two weeks, the team manager, a Mr. Harlow, had a report to the members about the players he had signed up for tryouts. The directors of the Baker Baseball Association were pleased with the progress being made. Ten men who ranged in territory from Sumpter, Ore.; Shannon, Ill.; Anaconda, Mon.; and

Salt Lake City, Utah, all had their transportation paid for by the club so they could come try out for the team. There was also discussion about the team name. The baseball team from Baker had generally been known as either the Miners or the Diggers as a nod to the importance of mining for the city. This year the team would be known as the Baker Gold Diggers. Plans were also made for a "smoker" and booster meeting. "The idea is to call all live wires and fans who are interested in the success of the club, and by that time quite a number of the players will be here and an opportunity afforded to all to meet them and get acquainted."[2]

The booster was held on a Friday night, April 4, at the Commercial Club. Billed as a Monkey Banquet and Baseball Booster, the paper described it as "a howling success." "In spite of the fact that a hundred extra chairs had been provided for the occasion, the seating capacity was insufficient to accommodate the fans and many stood up during the course of the evening, which was full of pepper and boosting spirit from start to finish." There was also a demonstration run by the fire department. Starting at precisely eight o'clock, the fire department, replete with all its equipment, made a test run from the fire station to the corner of Center and Main in fifty seconds.[3]

Leo would have been just a few months shy of eighteen at the time. There are no records to say whether he attended, but he was definitely surrounded by baseball that summer. He served as the equipment manager for the Baker High team, which allowed him to get to know Wade Williams better. Baseball was also another way Leo could stake out a new interest for himself that was different from those of his father. Playing baseball on a spring day anywhere in the United States makes you feel like you're part of the team. This must have been an especially good feeling to an American boy from a German Jewish background. On April 11, 1913, President Woodrow Wilson threw out the first ball for the opening game in Washington, D.C., between the Washington Senators and the New York Giants, and while the Senators were usually ridiculed as "first in war, first in peace, last in the American League," on that day they won.[4]

As American affection for baseball continued to grow, many players enlisted in the First World War. A picture of Christy Mathewson ran in the April 3, 1918, Baker *Morning Democrat* showing him visiting the troops at Camp Sheridan in Montgomery, Ala., and washing up his own plates. Later, during a drill, Mathewson would be exposed to poison gas that seared his lungs; he died seven years later, never regaining his former ball-playing stature. In Baker, baseball schedules were shifted because of the war. During 1918 a twilight league was organized. The YMCA, which had opened in 1913, leased the ballpark, and seven-inning games began at six o'clock. Professional men, clerks, butchers, civil service workers, the White Pine Company, the Oregon Lumber Company, Eccles Lumber Company, and the Methodist Athletic club all entered teams.

During the 1920s, the playing, showmanship, and selling skills of Babe Ruth had a huge impact on the game. By this time, Leo was spending time on the road and expanding his business. In almost any of the large or small towns he visited in the summer months from The Dalles, Ore., to Grand Island, Neb., Leo could probably find a game to watch. Aside from the personal enjoyment he took in the game, baseball had a professional impact on him as well. Between 1917 and 1929, newspaper, magazine, and billboard advertising quadrupled, with much of that new advertising focused on baseball.[5] Anything that made the magazine and newspaper industry boom was good news for Leo Adler.

There were few figures as sought-after or as willing to endorse products as Babe Ruth. In 1924, the Sultan of Swat came to Portland for a "Swat exhibition." There would be a contest between Ruth and Rudie Wilhelm, one of the leading golfers on the Pacific Coast. Wilhelm was attempting to drive the ball as far as Ruth hit it. Ruth also took time during his Portland stop to visit the Shriners' Children's Hospital.[6]

Leo was not a passionate follower of any one particular team, but he thoroughly enjoyed going to major-league games when he could. Any town in America is cast in a different light when looked at through its ball team. Because of his travels to large and small communities, Leo could see that baseball was a common and a unifying element in many towns. The American public had access to baseball not only through their home team and the scores they could read about in the daily newspaper. Now it was coming into their home through the radio.

Red Barber, one of the sport's great broadcasters (first for the Cincinnati Reds and later for the Brooklyn Dodgers), recalled what baseball over the radio meant to the listening public. "People who weren't around in the twenties when radio exploded can't know what it meant, this milestone for mankind. Suddenly with radio, there was instant human communication....The world came into our homes for the first time....We heard a drama that we ourselves played a part in."[7] The Chicago Cubs were the first to start broadcasting over the radio in the twenties. Other teams followed suit as they saw it didn't keep fans from coming to the ballpark to watch the game. Radio broadcasts of baseball also helped get women interested in the sport as well. The great broadcasters told not simply the score of the game but the story of the game, which helped to build a new base of fans.

Leo's business genius with magazine distribution led him into smaller communities that had a limited supply of magazines to choose from. Knowing that the country was ravenous for the game of baseball, he wisely realized that they might just as easily be hungry for the news of baseball. In the 1930s, Leo made a friendship with John George (J.G.) Taylor Spink, the publisher of the *The Sporting News*, a magazine that eventually became known as the "Bible of Baseball." It was the best source for statistics, box scores, records, and coverage of all levels of professional play. To gather detailed information, Spink deployed an army of correspondents and stringers in every baseball town, tirelessly directing their activities by persistent phone calls and telegrams. Spink had many of the large magazine markets covered, but Leo convinced Spink to let him bring *The Sporting News* into many of the smaller towns in the west. It was a great move for both Leo and Spink.[8]

Baseball also sparked Leo's civic instincts. In 1929, the Kansas City Monarchs, one of the premier teams of the Negro National League, began using a portable lighting system for its games; and the minor leagues started playing night games in the thirties.[9] Larry MacPhail, general manager for the Cincinnati Reds, was the man who brought night games to major league baseball. He enlisted General Electric to design the best possible illumination system and recruited President Franklin D. Roosevelt to switch on the lights via telegraph from Washington, D.C. Red Barber later described the evening when "a silence fell over the crowd as the magic moment of 8:30 approached. Precisely on time, President Franklin D. Roosevelt pressed a telegraph key in the White House.... A mighty roar went up from the crowd.... There was light—tremendous, almost blinding light."[10]

In February 1937, Leo became the director of the Baker Chamber of Commerce. At the age of forty-one, he was the youngest ever elected. He made a big splash quickly. On June 3, 1937, Baker celebrated the addition of outdoor lighting to its baseball field with a game between Baker and Ontario. The lighting system cost $6,000, with Leo covering $4,325 of that amount. Generous donations of labor and materials were also made by Eastern Oregon Light and Power, the city of Baker, and local electrician Carl York. Addressing local sensitivity to keeping money in the community during those days of the Depression, a newspaper article pointed out that most of the money for the flood-lighting system was spent in Portland because the special materials needed for it were not available in Baker.[11] For the inaugural game under the new lights, the Chamber of Commerce sold tickets at fifty cents apiece.

On that evening, the crowd was between 2,000 and 2,500. Many were attending a night game for the first time. Speeches were made over the new public-address system, another new innovation for the Baker field. The mayors of Baker and Ontario spoke. Leo also was introduced, and said to the crowd, "On behalf of the Baker Flood-lighting Corporation, I want to thank you for your co-operation and I hope we will see you here on many nights this summer." The Baker Miners beat Ontario 6 to 4.

An editorial that ran in the newspaper the following day noted, "One way for Baker to keep ahead of the procession of eastern

Oregon communities is to make this an attractive place to live and to come for entertainment.... Thursday night the finest floodlighting system in eastern Oregon was dedicated with a ball game. This improvement is made possible mainly through the public spirit of Leo Adler, who advanced the money to be repaid from gate receipts at public events."[12] The other big news item on that day was the marriage, in Paris, of England's former King Edward to Wallis Simpson. Under the headline "Let 'Em Alone," the *Democrat-Herald* described "Wally" as a combination of Helen of Troy, Joan of Arc, and Cleopatra all rolled into one and hoped that the public would turn its attention to other more serious matters, "of which there are plenty available."[13]

Leo's interest in baseball continued as national baseball moved from radio waves onto television screens. In the fifties, major-league baseball spread itself west of the Mississippi River. Oddly enough, an old friend of Leo's played an important role in the passage of one of baseball's emotional touchstones, the move of the Brooklyn Dodgers west to Los Angeles.

Norris Poulson was born to a Danish family on July 23, 1895, and grew up on a ranch near Haines in Baker County. He was a classmate of Leo's and was editor of the Baker High *Rosemary* yearbook for 1914. He went on to study at Oregon State College in Corvallis, and eventually moved to Los Angeles. He became a certified public accountant in 1933 and went on to pursue political interests, serving as a Republican congressman from California from 1943 to 45 and 1947 to 53. At some point in the early fifties, he was recruited by a group of Los Angeles power brokers including Norman Chandler, the owner of the *Los Angeles Times*, to run against the incumbent mayor, Fletcher Bowron. The group

Leo and Baseball: An Enduring Love

Los Angeles Mayor Norris Poulson (second from left) greets Bishop Francis Leipzip (right) at a firemen's convention in 1958. (Adler House Museum)

promised that campaign funds would be forthcoming and that they would make sure that the mayor's salary would be increased. They guaranteed that Poulson would have other perks, including "a Cadillac to strut around in." In later years, Poulson recalled that when this group made such a request, there was no choice but to run. He served as mayor of Los Angeles from 1953 to 1961.[14]

Walter O'Malley, the owner of the Brooklyn Dodgers, wanted to increase the profitability of his team. During the 1950s it was one of the richest teams in baseball and the second most profitable team in the National League. But attendance at ball games was shrinking, and the Dodgers' home at Ebbets Field in New York, where they had played since 1913, was too small to produce the kind of profits O'Malley was looking for. He tried to buy a bigger site, but the city turned him down. The Dodgers had made their home in Brooklyn since 1890, their name deriving from their description as "trolley dodgers." During the team's 1957 spring training in Vero Beach, Flo., Los Angeles Mayor Norris Poulson made a visit to the team with great fanfare, and Walter O'Malley began to look westward, specifically to what the city of Los Angeles could offer.[15]

Los Angeles had a great deal to offer. The city offered the Dodgers over 300 acres in the Chavez Ravine area. In exchange, Los Angeles would hold on to half the mineral and oil rights and receive the rights to Wrigley Field property, which the Pacific Coast League currently used. The City would also spend $2 million to level the proposed new stadium site. After much wrangling and heartache in Brooklyn, the Dodgers went west. At a welcoming luncheon in Los Angeles, the Dodgers' move was referred to as "the greatest catch in baseball." As the event's host, the actor Joe E. Brown called Mayor Norris Poulson "the Lord Mayor of Baseball." In a full career that included a public spat with Nikita Khrushchev during a 1959 visit, Norris Poulson would point to bringing major-league baseball to Los Angeles as one of his greatest accomplishments.[16]

It is interesting to ponder where Leo would have come down on the question of the Dodgers leaving Brooklyn. He may have been conflicted about it. The term "franchise shift" seems an icy description for pulling away a hometown team from a base of fans that supported it. It was the first time in a long while that fans had been so starkly reminded that baseball was a business. It seems likely that Leo would have been sympathetic to the fans' loss. But he was a businessman himself and a Westerner, and he was probably immensely proud that an old friend of his had been able to bring one of the great jewels in baseball's crown to the West for a new group of fans to see.

In 1959 the Los Angeles Dodgers and the Chicago White Sox squared off in what the *New York Times* referred to as "the first World series ever held in the Far West." The Dodgers were not yet in their new home and were playing in the Los Angeles Memorial Coliseum, where the track and field events for the 1932 Olympics had been held. At that point in his life, Leo probably had the pull to get some good tickets for the game, particularly since the mayor was a friend of over fifty years. Because the Coliseum was a publicly operated building, sportswriters were at pains to point out that it was the first "dry" Series game since Prohibition.[17]

Leo's chair with an appropriate note. The baseball in the foreground was autographed by Sandy Koufax. Photo by Walt Zimmerman, Baker Democrat Herald, *Oct. 13, 1972.* (Oregon Historical Society OrHi 104908)

Leo continued to attend World Series games into the seventies. Sometimes he would hook up with former Bakerites living in playoff cities, and occasionally friends from Baker would join him on the trip. Traditionally, when he knew the final four teams in the playoffs he would make hotel reservations in all four cities.

The Spark and the Light: The Leo Adler Story

Many people interviewed for this biography told a variation on the following story.

Leo found himself in one of the playoff cities and went to the hotel where he had made his reservations. Unfortunately, there had been a mix-up, and Leo found himself without hotel reservations in a city swarming with baseball fans. He hailed a taxicab and, after conferring with the driver about potential hotels (there weren't any), asked the driver to take him to a hospital that he had seen nearby. The driver complied.

Leo got out of the cab and asked the driver to wait. He strode into the hospital reception area and asked to see a listing of the doctors or hospital administrators. After scanning the list he recognized the name of a former Bakerite or a member of an Oregon Jewish family. He asked to see this person; after explaining his predicament and making a generous donation to the hospital, he was escorted back to the cab in a wheelchair to collect his luggage. Checked in as a patient for the duration of the World Series, Leo had found his lodgings. He thought the food was just fine, and it didn't bother him that he had to be wheeled to his cab to get to the games. If it wasn't the best room he ever had, it was certainly the one he enjoyed talking about the most.

In 1961, Leo's baseball interests were refocused on Baker. In March, the Baker County Baseball Association decided to liquidate and turn over its funds to an emerging local Little League group. The BCBA had a good strong run of semi-pro seasons from 1952 to 1957, when it became inactive. The semi-pro players had been guaranteed jobs locally. Some were imported specifically for baseball, while others were local. To keep the team going took good season ticket sales, contributions, and promises of work for the ball players. Strong contributors to the BCBA included the banks and lumber mills of Baker, Cal-Pac, and Basche-Sage Hardware. During their heyday, a dollar spent on the Baker Loggers seemed a dollar well spent. The team won the tri-state league championship three times between 1952 and 1957, and in the other two years went to the playoffs but were defeated in the final round. Both Henry Levinger and Leo Adler had served time on the BCBA board of directors.

In the winter of 1960 and the spring of 196l, the Baker Little League was formed with the intent of having six major league and six minor league teams fully uniformed, with full equipment and ball fields upon which to play. Before that time, there had not been an organized way for youths to participate in the game of baseball. Upon the liquidation of the BCBA, the association's assets of $1,835.93 were passed on to the Baker Little League, which planned to build an official park with the funds.[18]

There was a park in South Baker known as the Elks Park. It was in a pretty area bounded on the west by the Powder River—a perfect site for a ballpark. The Elks were approached and kindly consented to the construction of a new field there. The Little League field was built and in June 1961, it was dedicated with a new name, Wade W. Williams Park. After his coaching in Baker, Wade Williams enlisted in the army and later began coaching high-school baseball in Portland in 1921. He eventually coached baseball and football at Lincoln High School. A few of the players he coached that went on to the pros were Johnny and Vince Pesky, Eddie and Joe Erautt, Johnny Leovich, Dick Sinovic, and Pete Ward. Williams was later hired as a scout for the Portland Beavers. He also coached at Lewis and Clark College after his retirement. He was considered by many as one the finest coaches in Oregon for developing young talent. He was often asked about whether the boys he coached might be major league prospects; he would reply, "We don't talk in terms of major league prospects. Play the game for all you're worth in the league you're in and 'let it come.'" Williams' advice applied to far more than baseball, which may have been another element of what made him such a strong coach. The *Oregon Journal* commented that the naming of the new field was a fitting honor for his Baker friends to bestow on him.[19]

The Wade Williams Park was active, so active that soon many of the people associated with Baker Little League and other baseball programs in the city began dreaming bigger dreams. Ideally, they would have a site that could hold two regulation-size fields and two Little League-size fields. The regulation-size fields would give the students who attended the local Catholic school at St. Francis Academy a place for their football and baseball teams to practice. As a private school, St. Francis could not use the facilities of the public high school, whose teams were already practicing on them.

With his gift of an ambulance to Baker in 1964, Leo's civic charity had moved up to a new level. A group of citizens, including Little League interests, members of St. Francis (Art and Francis Chaves), Gene Rose (who had played ball on the University of Oregon team), and other baseball enthusiasts around town, began dreaming and planning ways to make this larger baseball facility a reality. They started out with no site and no money for the field, but they had energy. After hearing about the project, Bishop Leipzig gave his endorsement. The group began its homework in earnest and with some trepidation; they knew it was going to cost a lot of money.

Leo and Baseball: An Enduring Love

Two Baker-based Bureau of Land Management employees, Dennis Erickson and Don Woodman, made a scale model of the proposed facility in their spare time. Complete with working field lights, it included a sign that proclaimed it Leo Adler Field. Rumors about the new field were flying around the town. Gene Rose made a presentation to Leo, who peppered Rose with questions as soon as he saw the scale model: "Who's on your board? How much money do you have? How much work are you willing to do?" Rose answered all his questions, and Leo finally said, "How much is this going to cost me?" Rose had been worried about voicing what seemed to him an enormous amount, but he had barely gotten the words "$18,000" out of his mouth before Leo was asking him where he wanted him to send the check.[20] An equivalent gift in 2004 would be roughly $110,000.

On July 11, 1964, the gift was announced in the Baker *Democrat-Herald* with the headline "'Mr. Baker' gives $5,000 for New Baseball Field" (it was an initial payment) and a photo that shows him with Wade Williams and Dick Sheehy, the president of the Baker Little League. Plans for the new field included lights, a covered grandstand, and a football field in the outfield area. A site was found north of the armory. The Little League organization would lease the proposed lots from the county. The proposed field would mean a $30,000 improvement to the city.[21]

As work continued on the project, other contributors got involved. Bishop Francis Leipzig contributed $2,000, and the St. Francis Cathedral parish contributed $2,000. Leo wrote another check for $7,000, which was described as a surprise "but also another example of his outstanding generosity to civic projects, charities and character building organizations of the community."[22]

The Spark and the Light: The Leo Adler Story

From left: Dick Sheehy, Leo Adler and Wade Williams at the fourth anniversary of the Wade Williams Field. Baker Democrat Herald *photo, July 11, 1964.* (Oregon Historical Society OrHi 104910)

Leo Adler Field. (Adler House Museum)

Leo and Baseball: An Enduring Love

Leo and young players on dedication day for the Leo Adler Field. Photo by Holman Studios. (Adler House Museum)

Other people and organizations got involved through contributing their money, time, or talents. To commemorate its one-hundredth anniversary, First National Bank donated ten trees. Before the site was Leo Adler Field, Gene Rose remembered it as "a huge hole in the ground." Aaron Logsdon of Logsdon Sand and Gravel had agreed to help out with fill dirt from his gravel pits. He had initially said he wouldn't be able to offer any of his better earth-moving equipment, but after seeing a group of men working one weekend he was either so inspired or so pained by their efforts that he brought in the good equipment, some volunteers who knew a bit more about using it, and 23,000 yards of fill dirt.

The dedication of Leo Adler Field. From left: Gene Rose, LeRoy Merrick, President of Baker Little League, Leo Adler and Bishop Leipzig. Baker Democrat Herald, *June 22, 1966.* (Oregon Historical Society, OrHi 104912)

Logsdon greatly admired what Leo was doing for the community.

1966 was an eventful year for Leo in many respects. Now seventy years old, he was moving into the "honors" portion of his life. In March, he was given a Human Rights Award by the Publishers Division of the Anti-Defamation League. A long-time and generous supporter of the Anti-Defamation League, he received the award at a banquet at the Waldorf-Astoria Hotel in New York on March 9, 1966. He was to be honored "for distinguished service in the cause of human rights and his outstanding record of concern for his fellow Americans."[23]

On June 21, 1966, Leo turned seventy-one and Leo Adler Field was dedicated. Oregon Governor (and, from 1967 to 1997, Senator) Mark O. Hatfield was there for the dedication. Governor Hatfield described Leo as "a man that is not afraid to stand up

Leo and Baseball: An Enduring Love

Leo Adler (left) and Bishop Leipzig. Photo by Holman Studios. (Adler House Museum)

and be counted—a man that is willing to say 'I will do this,' and then carry it out." It was a very full day, starting with an early-morning breakfast, a luncheon for 150, a picnic in the park, and finally the evening dedication of the field. In his remarks at the dedication, Gene Rose declared:

> *On this field, it matters not whether the boy is black or white,*

but can he hit the ball to right field? People won't ask whether he is Catholic, Protestant or Jewish, but can he execute the squeeze play? The Rosenburgs will play beside the O'Connor's and the Golkowskis beside the McDonalds. The poorest man's son will strike out the richest man's boy. On your field, a lesson in democracy is taught in every game, for baseball draws no lines of race, color or creed.

There were over 300 members of the 28 Little League, Babe Ruth, and Junior Legion teams in attendance, along with 1,000 other spectators. The dedication concluded with Leo presenting the keys to the field to Bishop Leipzig and to LeRoy Merrick, president of the Baker Babe Ruth and Little League teams. In passing on the keys, Leo noted that the park was a community effort, and that he was proud to be able to play a part in making it become a reality.

Gene Rose said that Leo provided the spark that created the flame that helped to build the baseball field. A committed group of Baker citizens did the preparation, providing the kindling for that spark, and Leo understood that quite clearly. As "Mr. Baker" and as the name at the top of so many donor lists in the county and state, Leo realized that the main thing that he had to offer was his money and his wide array of connections. He also wanted some certainty that his money would be planted in well-prepared organizations and projects; the Leo Adler Field project was clearly that. While Leo gave to the community, the community also gave back to him with its willingness to tackle new projects and think big. In September of the same year, Leo received a special award from his old friend J.G. Taylor Spink of the *Sporting News* in com-

Leo and Baseball: An Enduring Love

Governor Mark O. Hatfield and Leo Adler with young players. Photo by Holman Studios. (Adler House Museum)

memoration of his service and efforts for the new Leo Adler Baseball field.[25] Both Leo and Baker were receiving good press coverage for taking on a big community project and doing it the right way, with strong financial backing and strong community involvement. The Portland *Oregonian* made mention of the new field. "While Portland wrestles with its stadium problem, it's encouraging to note what community effort has wrought in Baker—by rough count at least 1,000 Baker citizens from a population of 9,500 in one way or another helped complete Leo Adler field."[26]

Leo continued to attend World Series Games through 1977, when he was eighty-two. In his typical understated fashion, he told one friend that he stopped going when the price of hot dogs went past $5. At the 1976 Series he recalled sitting next to Pee

Wee Reese of the Brooklyn Dodgers, who introduced himself. Leo also had collected signed baseballs from many players, including Sandy Koufax, who was a particular favorite of his. The most memorable Series for Leo was 1969 when the New York Mets beat the Baltimore Orioles. Ecstatic fans poured on to the field and began tearing up pieces of the turf as prized relics. At a time when America was involved in the Vietnam War and Neil Armstrong had just landed on the moon, many saw the Mets Series win as a sign of hope. The great violinist Isaac Stern said, "If the Mets can win the series, anything can happen, even peace." New York Governor Nelson Rockefeller said, "the magnificent Mets have performed a baseball miracle. But they've done a lot more. They've taught us again the great lessons of this county—that you never say die, you don't give up."[27]

And perhaps those two quotes sum up what Leo took from baseball, a continuing hope that things were improving and the belief that you keep giving your best with all your heart. Some have said that baseball is all about learning how to cope with and overcome failure, because even the greatest hitters miss the ball seven out of ten times. As a salesman from a very young age, Leo knew all about the importance of continuing to step up to the plate, to keep pitching new publications and to seek out new fields for expansion. Perhaps baseball was such a joy for him because it was pleasure to watch someone else step up to the plate and take a swing.

Closing the Circle

On a February evening in 1967, both Leo Adler and Sanford Heilner received special honors from the Exalted Ruler of the Baker Elks. Leo received a pin commemorating fifty years of membership, and Sanford received one for sixty years of membership. If their fathers, Carl Adler and Sigmund Heilner, could have looked down on their sons that night they would have been astounded to see what their boys had achieved, just one generation removed from their German roots. Sanford Heilner accepted his sixty-year pin at the age of eighty-one. He had continued in the family business running Neuberger and Heilner until he retired and passed the store on to his cousin Gert Neuberger, who emigrated to Baker from Germany prior to the Second World War. When Leo received his pin at the age of seventy-one, he was the wealthiest man in the community.[1] He was known around the state and in many places outside the state as "Mr. Baker." While all parents dream big dreams for their children, surely Carl and Laura Adler would have been amazed to know what their son had accomplished for himself and for his community.

Sanford Heilner (center) and Leo Adler (right) receive their sixty-year and fifty-year pins from the Baker Elks. Baker Democrat Herald, *Feb. 24, 1967. Holman photo.* (Oregon Historical Society OrHi 104911)

Leo retained the lessons his family had taught him with regard to his community and his religion. Already a strong supporter of the Israel Bond drive, when Israel conducted pre-emptive strikes against Egypt, Jordan, Iraq, and Syria in what became known as the Six-Day War in June 1967, Leo stepped up his financial support of Israel by buying even more Israel Bonds and making contributions where needed.[2] The strike enabled the nineteen-year-old state of Israel to take control of the Sinai Peninsula, the western bank of the Jordan River, the Gaza Strip, and the Golan Heights, which in turn led it to grow to three and a half times its prewar size. Because of his financial support, Leo was awarded with a citation of merit from the State of Israel as well as an autographed photo of Golda Meir, prime minister of Israel from 1969 to 1974. Many people interviewed for this biography pointed out that Leo was not religiously observant, particularly that he had an immense fondness for ham, or what he liked to call "pink chicken." Although he may not have been strictly observant of his own faith, he had an appreciation of his background. He was very grounded in who he was and where he came from. His understanding of his roots continued to inform his philanthropy and his sense of community.

On January 14, 1968, Leo received an award that his parents could never have imagined for him. Along with Anthony Brandenthaler, a local Baker industrialist, Leo received papal honors in the form of the Knighthood of St. Sylvester. The honor was conferred to the men at a Sunday mass by Bishop Leipzig for their

Autographed photo of Israel's Prime Minister, Golda Meir, to Leo Adler. (Adler House Museum)

civic and religious cooperation in the community and within the state. It was noted that it was the first time in the history of the Diocese of Baker that a Protestant and a Jew had received such an award. The honor was named after St. Sylvester, who had been Pope Sylvester I from 314 to 335. The first ecumenical council of the Christian Church was held at Nicaea during his pontificate.

In a strange way, the ecumenical honor seemed to anticipate what the needs of the country would be in the coming year. On April 4, 1968, Dr. Martin Luther King was assassinated in Memphis, Tenn. Rioting and looting occurred in cities throughout the United States, including New York, Washington, Chicago, Detroit, and Oakland. News of the rioting in the United States left G.I.s serving in Vietnam feeling angry and confused. Dr. King's funeral was held in Atlanta on April 10, with network television coverage for seven and a half hours. Because that year the observances of Passover and Easter were unusually close (April 12 and April 14, respectively), religious men throughout the country spoke about the tragedy of Dr. King's death. What with the war in Vietnam and assassination of Dr. King, the country seemed to be in danger of coming apart.[3]

But Leo Adler did what he often did. He kept working. On April 15, he left for meetings in New York, Washington, and Philadelphia. In New York he attended a Time, Inc. stockholders meeting as well as a meeting with magazine and book publishers. In Washington he talked with Oregon congressmen and members of the Civil Aeronautics Board, and attended the annual U.S. Chamber of Commerce convention. In Philadelphia, he met with the Curtis Publishing Company, a firm he'd been doing business with since he was ten.[4] Few people would have described Leo as a

CLOSING THE CIRCLE

Leo Adler receives the Knighthood of St. Sylvester from Bishop Leipzig. Photo by Holman Studios. Baker Democrat Herald, *Jan. 16, 1967.* (Adler House Museum)

courageous man, but going to those cities at that time did take some courage.

1968 was also a presidential election year and in hopes of winning the Oregon primary, Senator Robert Kennedy made a campaign swing through Oregon with a stop in Baker on May 22. It was a quick stop, but Kennedy took time to joke with local children that he was running for president just so he could come to Baker. When he asked the savvy children if they believed him, they gleefully shouted "No!" Mrs. Alan Jay Lerner was spotted in the crowd. Preliminary production had begun on the movie musical *Paint Your Wagon*, which was to be filmed in the Eagle Creek area throughout the summer and was likely the reason Mrs. Lerner was part of the crowd. Senator Kennedy lost the Oregon primary; just two weeks later he was assassinated while campaigning for the California primary.[5]

It was a strange summer for the country and for Baker, likely made even stranger by the fact that a $13 million movie musical (its final cost was $20 million, a phenomenal amount in that day) was being filmed nearby at Eagle Creek in the Wallowa Whitman National Forest. The *Paint Your Wagon* film production team chose Eagle Creek because it gave them room to build two complete cities, both with identical backgrounds. The production brought many things into Baker. In an article he wrote for the *New York Times*, Rex Reed described a few of the things that came to Baker: a 250-person production crew, 300 extras, the Nitty Gritty Dirt Band, 250 horses, 30 water oxen, 150 hippies, Alan Jay Lerner, Joshua Logan, Lee Marvin, Clint Eastwood, and Jean Seberg. It also brought an estimated $50,000 a day into the general economy of Baker. Extras earned $22.50 a day and those with more than three lines earned $90. Laborers on the production earned a minimum of $225 a week for a six-day week. Even if there were several hundred unusual new people in town, the film was helping to bring a lot of money into Baker.[6]

Lots of people wanted to get involved with the project, including Leo's old friend, Senator Wayne Morse. The collections of the Oregon Historical Society show Senator Morse suited up in what was described as gambler's garb, for a ten-second cameo. Later that year Wayne Morse lost the Senate seat he had held since 1945 by less than two hundred votes to an energetic young man named Robert Packwood.[7] Richard Nixon was elected president. With a new Republican president, there would surely be more

Oregon Senator Wayne Morse as an extra in the movie, Paint Your Wagon. (Oregon Historical Society CN 013764)

Senator Robert Packwood (left) and Leo Adler discuss postal rates. Baker Democrat Herald, Aug. 20, 1969. (Oregon Historical Society, OrHi 104913)

changes in store for a country that had just come through an extremely difficult year.

On February 8, 1969, the *Saturday Evening Post* published its last issue. The passage of this venerable American magazine must have given Leo a twinge, since it had been a long-time friend to him over the sixty years he had sold it. While he may have felt sad at the loss of the magazine, it was better to see a friend go easily than with great struggle. And Leo could clearly see that the world was changing. That same month Leo made an offer to donate another new ambulance to the city. It would join the 1964 model that he had donated earlier. The city gratefully accepted the offer. In August of that year, Senator Robert Packwood made a stop in town and took time to discuss with Leo the U.S. postal system and some of its problems. He also took time to address a luncheon group during that visit.[8] Just as he had for the past twenty years, Leo maintained his strong access to the Oregon congressional delegation.

Leo's lobbying abilities could not hold back postal increases on second-class mail, which affected his business greatly. In January 1971, postal rates went up; at the same time air and rail access to Baker was cut back. Leo felt that the changes would cripple mail subscribers in rural areas, the bulk of his customers. His business shipped between 150 and 200 sacks of mail a day out of the Baker Post Office, and of $270,000 collected in postal receipts in 1970, Leo's business made up $90,000.[9] It was a problem that would continue to nettle Leo for the rest of his working days.

Leo continued his role as one of the best fund-raisers in Baker County and was active with the Oregon Heart Association, United Good Neighbors, and St. Elizabeth's Hospital in Baker. He was also a member of the Boise District Council for the Small Business Administration. Although he never had quite as many accounts as he had in his heyday during the forties, work kept him as busy as he wanted it to and his office staff kept things moving along. Zella Smurthwaite was still the office manager and Nedra Roske continued as the accounts manager.

While office technology had changed a great deal during the time that Leo had been running his business, it hadn't changed much in the offices of the Knights of Pythias building where the staff had been since the late 1950s. His accountant and friend Norm Kolb would occasionally discuss updating the equipment. Leo was approached numerous times by eager salesmen about putting in a sophisticated computer system. During one visit to Leo's office, Norm asked him what he thought about the possi-

Nedra Roske, long-time accounts manager for Leo Adler. (Adler House Museum)

bility of getting one. Leo pointed at Nedra Roske, who did his books, and said, "That girl can smell a penny from a block off. There is no computer in the world that can do that." Leo was satisfied to conduct business as he always had with the people he knew and trusted.[10]

In March 1971, Leo was named Baker's outstanding citizen. A long article in a special supplement to the Baker *Democrat Herald* described the range of activities that he had been involved in throughout his lifetime, the awards he had received, and the various gifts he had given to Baker. When people marveled at his ongoing generosity, his measured response was "Well, someone has to do these things."[11] The coverage that Leo received about his achievements and philanthropy reflected well on Baker, and it was also a good way to sell the merits of the city to the state and the inland Northwest. Leo's accountant Norm Kolb recalled a successful client of his who started a restaurant on a shoestring in Baker and then opened others in La Grande, The Dalles, and Portland. When asked how it was that he came to Baker, the man said, "I was looking around for places to go and I picked up a trade association magazine, and it had an article about Leo and his business in it. I figured that if Leo Adler could make a go of a business like that in a smaller community, maybe I should take a look at it."[12]

In October of that year, Leo shared with the City council news he had heard while traveling to attend the World Series. Hughes Air West was planning to announce that effective November 1 it would be discontinuing all westbound flights. Baker travelers would now need to fly to Boise to make all their plane connections. This infuriated the Baker business community, and an emergency meeting of the aviation committee of the Chamber of Commerce was called. Leo made calls to Rep. Al Ullman for further assistance, who quickly moved to gather more information. The congressman wrote a letter to the general manager of Hughes Air West requesting that the situation be rectified. Leo was once again able to mobilize his connections to make the situation move more smoothly, even though it was a hard time nationally for airlines.[13]

Zella Smurthwaite, Leo's office manager. She had worked for Leo since 1921. (Adler House Museum)

Later that same month, one hundred people gathered to pay tribute to Bishop Francis Leipzig, who had decided in June to retire. When he called Leo to tell him that he was leaving Baker to accept a position in Portland doing research work for the Archdiocese there, Leo expressed his regret and then asked the bishop if he would be taken care of. Leipzig assured Leo that his finances were sufficient. Special guests at the banquet included Oden Hawes, executive secretary of the Oregon Schools Activities Association; Anthony Brandenthaler; and Leo Adler. The Most Rev.

Leipzig was praised for the publicity he had helped focus in Baker's direction through his work on the Vatican II council, his work as chaplain of the nation's fire chiefs, and his great love of high school sports. The reporter for the *Democrat Herald* described it as an evening of lumps in the throat and flowery prose.[14]

With the retirement of another old friend, and as more honors continued to be heaped on his head, Leo's thoughts could have logically turned toward retirement as well. He did think of it, but he had certain conditions in mind for anyone who might want to buy the business. He wanted any buyer of the business to commit to remain in Baker for five years so that his twenty-five employees would have time to transition. But doing business as he had done it in the past was becoming more difficult with the continuing changes in postal rates and changes in air and rail freight to Baker. After going to a convention in Banff, Canada, and attending a meeting focused on the problems that reshippers were facing, Leo saw that those that remained in business would need to find ways of transportation other than U.S. mail. That could be a problem in Baker.[15]

In March 1974 the country was roiling with continuing new revelations about the Watergate controversy. Later that month, Leo sent a brief note to Rose Mary Woods, who was executive assistant to President Nixon. At this time, Miss Woods was a household name because of her claimed accidental role in erasing a crucial eighteen-minute section of taped conversation in the Oval Office.

Dear Miss Woods:

The first part of this week I was in San Francisco for a

magazine and book convention where I saw our good friend Jack Drown and we talked very frankly.

It was through Jack that I met you and Mr. Nixon when he was Vice President.

Knowing that I travel around the country a lot and keep my eyes and ears open, Jack wanted me to convey to you what my opinion is. I hope the President will not resign.

Will you please convey this to him?

Cordially,
Leo Adler

Rose Mary Woods responded to Leo's letter on April 8.

Dear Mr. Adler:

Many thanks for your letter of March 28, telling me of your recent meeting with our mutual friend, Jack Drown. It was deeply gratifying to read your words of continuing support for the President, and I can assure you that I passed your very encouraging message along to him. Your comments serve to strengthen my belief that this Administration will succeed in achieving the great goals for America and the world to which it is dedicated.

You may be sure the President joins me in extending his appreciation and very best wishes to you.

Sincerely,
Rose Mary Woods[16]

This exchange once again shows Leo's personal and quiet way of making contact with politicians. He starts out by explaining

Leo (center) received life membership to the Oregon Fire Chiefs Association. Association President Martin Krupeka (left) makes the presentation while Association Chaplain Francis Leipzig looks on. Baker Democrat Herald, *July 2, 1974.* (Oregon Historical Society OrHi 104917)

his connection to a friend of Woods and then mentions even earlier contact that they had back in the Eisenhower administration. It was a subtle, thoughtful approach. As was often the case with Leo, it doesn't give any direct indication of his political affiliation, but it does show his concern for the state of the country.

As he showed his concern for the country, he continued in his concern for Baker with the gift of a third ambulance at a cost of $20,000, and he received another honor for the contributions he had made to the city of Baker through the fire department. At the Oregon State Fire conference in Seaside, not too far from Astoria where his father had developed his own firefighting interests, Leo received an honorary life membership from the Oregon Fire Chiefs

Association. Leo had always thoroughly enjoyed his work with the Baker Fire Department, and the picture of him with Bishop Leipzig and the association president shows him absolutely beaming.[17] Several weeks after Leo received the award, his old friend Wayne Morse passed away on July 23, while he was trying to win back his old Senate seat from Senator Packwood. It was a shock to all but a few who were very close to Morse. President Nixon resigned in August that same year.

The problems Leo had with his mail continued. In December 1976, The U.S. Postal Service abruptly eliminated a round-trip mail run from Boise to Baker. After letters to Sen. Robert Packwood and Rep. Al Ullman, chairman of the Ways and Means committee, the problem was resolved with a special congressional act. Senator Packwood told Leo that he thought the run would be safe until summer of 1977.

In October 1977, at the age of eighty-two, Leo Adler announced that he was retiring from the magazine distribution business. Norma Giles, Zella Smurthwaite's niece, recalled that Zella found out that the business was being sold while Leo was out of town. She opened Leo's mail for him, as was her custom when he was gone. A letter from *TV Guide* said the magazine had enjoyed doing business with Leo through the years, and that it would seem strange not doing business with him any more. Zella read the letter and then had Norma read it, saying "It sounds like they are pulling *TV Guide* from Leo. I don't understand this at all." She then called *TV Guide* and was told that Leo had sold the business. He hadn't told Zella or anyone on the staff, which upset Zella very much; she thought that he should have at least told her what was going on.[18]

The Spark and the Light: The Leo Adler Story

The notice that Leo sent out was a simple four-paragraph statement reporting the sale and thanking the publishers, distributors, and staff he had worked with over the years. While it was stunning for magazine distributors to think that Leo would no longer be in business, he was eighty-two years old and likely ready to stop wrestling with the day-to-day problems of his business. Concerned about his staff, he had found a buyer for the business who was willing to make the commitment to stay in Baker for five years. Joe Meier, who had worked in the circulation division of Time for twenty years, bought the business and moved his family from Connecticut to Baker. Seeking out a buyer like Joe Meier to take over the business was for Baker's benefit. Norma Giles recalled that when Leo went out of business, many publishers had expected to divide up his accounts among other wholesalers,

Leo Adler shows Joe Meier one of the early building blocks of his business. Baker Democrat Herald, *Oct. 17, 1977.* (Oregon Historical Society OrHi 104919)

which would have scattered the work to areas far from Baker.

Joe Meier couldn't recall when he first met Leo, but he did recall meeting him at a convention in Las Vegas. Leo was particular about who he wanted to take over the business and he probably liked Meier's connections with Time, not just for his experience but also because Leo had a healthy amount of Time stock in his portfolio. Meier bought the business for $90,000 and immediately changed the name to Inland Empire Periodicals. In later years, he regretted changing the name of the business so quickly.[19]

On January 21, 1978, Leo was honored with a huge banquet put on by the Baker County Chamber of Commerce. Three hundred eighty guests came to pay their respects as friends spoke of his charity. His brother Sanford spoke of their younger days, Baker Fire Chief Bob Young recalled what a friend he had been to the fire department, and toward the end of the evening City Manager George Hiatt announced that Leo had given the city money for yet another ambulance, an item they likely wouldn't need for another two years. Joe Meier also made a presentation that brought down the house. "We can't give a trophy or a plaque to a guy who's got a warehouse full of them." He joked that the March issue of *Penthouse* magazine would be devoted to Leo and held up a *Penthouse* magazine cover that had Leo taped between two beautiful women. The smile it brought to Leo's face was said to be worth the price of admission.[20]

At the end the evening, boys and girls armed with news sacks handed out copies of "The Adler Times," an eight-page supplement the *Democrat Herald* put out in his honor. It included letters from well-wishers around the state. Shirley Tanzer, director of the Jewish Historical Society of Oregon, had interviewed Leo and

Leo Adler looking over "The Adler Times" at his retirement banquet. Baker Democrat Herald, *Jan. 23, 1978.* (Oregon Historical Society OrHi 104918)

many other members of the Baker Jewish community in the summer of 1977. She wrote, "Leo and his brother Sanford have followed in the family tradition of civic concerns. The breadth of their generosity is not confined to Baker, but to Oregon, the United States and specific international humanitarian institutions. This is fulfilling the 'mitzvot' [acts of loving kindness] of the Jewish religion. They can be proud of their accomplishments." The Most. Rev. Francis Leipzig recalled their annual birthday dinners with Norris Poulson. Thomas Vaughan, director of the Oregon Historical Society, recalled meeting Leo for the first time in 1955 when he became a new board member.

> *In mid afternoon a man came into the room I knew instantly had to be Leo. A heart of gold in a body of oak with good will*

and good cheer radiating from his face. Stepping forward to make the introductions I was swept aside and practically knocked down by a sudden stampede. There was Leo, rushing forward to meet his friends and they were crowding forward to greet him, a tried and true friend of old. I suddenly realized that Leo was not only Mr. Baker but a great and generous public servant of the American West known to many as Mr. Oregon.[21]

There were also good wishes from Senator Mark Hatfield, Rep. Al Ullman, and Governor Bob Straub. Albert Rachoi, president of International Circulation Distributors, wrote to say, "It will be difficult to think of our business with an inactive Leo Adler." Leo was now officially launched into his retirement years. But what would retirement mean for a man who had worked for the past seventy-seven years?

Leo (right) and Sanford Adler at the entrace to Leo's offices in the Knights of Pythias building. (Adler House Museum)

A Bright Twilight

Although Leo was officially retired in January 1978, his life didn't look terribly different after his retirement than it did before it. At first he still went to his office in the Knights of Pythias Building every day, usually working about six hours as he took care of correspondence, reading, and some of his other interests.[1] This made things a little difficult for Joe Meier as he was working to get his arms around the business. When he was interviewed for this biography, Joe Meier described Leo as having the books, or the accounting for the business, in his back pocket. He didn't mean this unkindly; it was an accurate reflection of the way Leo had structured his business.

Throughout all his years in business, Leo was a sole proprietor. After the 1958 fire that caused him to move to the Knights of Pythias building, Leo was audited by the Internal Revenue Service; while he made it through the audit, he felt that the Boise tax attorney representing him was too aggressive. He hired Norm Kolb after the audit was completed. Kolb recalled that tone was very important to Leo. Leo was not a controlling personality, but he needed to have a sense of ease with any dealings that were done in his name. He needed to trust the people he was working with. At the time of his retirement, half of his thirty-member staff had been working with him for more than twenty-five years. He remained a sole proprietor because it allowed him to see what his business was doing and it also allowed him to keep his assets reasonably liquid, which would understandably be important to a man who had lived through the majority of the twentieth century.[2]

When the business was sold, Joe Meier brought many technological changes. Zella Smurthwaite and Nedra Roske, both in their late seventies, were encouraged to retire. Norma Giles became the new office manager and began to learn more about the new technology. The office staff was further reduced as Meier began working with the business.

Leo continued with his past interests. He still read several newspapers a day: the local *Democrat-Herald* and *Record-Courier*, the *Oregonian*, the *Idaho Daily Statesman* and the *Wall Street Journal*. His retirement gift of a radio scanner helped him keep track of what was happening in the fire department. He also kept track of the money that he had earned over his lifetime. Ralph Giles, who daily picked up Leo's mail from his post-office box, recalled that Leo had a keen sense of when his series of dividend checks should be arriving, and would begin to worry if they seemed off schedule.

Leo had done quite well through the years with his stock investments, and he made a point of keeping his money local. Two people who were important to him in that area were Roger Ager of the Trust Department of U.S. Bank and Gary Schmitt, the manager of U.S. Bank in Baker from 1977 to 1989. Schmitt recalled that Sanford and Leo Adler were the first people in town to invite him and his wife over for dinner. Leo would come into the bank weekly and sit down for a chat with Schmitt. This is not to say he didn't enjoy talking with the tellers, because Leo still enjoyed the company of women. Any time Leo was getting ready to give a large donation, he would ask Schmitt out to dinner. Schmitt recalled that Leo enjoyed seeing his resources put to the use of the community.[3]

Roger Ager met Leo in 1980. Based in Bend, Ager tended to call in eastern Oregon once a quarter. If Leo was interested in a visit and available, Ager would stop by and see him. Leo kept substantial deposits at the Baker U.S. Bank. At one point Roger suggested that Leo could put his money in a different kind of account that could bring him more income. Leo's response was, "Yeah, but if I keep a lot of money here, you'll pay attention to me."

When Ager visited Leo, he would see him at his home, where his round oak table was always covered with mail and newspapers. He always had his fire department scanner turned on. Leo was a consummate reader of the *Wall Street Journal* as well as several other papers mentioned earlier. Early in their relationship, Ager remembers, Leo would call him to ask if he had seen a particular article in the *Journal*. Ager read the *Journal* at that time, but not as carefully as Leo did. After the third such call, Ager realized that Leo was checking up on him to see if he was on top of things and engaged with what was going on in the wider business world. After that, he made a point of reading the *Journal* more carefully. This same careful reading eventually crossed over to the other papers Leo read as well.

Ager remembered Leo as being "very pleasant, not gruff, always inquisitive. He could see the subtle nuances and read between the lines. He could also see the political underpinnings of a given situation. He was very well respected." As a client Leo didn't expect anything out of the ordinary. He would usually simply say to Ager, "just stop by when you are in town," and Ager would stop by for a chat. Leo was always very specific in the questions he asked.[4]

As a new relationship was beginning, a lifelong one closed. Leo's brother Sanford died in December 1980 at the age of eighty-eight. Sanford had long been involved in a variety of community affairs, but not to the same degree as Leo. After retiring from twenty-seven years as Baker's postmaster in 1962, Sanford continued his involvement with the Baker Elks, Lions, and Masons. He was also active with the Salvation Army. As many of the older members of the Jewish community passed on, Sanford took the role of elder in conducting services for what remained of the Jewish community of Baker. Sanford's wife Louise had passed away in July 1979. They had been married just over fifty years and were known around Baker as gracious entertainers and enthusiastic travelers. Louise was remembered by those who knew her as "a real lady." In 1961 she published a cookbook called *Galloping Gourmet*, which she dedicated, "For my husband Sanford Adler, who has survived this cooking for many years." In the later years of her life, Louise experienced severe back pain, but she would still dress up for an evening of dancing with her husband. She wouldn't dance, but she would enjoy spending the evening out with friends and watching her husband cut a dapper figure on the dance floor. Louise also helped to preserve and maintain the Adler family history, which is now housed in the collections of the Oregon Jewish Museum in Portland. Both Sanford and Louise were buried in the Mount Hope Cemetery in Baker, the first of the Baker Adlers to take their rest there.

Mary Louise Adler (1895–1979) helped maintain the Adler family history after Laura and Theresa Adler passed away. A gracious hostess, she wrote a cookbook, The Galloping Gourmet.

Sanford and Louise had no children, but they left a gift to the students of Baker. In 1982, the Sanford and Mary Louise Adler Scholarship was established. It contributed toward the education of selected students living in Baker County who were attending state-funded colleges. Although the scholarship looked at several criteria including the scholarship, character, and dedication of the applicant, financial need was a very important element. Applicants had to show that they would be able to continue their educational program without the assistance of the scholarship.

Leo was shaken by the death of his brother. It was said that Sanford had been making a visit to Leo when he slipped and fell; sadly, he never made a full recovery from the fall.[5] With Sanford's passing, an important link to Leo's Jewish heritage was gone. While Leo had long been socially and financially active with the wider Jewish community in Oregon, Sanford had been the more religiously observant son.

Although Leo had long been involved with fundraising for St. Elizabeth's hospital, Sanford's death may have made him redouble his efforts. He also had some of his own health difficulties in the early 1980s, including a convalescence at Portland's Robison Jewish Home. As a well-established member of the local hospital board, Leo was especially helpful to the hospital when large equipment was needed. Sister Martha Joseph Rooney, who worked with St. Elizabeth's between 1976 and 1990, recalled meeting Leo through hospital board meetings. He was often with Henry and Mary Levinger, who were also involved with the hospital. She recalled him as being a gentle man with a vigorous mind who enjoyed chatting with people. "He never blew his horn, but was anxious to do what was best for the community." She recalled that when he was in meetings, he listened very carefully and took part in the areas that he was involved with. "He never tried to drive the agenda." In May 1983 he gave the hospital the gift of an ultrasound machine. Later that year, the Sisters of St. Francis presented him with the inaugural St. Francis Humanitarian Award. At that point, Leo had contributed more than $258,000 to the hospital for medical equipment. Sister Martha Joseph would occasionally visit Leo and tell him that they prayed for him because, as she said, "We pray for all our donors." Remembering him in 2002, she said "His reward in the next life will be great" because he had great love, "love for his family, friends and community."[6]

As Leo moved into his late eighties and nineties, people seemed to be standing in line to thank him for all the things that he had done. He started a scholarship fund at Eastern Oregon State College; he donated a laser to St. Elizabeth Hospital; and "Leo Adler Hall" in the Oregon Trail Regional Museum was dedi-

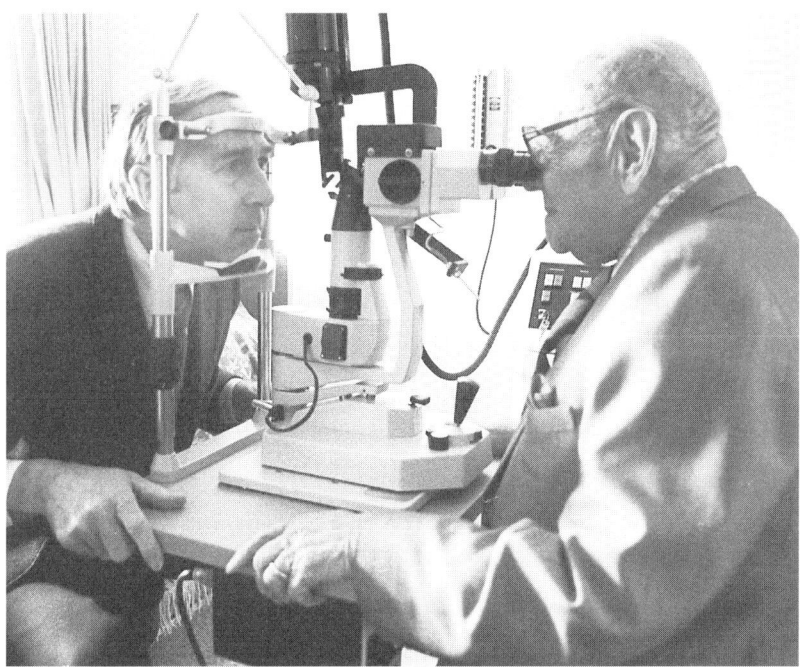

*Leo and Dr. Gordon Leitch with a new laser machine, purchased by a donation from Leo. Photo by S. John Collins. (*Baker* Democrat Herald, Dec. 8, 1987)*

cated and a portrait of him was unveiled. With the assistance of his longtime friend Bob Young as a driver and companion, Leo accepted the accolades not so much for himself as for the Baker community, secure in the knowledge that Baker was striving in new ways, even during the tough economic times of the mid-1980s. According to county records, between 1983 and 1986 Baker County had the highest jobless rate in Oregon, with unemployment at a high of 23 percent at one time.[7] In later years, Portland columnists referred to it as the Appalachia of Oregon[8] and said that with the collapse of the lumber industry, the community was being bled to death.[9] Interviewed when he was ninety years old in 1986, Leo told a reporter, "Sure I'm optimistic but I've been around long enough to know that if people go around saying we're going to hell everyone else will start believing it. Baker's a good town. I'm cheerful, I think we're going to come back."[10] And he was right. Baker found its way to the future by looking to the past.

In 1986, Neil Goldschmidt was elected governor of Oregon. A native of Eugene, Goldschmidt became mayor of Portland (1973-79) at the age of thirty-two and in 1979 became U.S Secretary of Transportation under President Jimmy Carter. After Carter lost the presidential election in 1980, Goldschmidt came back to Oregon to work for the Oregon-based shoe company Nike. When he entered the governor's race, his opponent was Norma Paulus. Twice elected as secretary of state, Paulus had deep roots in eastern Oregon, spending her youth in Burns, and striving to become the first woman elected governor of Oregon. Goldschmidt made strong connections in Baker and campaigned hard. He received 3,193 votes to Paulus' 2,847 in Baker County[11] and he won the Oregon governor's race 52 percent to Paulus' 48 percent. Baker resident Mike Nelson had worked hard on the campaign and was asked to be part of the Goldschmidt transition team. Nelson was later elected to the Oregon House of Representatives.

The Goldschmidt administration rolled out a series of programs under the broad title of the "Oregon Comeback." One of them was the Regional Strategies program, which was designed to jump-start economic development across the state. Each region was challenged to identify an underutilized resource at its disposal. Because of its strong contacts in the Goldschmidt administration, Baker began work on its plan almost immediately in November 1986. The Baker Economic Development Commission was created and an economic development director was hired.

A Bright Twilight

Chaired by local U.S. Bank Manager Gary Schmitt, the commission put together a proposal that created a nationally recognized interpretive center focused on the Oregon Trail. The 150th anniversary of the 1843 wagon trains coming across the Oregon Trail would be celebrated in 1993. With fifteen miles of trail and wagon ruts, Baker's past was turning into one of its biggest resources.

The Interpretive Center was a leap of faith for the city at that point, and there was controversy over whether that was a proper direction to take. While the economic development director's position was created, the fire department's force was reduced. Leo was not thrilled about what was done at the fire department, but his general attitude toward the project was, "Go do what you think is right."[12]

Leo sitting on his bed after returning from his Portland convalescence. Photo by S. John Collins. (Baker Democrat Herald, *Feb. 25, 1982)*

THE SPARK AND THE LIGHT: THE LEO ADLER STORY

From left: Former Oregon Gov. Neil Goldschmidt, Mike Nelson and Brian Cole congratulate Leo on the opening of the Leo Adler Theatre at the Oregon Trail Interpretive Center. Photo by S. John Collins. (Baker Democrat Herald, Oct. 13, 1992)

The development of the Oregon Trail Interpretive Center seemed like the type of project Leo could have dreamed up in his younger days. The Baker application for the project was the first submitted to the Regional Strategies program and the third one approved. The proposal asked for $600,000 in state lottery funds, and in 1987 representatives from Baker went to Washington, D.C., to start the process of asking for federal money. The state was committed to the project in the spring of 1988, and later that year the project received $1.3 million in federal funding with the assistance of Rep. Les AuCoin and Sen. Mark Hatfield.[13] The initial group of local Baker men and women who had been working on the Oregon Trail Interpretive Center now had state and federal funding; the next piece they needed was local community funding, and who might they turn to for that?

In November 1988, Leo hosted a luncheon at the Kopper Kitchen in Baker. Representatives from five different community organizations joined him. At some point during the event, likely during the sweetness of dessert, it was announced that Leo was donating a combined $254,000 to the groups assembled before him. The Baker *Democrat Herald* covered the event and listed the organizations he gave to:

$25,000 to the Baker School District's high school baseball program
$103,000 to the Oregon Trail Interpretive Center
$25,000 to the Baker County Library for the purchase of books
$51,000 to the Oregon Trail Museum
$50,000 toward the city's ambulance reserve fund

These contributions were in addition to Leo's other usual contributions to a range of charities. This particular piece of largesse came from the sale of Crowell-Collier stock that Leo had purchased in 1950 for $28,000 on the advice of a friend. In a leveraged buyout, the Macmillan Publishing bought up all shares held by stockholders. Leo's portion had grown to $856,412. That year he made contributions of $428,206, including the $254,000 he gave to those assembled at lunch. When people commented on his generosity, he replied, "I just feel I owe it to the community because I got my start here."[14]

Many people interviewed for this book remarked on Leo's positive character. He was not a man to be highly critical of others. Consequently, few things made him as angry as when people criticized him for the way he was spending his money. His accountant and friend Norm Kolb recalled that the only time he'd ever heard Leo swear was when a friend criticized him for a project in which he was involved. The friend came to Leo and told him he was making a terrible mistake. Leo said to Norm, "God damn it, Norm, it's my money and I'm gonna do this."

For a man known to be very even-tempered, when his temper did flare it was always a surprise. At some point in the 1980s, Leo's television gave up the ghost and needed to be replaced. Bob Young took care of this for him, buying a new color TV with a remote-control channel changer that added $40 to the price. When Leo saw the remote control, he hit the roof. He said quite forcefully that he didn't want a remote control, that his doctor had told him that it was good for him to get up out of the chair and change the channels himself. Stunned by Leo's reaction, Young returned the remote control unit and Leo continued to get some form of exercise by struggling out of his chair to change the channel. Looking back on it, Young would describe Leo as being generous with everyone but himself.

Leo continued to live in the kitchen area and back bedroom of his home. He never went upstairs, and the downstairs had accumulated the detritus of living in the same place since 1899. Among his mother's beautiful furniture and decorations, people would comment on the oddity of seeing broken lawn mowers in the parlor. A lifelong bachelor, Leo didn't appear to be particular about his physical surroundings. Home healthcare workers had to firmly insist that he buy a new rug when his old rug was described as a trip hazard.[15] His sister Theresa's piano was still in

A Bright Twilight

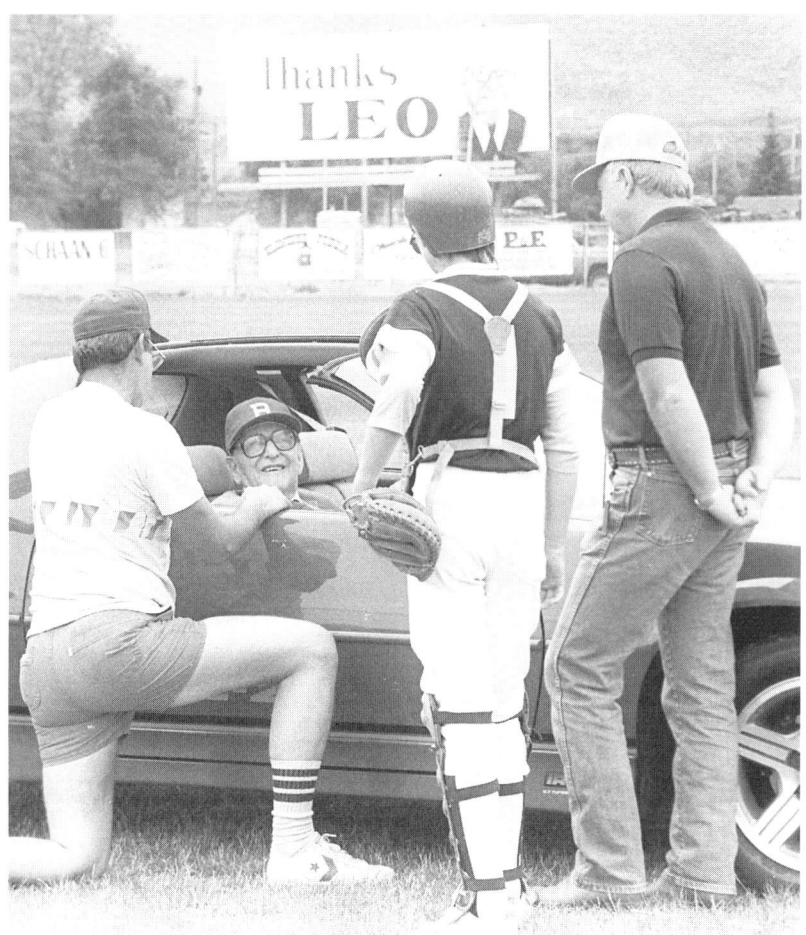

Leo chats with some ball players who are gathered in honor of the many gifts he has made over the years. Photo by Gerry Steele. (Baker Democrat Herald, *July 6, 1989)*

the front room and Leo enjoyed it when the grandchildren or in-laws of friends would come and play it even though it had been a long time since it had been tuned. He also enjoyed visits with the children and grandchildren of friends and tried to be hospitable, even if the maple bars or bananas he was offering generally were

Henry Levinger (left) and Leo enjoy some cake in honor of Leo's ninety-fifth birthday. Photo by S. John Collins. (Baker Democrat Herald, *June 25, 1990)*

not at their freshest state. Norma Giles recalled hearing one of her grandchildren tell another friend, "We're going down to Leo's to get a black banana."[16]

After some problems in the early eighties, Leo's health continued at an even keel for the next decade. Choosing his words carefully, his doctor described Leo as "not a medically compliant person."[17] In his later years, Leo stepped back from the drinking that he had done as a younger man. Even though he lived alone, he was surrounded by people who were looking out for his care, including Bob Young, Norma and Ralph Giles, and his long-time friends, Hans Neuberger or Henry and Mary Levinger, who lived just behind him.

In 1990, just before her eighty-ninth birthday, Zella

Smurthwaite passed away. Throughout his life, Zella was the woman with whom Leo shared the longest, closest bonds. In various drafts of his will throughout his lifetime, Zella was always provided for. Many people interviewed for this biography described Zella as Leo's mistress, while many others would not use that word. There are a variety of definitions for the word mistress, only one of them with a sexual connotation. Perhaps the most apt definition of the word to describe Zella's relationship with Leo is "a woman who has ultimate control over something." She had ultimate control of the day-to-day work of his office, and she had his trust. They were able to work together for fifty-eight years, an accomplishment in any sort of relationship. Although he was very upset by her passing, Leo was afraid to go to her December funeral, for fear of slipping and falling on the ice as his brother Sanford had done. Various people offered to assist him, yet he couldn't bring himself to go. Norma Giles tape-recorded the funeral and Leo took comfort in listening to it.[18]

Leo continued his strong record of giving. The fire department received another new ambulance. The Oregon Trail Interpretive Center opened in May 1992 to great fanfare and enthusiasm throughout the state of Oregon and pulled many Oregonians eastward to see the beauty of Baker County. A proposal was brought before City Council to change the name of Campbell Street to Leo Adler Boulevard. Because Campbell Street had been named after a historic Baker resident, the renaming proved controversial. As the controversy arose, Leo pulled away from the idea because he loathed anything that might divide the community. He continued to feel that if a community doesn't pull together, it pulls apart.[19]

The Spark and the Light: The Leo Adler Story

Pencil portrait of Leo Adler by Tom Novak. Photo by S. John Steele. (Baker Democrat Herald, Dec. 29, 1993)

Leo received further accolades that year in November when the Leo Adler Theater was dedicated at the Oregon Trail Interpretive Center. Former Governor Neil Goldschmidt came for the festivities and spoke these words at the event: "Leo has always been like a lighthouse in eastern Oregon, because we knew we could always find our way home to eastern Oregon by Leo's light, by his commitment. . . . He is a true pioneer. Somebody not afraid to step out ahead of his flock. Today, we honor somebody who has honored us over and over again."[20]

Leo sat in his wheelchair and quietly took it all in, looking over what his seed money had helped to grow. Since his work with the American Pioneer Trails Association in 1943, he had been involved with the Oregon Trail for over fifty years. With the Leo Adler Theater, he was now a permanent part of the rich legacy of a splendid facility that explained the rigors of the Oregon Trail to current and future generations.

Over the next year, Leo's health declined, with trips in and out of the hospital. He spent his ninety-eighth birthday in a hospital room, with visits throughout the day from friends and the children and grandchildren of friends. In the fall, Leo's friend and former attorney Gene Rose paid him a visit. Rose was in the process of moving back to Baker after living in Ontario since 1968. Leo talked about how beautiful Baker was in the fall. Then he said to Rose, "This is a great town, isn't it?"[21]

On November 2, 1993, Leo Adler passed away of causes related to old age at St. Elizabeth's Hospital. The flags of the city were flown at half-mast. As seems fitting for a Jewish man who had received papal honors for his work with various religious and civic groups, the funeral service was held at the Church of Jesus Christ of the Latter-Day Saints. Norma and Ralph Giles helped to organize the service, ward Bishop Don Morgan conducted it, and Norma gave the eulogy.

Bishop Don Morgan reminded the almost 200 mourners, "When you are in the service of your fellow man, you are in the service of your God." He also recalled an early experience with Leo after he had moved to Baker in the seventies. He hadn't been in business six months when Leo came in; he recalled, "I didn't know Leo Adler from anybody, but he wanted to know how I was doing. He was concerned that as a businessman, I'd be able to make it and to prosper." When Morgan learned who Leo was, the visit gave his morale a boost. After talking with another businessman in the week after Leo's death, he learned that the same thing had happened to him. It might have been a practice of Leo's, to come around and visit new businesses to encourage them.[22]

Norma Giles gave a touching and beautiful eulogy, saying good-bye to a man she had known all her life. Calling him the most honest man she had ever known, Giles noted that a great era had ended in their community. She closed her remarks saying, "We will miss Leo, but his generosity will undoubtedly continue."[23]

Afterword: Reaping What Was Sown

Norma Giles was quite right about the continuity of Leo Adler's generosity. A week after Leo died, the Baker City *Herald* ran an article estimating Leo's wealth at $20 million, the vast majority of it left to the benefit of the future generations of Baker County in the form of the Leo Adler Trust. The money would be divided, with roughly $12 million, or 60 percent, going to the Leo Adler Foundation and the remaining $8 million, or 40 percent, going to the Leo Adler Community Fund. The foundation would provide scholarships in the form of grants or loans to graduates of Baker, Pine Eagle, Huntington, Burnt River, and Powder Valley high schools. The Community Fund would support the work of many of the organizations that Leo had favored during his lifetime. He also left particular remembrances to various people and organizations.

The community and the state of Oregon was stunned not only by the generosity of the gift but by the size of it. Leo was known to be a very wealthy man, but because of the simple and some would say shabby manner that he kept himself and his home, no one suspected that he had left that much money. Many people interviewed for this biography firmly believed that Leo didn't know how much money he had. The trustees of the Leo Adler Trust, Roger Ager of U.S. Bank, Henry Levinger, and Norm Kolb, knew better. Leo had always been an astute man with numbers. The type of giving that he enjoyed didn't really come under the category of a conspicuous display of wealth. He liked giving things to his community that many people don't see when they are looking for wealth, such as lights for a baseball field, a fire truck, new equipment for the hospital, money for books for the library, and the connections and seed money to help things happen for Baker City. At the time of his death, Leo was receiving dividend income from an array of seventy-seven stocks that included holdings in Albertsons, Boeing, Chevron, James River, Neiman Marcus, the *New York Times*, Tektronix, and Time-Warner Inc. His dividend and interest income from his investments amounted to over $420,000 in 1993. Leo knew what he had; he simply was not impressed by it.

Although his own formal education had stopped when he finished high school, the majority of his money would now go toward assisting with the education of future generations from his community. In 1995, the first year that scholarships were granted, 207 Adler scholars received an average of $2,936. The first person to receive a scholarship was Michael Thompson. A 1968 graduate of Baker High School, Thompson worked as a Baker City firefighter for fifteen years before enrolling in nursing school. He planned to use the money to enroll in a master's program to obtain his family nurse practitioner certifications. His daughter Emily was a 1995 graduate of Powder Valley High School, and

Afterword: Reaping What Was Sown

she received an Adler award as well to attend Eastern Oregon State College in La Grande.[2] From its first granting year in 1995 through 2003, Adler Scholarships have granted $7,525,000 to 3,638 scholars, many of whom renewed their grants through their five years of eligibility. In the 2003–2004 academic year, 467 Adler Scholars were attending 117 colleges, universities, and vocational schools.

Leo left his formerly magnificent home and its contents to the Baker County Museum Commission. Leo had been generous to the area's historical organizations in the past. He tended to give gifts of $10,000 each year to either the Baker County Museum Commission or to the Baker County Historical Society. But the gift of the family home was a surprise, especially since, as one commission member described it, it was a gift with "no strings attached."[3] Chary Mires and Colleen Brooks were appointed by the Museum Commission to develop a plan for what to do with the house. Chary Mires took her first tour through the Adler home and recalled that it left her "speechless for several days. Whatever I expected, that wasn't it." On the first floor, the turn-of-the-century wallpaper had been painted over, as had the wood floors. On the second floor, the walls were black with soot, but on the whole the area was magnificently preserved. Pieces of the the ceiling had fallen down, but she picked up all the pieces she could find and saved them in a plastic bag for future reference. The scope of the project was beginning to dawn on her.

Chary Mires and her husband had moved back to Baker in 1989 after living in Ontario for many years. She joined the Museum Commission in 1989 and by 1991 she was the commission's secretary and had begun writing grants for various historical projects. By 1994 she was chair of the commission and had helped accomplish several projects with the Oregon Trail Regional Museum, which was housed in the former Baker Natatorium. She had been part of the renovation of the museum's ballroom and the pouring of the cement floor to cover over the pool. She had tackled big projects before, but this project was bigger than anything she'd imagined.[4]

There were a range of options for what could be done with the house. It could be demolished and the property sold, the house could be sold as is, or it could be sold with the condition that it should remain similar externally to its original condition. Carolyn Sherreib of the Oregon Trail Regional Museum thought it should become a historic house, and there was community support for this idea. Colleen Brooks and Chary Mires sat down over a pot of coffee and plotted out how it all might happen. They gave the project a timeline of three to four years. They held a yard sale and raised $1,000 to pay Peter Baer, a contractor from Bend who was interested in the project, to come up with preliminary estimates of what it would cost to restore the house. The price he came up with was $212,483.

Chary Mires laughed at the memory of how she and others interested in the preservation of the house tried to take the easy way out by asking the Leo Adler Community Fund for the full amount up front. Letting their mantra of "How would Leo want this money spent?" guide them, the trustees gave the Adler House Museum $25,000 in their 1995 granting cycle. That was enough to take care of the immediate critical work that needed to be done. Inspectors had discovered that the house was no longer touching the main beam. Walls on the first level were cracking, so the structure had to be leveled. In 1996, the Adler House Museum received

Afterword: Reaping What Was Sown

The Adler home, now the Adler House Museum. Photo by Adair Law.

$50,000 from the Adler Community Fund, which covered the work that would be done in the coming year. All the rotted windows and casings were replaced with custom-made work, a huge undertaking in this home. A new roof was put on the house, and deteriorated mortar between the foundation rocks was replaced. Damaged wood on the exterior of the house was replaced with wood salvaged by work crews from the Powder River Correctional Facility. The wood came from a home that was slated for burning as a practice exercise for the fire department.[5] New stairs were built, and the community could begin to see the improvements.

On June 21, 1997, Leo's Birthday Party and Sale was held on the grounds of the house. Many of the possessions that were less critical for the house museum were sold to raise money for the continuing work, which would soon be moving into interior design. Through the years, the yard sales paid for the utilities while the work on the house was in process. Chary Mires, Colleen Brooks, Jane Hutton, and Scotty Haskell referred to themselves as the "gang of four," and they all continued to push the project forward. Interior decoration of the house quickly moved into high gear. Pieces of furniture from the Adler family were restored and gradually moved back into the house. It was decided that the house would be restored to the era between 1910 and 1915. Most of the research for the restoration was done at the Baker County Library, just a block away from the Adler House. Pictures of Baker homes from that period gave them background, and the group also did research in various historic houses in the state of Washington, which gave them inspiration.

Deciding on the type of wallpaper was the most difficult part of their research. Few manufacturers made styles that were suitable for this type of restoration, and as Mires noted, "We didn't want to have someone come in and say, 'My sister-in-law has that in her house.'" Their research took them to Bradbury & Bradbury Art Wallpapers in Benecia, Calif. The company was and is known for its collection of historic wallpapers representing designs created in Europe and America in the nineteenth and early twentieth centuries. Some designs were reproductions, some were adaptations of stenciled and hand-painted decorations. Mires tracked down a design she liked and paid for a sample with her own funds. When she asked for a larger sample, she was told that they were no longer making that wallpaper, and they weren't sure who the forms and stencils had been sold to. Further research led her to

Afterword: Reaping What Was Sown

make contact with the Boston Design Center, which told her that Cockshutt & Allen in Melbourne, Australia, was now manufacturing that wallpaper. She contacted the company and asked for samples of what she was interested in. When the samples arrived in Baker City, a cry of "That's it!" arose among the Gang of Four. Unfortunately, the price tag of $10,000 was beyond anything they had imagined for this aspect of the renovation. But if there was one area Chary Mires had gained new confidence, it was in writing grants. Through her research she discovered a gentleman who had a foundation dedicated to supporting historic homes. Mires received a call one day to tell her that the check for $10,000 was in the mail. She in turn heaved a great sigh of "Thank you, Leo!" The Collins Foundation of Portland also assisted in the restoration of the house with a grant of $37,500. The Adler Community Fund had funded two-thirds of the project, and the resourceful citizens of Baker figured out how to come up with the rest. The grand opening was set for June 21, 1998, on what would have been Leo's 103rd birthday.[6]

Because of delays in moving the wallpaper off the dock in Melbourne, not all the rooms were able to show the full flower of their restoration. The front parlor and the family and formal dining rooms were not papered, but they were still transformed by the work that had been accomplished. At a special reception for about sixty people, Baker City Mayor Karen Yeakley played a few tunes on the piano that Leo's sister Theresa had so loved throughout her life. On the day the house was opened to the public, 250 people came through. It was an amazing accomplishment and one that would have tickled Leo immensely. Although he could certainly dream big dreams, he probably never would have dreamed that the home he had lived in for so many years could be transformed into such a jewel.

Leo knew that it often took some initial money to tap the less well-known or understood treasures of an area. He knew that while money is important, it is not the only thing that carries a project through to the end. It also takes energy, enthusiasm, and occasionally some hard-headedness to see a project through; those are things that money can't buy. Recipients of Community Fund grants take seriously the responsibility of spending the money in a thoughtful manner. In the process of working on the Adler House Museum, Chary Mires commented that she was surprised to learn that it was easier to raise money than it was to spend it.[7] Could this be another lesson Leo has passed on to the community posthumously?

The Community Fund continues to support charities that Leo favored throughout his lifetime, along with several others. From 1995 to 2002 St. Elizabeth Health Services has received $410,000 from the fund. Ten area churches receive annual gifts from Leo as they did when he was alive. His generosity will always be deeply woven into the community. As of Dec. 31, 2003, the Community Fund has given out 542 awards for a total of $5,750,000.

The community returns thanks in many ways for the gift Leo gave them. His June 21 birthday is celebrated in a variety of ways, often with an article in the newspaper and sometimes with a parade along Main Street with many of the organizations that have been affected by his generosity. Occasionally there have been hot dogs and baseball games. Some community members joke that the bars in town should make sure they have a bottle of Old Granddad Whiskey in Leo's honor.

Afterword: Reaping What Was Sown

As Adler Scholars return to their eastern Oregon homes or strike out into new homes around the country and around the world, what of Baker City and what of Leo Adler will they carry with them? Will they work to become the spark and the light for their communities in the same way that Leo was for his? Only time will tell, but it will certainly be a story that Leo Adler never would have tired of hearing.

Endnotes

Coming To America

1. Adler Family File, Ind. 46. File 1. Documents. Oregon Jewish Museum, Portland, Oregon.
2. The names of family members were pieced together from translations of correspondence in the Adler Family scrapbook at the Oregon Jewish Museum.
3. Steven Lowenstein, *The Jews of Oregon, 1850-1950*, Jewish Historical Society of Oregon, Portland, 1987, p. 4.
4. William Toll, *The Making of an Ethnic Middle Class: Portland Jewry Over Four Generations*, State University of New York Press, Albany, 1982, p. 9.
5. Norma Giles funeral eulogy transcript.
6. Adler Family File, Ind. 46. General correspondence. Oregon Jewish Museum, Portland, Oregon.
7. Adler Family scrapbook, p. 46.
8. Leo Adler Oral History, Oregon Jewish Museum. According to Leo, his father Carl came around Cape Horn. Norma Giles funeral eulogy says Carl crossed at the Isthmus of Panama.
9. Samuel Suwol, *Jewish History of Oregon*, 1958, p. 4. Lowenstein, p. 44.
10. Baker *Morning Democrat*, Oct. 21, 1892. Obituary for Leopold Hirsch.
11. Salem *Oregon Statesman* on Feb. 16, 1864, p. 3, col. 4
12. 1880 United States Census (A. Hirsch. East Salem, Marion, Oregon. NA Film number T9-1082, p. 32B)
13. Eugene, *Oregon State Journal*, Nov. 22, 1873, p.2, col. 5.
14. 1880 United States Census, (S.H. Friendly. Eugene, Lane. NA Film number T9-1081, p. 254D). Lowenstein, p. 39.

15. *Current Biography*, "Fred Friendly," The H. W. Wilson Company, 1987.
16. Eugene, *Oregon State Journal*, Nov. 22, 1873
17. 1880 United States Census (Anna Adler. Eugene, Lane. NA Film number T9-1081, p. 254D)
18. Leo Adler Oral History, 979.165 A237D #9677, Oregon Historical Society, and Leo Adler Oral History, Oregon Jewish Museum. Toll, p. 11. Adler Family, Ind 46, certificates, Oregon Jewish Museum.
19. Adler Family scrapbook, p. 46. Oregon Jewish Museum.
20. Adler Family, Ind 46, correspondence, 1870. Oregon Jewish Museum.
21. Dan Cohn-Sherbok, *A Concise Encyclopedia of Judaism*, p. 111.
22. Obituary notices for Carl Adler mention that he worked in Eugene and Astoria prior to moving to Baker City. Baker *Herald*, July 29, 1918 p. 8, and Baker *Morning Democrat*, July 30, 1918, p. 8.
23. Adler Family, Ind 46, General correspondence, 1872-1877. Oregon Jewish Museum.

BUILDING THE CRYSTAL PALACE

1. John Scofield, *Hail, Columbia!*. Oregon Historical Society Press, Portland, 1993, p. 258.
2. Ibid., p. 259
3. Lewis McArthur, *Oregon Geographic Names*, Sixth ed., Oregon Historical Society Press, Portland, 1991, p. 30.
4. Alfred A. Cleveland, "Social and Economic History of Astoria," *Oregon Historical Quarterly*, 4 (1903):139-141.
5. Ibid., p. 141.
6. Ibid., p. 142.
7. Adler Family, Ind 46, "Bank records, Stocks, Deeds-1871-1927," Jan. 1, 1878 resources. Oregon Jewish Museum. Toll, *Making of an Ethnic Middle Class*, pp. 11-12.
8. *Daily Astorian*, Aug. 4, 1877.
9. Ibid., Aug. 17, 1877.
10. Ibid., Aug. 26, 1877.
11. Adler Family, Ind 46, General correspondence, 1872-1877. Oregon Jewish Museum.
12. Ibid.
13. *Daily Astorian*, Nov. 25, 1879, p.3.
14. Adler Family, Ind 46, certificates. Oregon Jewish Museum.
15. Adler House Museum, Baker City, Oregon. Hirsch Baer scrapbook.
16. *Salem: A Pictorial History*, p. 37.
17. *Daily Astorian*, Feb. 7, 1882, p. 3.

18. Adler Family scrapbook, Oregon Jewish Museum, p. 12.
19. Ibid., p. 15
20. Adler Family scrapbook, p. 13
21. *West Shore*, June 1883, 9:136.
22. *Daily Astorian*, July 2, 1883, p. 3.
23. Ibid., July 4 1883, p. 3.
24. Cleveland, p. 143-44.
25. *Oregonian*, July 4, 1883, p. 1.
26. Ibid.
27. Ibid.
28. Ibid.
29. Thad S. Trullinger, "The 1883 Astoria Fire," *Cumtux: The Clatsop County Historical Society Quarterly*, 9 (1989): 17.
30. *Oregonian*, July 4, 1883, p.1
31. Cleveland, p. 143-44
32. Trullinger, p. 17-18.
33. Trullinger, p. 16.
34. Cleveland, p. 144.
35. *Daily Astorian*, Aug. 1, 1884.
36. *Daily Astorian*, Sept. 23, 1887.

MAKING A HOME IN BAKER CITY
1. Adler House Museum, Hirsch Baer Scrap book. Lowenstein, *The Jews of Oregon: 1850-1950*, p. 16.
2. Lowenstein, p. 9.
3. Ibid, p. 10.
4. Ibid., 12-13.
5. Ibid., p.13, 15.
6. Ibid., p. 13.
7. Ibid., p. 16.
8. *West Shore*, Feb. 1885, p. 36, 45.
9. Lowenstein, p. 16.
10. Gary Dielman, "'May Live and Die a Miner': the 1864 Clarksville Diary of James W. Virtue," *Oregon Historical Quarterly*, 105 (2004): p.62.
11. McArthur, *Oregon Geographic Names*, p. 38.
12. Andrews, "Baker City in the Eighties," *Oregon Historical Quarterly*, 50 (1949): 84
13. *An Illustrated History of Baker, Grant and Malheur Counties*, p. 170.
14. Ibid., p. 170.
15. Andrews, "Baker City in the Eighties," p. 83

16. Sanford Heilner Oral History, p. 12. See Baker City *Herald*, Oct. 29, 1998. The article "Murder on Main Street" by Gary Dielman has further details.
17. Wesley Andrews mentions the Crystal Palace (p. 90 and p. 93), as does Walter L. Scott in *Pan Bread 'n Jerky*, p. 106.
18. Adler House Museum collections. Oregon Jewish Museum, Adler collections, certificates.
19. Baker *Morning Democrat*, Oct. 21, 1892.
20. Baker *City Directory*, 1893, p. 27.
21. Interview with Chary Mires. The date was discovered in the process of doing research for the Adler House restoration.
22. Elizabeth Baer Oral History, p. 11.
23. Leo Adler Oral History, Oregon Jewish Museum, p. 4. Sanford Heilner Oral History, p. 8-9. Elizabeth Baer Oral History, p. 15.
24. Baker *Democrat Herald*, Oct. 27, 1971.
25. Baker *Morning Democrat*, July 3, 1907.
26. Toll, p. 62.
27. Richard Ohmann, *Selling Culture: Magazines, Markets, and Class at the Turn of the Century*, p. 28.
28. Ibid., p. 28.
29. John Tebbel, *The American Magazine: A Compact History*, p. 185.
30. Ibid., p. 190.
31. Leo Adler Oral History, Oregon Jewish Museum, p. 7. Leo Adler exhibit, text by Scotty Haskell, Oregon Trail Regional Museum. Leo Adler Oral History, Oregon Historical Society, p. 2. Leo Adler funeral eulogy by Norma Giles.
32. Leo Adler Oral History, Oregon Historical Society, p. 3.
33. Astoria *Daily Budget*, Aug. 25, 1911.
34. *Our Teams*, June 1910, p. 5, 8, 9.
35. "The Adler Times," supplement to the *Democrat Herald*, Jan. 23, 1978, p. 1.
36. 1914 Baker High School Rosemary, no page numbers.
37. Leo Adler Oral History, Oregon Jewish Museum, p. 23.
38. Baker *Morning Democrat*, May 23, 1908.
39. Leo Adler Oral History, Oregon Jewish Museum, p. 9.

Magazine Specialist

1. Adler family files, Oregon Jewish Museum.
2. Baker *Morning Democrat*, Nov. 10, 1914, p. 8.
3. "The Adler Times," supplement to the *Democrat Herald*, Jan. 23, 1978.
4. Baker *Morning Democrat*, Jan. 14, 1917, p. 6.
5. Baker *Herald*, Aug. 21, 1916, p. 1.

6. Baker *Morning Democrat*, May 9, 1915, p. 1.
7. Ibid., May 21, 1913.
8. Aaron Delwiche, "Of Fraud and Force Fast Woven: Domestic Propaganda During The First World War." Found on http:// www.firstworldwar.com/features/propaganda .htm.
9. Baker *Morning Democrat*, Feb. 25, 1917, p. 3. *Oregonian*, March 28, 1917, p. 11.
10. Baker *Morning Democrat*, April 3, 1917, p. 1.
11. Elizabeth Baer Oral History, p. 11.
12. Delwiche.
13. Eugene E. Snyder, *Portland Names and Neighborhoods: Their Historic Origins*, p. 65.
14. Baker *Morning Democrat*, Nov. 30, 1917, p. 1.
15. Leo Adler Oral History, Oregon Historical Society, p. 3.
16. Baker *Morning Democrat*, Jan. 9, 1918, p. 1.
17. Ibid., Jan. 27, 1918, p. 2.
18. Baker *Herald*, July 29, 1918, p. 8.
19. Carl Adler's will, July 22, 1918.

Opening New Territory
1. Leo Adler Oral History, Oregon Jewish Museum, p.8.
2. Baker *Democrat Herald*, Feb. 6, 1940.
3. 1992 Leo Adler Interview, Michael Oman-Reagan, p. 2.
4. Baker *Democrat Herald*, Feb. 5, 1935. The article mentions that Zella has been working with Leo for fourteen years.
5. Interview with Ralph and Norma Giles, June 22, 2002.
6. *An Illustrated History of Baker*, Grant and Malheur Counties, p. 178.
7. Adler Files, Certificate file, Oregon Jewish Museum.
8. Adler Family Scrapbook, p. 53. *Baker Democrat-Herald*, June 25, 1969.
9. Norma and Ralph Giles interview.
10. Leo Adler Oral History, Oregon Jewish Museum, p.15.
11. Baker *Democrat Herald*, Aug. 24, 1929, section 3.
12. A listing of the members of the Executive committee appeared in the Baker *Morning Democrat*, July 3, 1928, p. 8. The committee members of the Baker Community Hotel Company were Fred Soll, General Chairman; Leo Adler, wholesale newsdealer; Lucian Arant, editor of the Baker *Herald*; C. J. Bartlett, physician and surgeon, Baker Clinic; C.C. Basche, secretary-treasurer, Bascher-Sage Hardware Co.; C.L. Blakely, physician and surgeon, Baker Clinic; W.H. Browning, agent, Equitable Life insurance Co.; W.C. Calder, Timber Lands; Chares S. Dreisbach, proprietor, Dreisbach Grocery Co.; Will H. Evans, business manager, *Morning*

Democrat; George H. Foster, secretary, Eastern Oregon Building and Loan Association; E.R. Gurney, vice president, Baker White Pine Lumber Co.; Adloph Hansen, president, Hansen Weis & Co.; Fred Kerr, secretary-treasurer, Universal Motor Co.; Frank C. McCulloch, attorney; T. G. Montgomery, Citizen's National Bank; N.A. Muegge, proprietor, Muegge Drug Co.; C.L Palmer, retired; G. W. Palmer, Palmer Brothers; Charles Palmer, Palmer Brothers; O.T. Tinkle, manager, Pacific Telephone Co.; W.P. Smith, Smith Packing Co.; Joseph Stoddard, treasurer and manager, Wholesale Dept., Stoddard Lumber Co.; J.W. Stuchell, manager, Baker Grocery Co.; John A. Trotter, proprietor, Trotter Clothing Co.; F.C. Vaughan, Foster & Vaughan.

13. Baker *Morning Democrat*, July 8, 1928, p. 8.
14. Baker *Democrat Herald*, Aug. 24, 1929, section 3.
15. *Oregon Journal*, Aug. 24, 1929, Sect.1, p.10.
16. Baker *Democrat Herald*, Aug. 24, 1929, section 3.
17. Ibid., Feb. 23, 1932.
18. Ibid., March 11, 1932.
19. Ibid.
20. Multnomah County Library pamphlet, *Chronology of the History of Aviation in Oregon*.
21. Baker *Democrat Herald*, Oct. 14, 1932.
22. Leo Adler Oral History, Oregon Jewish Museum, p. 9.
23. Adler Files, scrapbook, p. 85.
24. Laura Adler Will and Probate. Baker County Circuit Court Records.
25. Adler Files, scrapbook, p. 43.
26. Editors of Time-Life Books, *Hard Times, the 30s* (Time-Life Books:, New York, 1998), p. 29.
27. Ibid., p. 104.
28. Baker *Democrat Herald*, Aug. 12 and Dec. 7, 1933.
29. Ibid., Feb. 6, 1934.
30. Ibid., Feb. 5, 1935.
31. Ibid., April 24, 1935.
32. Avis D. Carlson, "Dust", *New Republic* 82 (May 1, 1935), p. 332-3.

BECOMING MR. BAKER
1. Baker *Democrat Herald*, June 4, 1935.
2. Ibid., Jan. 28, 1936.
3. Much of the information on the Butterick Company comes from Christopher Wagner's Historical Boy's Clothing Web site, http://histclo.hispeed.com/pat/comp/pc-butt.html.

4. Information about Kable News Company came from http://www.kable.com and http://www.mtmorris-il.org/village_more.htm.
5. *New York Times*, July 3,1936, p. 1;, Feb. 8, 1940, p. 28.; and Jan. 21, 1961.
6. http://www.accomics.com/accomicsgoldenage/fawcett.htm.
7. Baker *Democrat Herald*, Dec. 26, 1936.
8. Johannah Fleetwood interview.
9. Baker *Record-Courier*, Feb. 4 and March 25, 1937.
10. Baker *Democrat Herald*, May 19 and Aug. 13, 1937.
11. Ibid., Sept. 21, 1937.
12. Stan Ingram, *Anthony Lakes, a Tale of Two Skis*, Baker, Oregon, 1971, p. 17.
13. Adler family scrapbook, Oregon Jewish Museum, p. 87.
14. Steve Neal, ed., *They Never Go Back to Pocatello: The Selected Essays of Richard Neuberger*, Oregon Historical Society Press, 1988, p. xxvi.
15. Baker *Record-Courier*, May 25, 1939.
16. Baker *Herald*, July 19, 1984. "Phil Harris," in *Almanac of Famous People*, 7th ed. Gale Group, 2000. *Current Biography*, "William O. Douglas," 1950.
17. Baker *Democrat Herald*, Feb. 6, 1940.
18. Barbara Anne Sturgill interview.
19. Ibid.
20. David M. Kennedy, *Freedom from Fear: The American People in Depression and War, 1929-1945*, pp. 465, 468, and 469.
21. Ibid., p. 477.

The War Years

1. Lawrence R. Samuel, *Pledging Allegiance: American Identity and the Bond Drive of World War II*, p. 10.
2. Ibid., p. 11, 13, 15.
3. Ibid., p. 17, 18.
4. Ibid., p. 19.
5. Henry Levinger Oral History, Oregon Jewish Museum, p. 2.
6. Ibid., p. 8.
7. Ibid., p. 16.
8. Bob Young interview, p. 4.
9. Kennedy, p. 620.
10. Baker *Record-Courier*, April 23, 1942.
11. Ibid., Feb. 3, 1943.
12. Ibid., June 4, 1942.
13. Ibid., Feb. 3, 1943.
14. Johannah Fleetwood interview.
15. Barbara Sturgill interview, p. 11.

16. Baker *Record Courier*, May 6, 1943. *Baker Democrat Herald*, Oct. 26, 1943.
17. *Columbia Encyclopedia*.
18. Baker *Democrat Herald*, Oct. 4, 1944.
19. Mason Drukman, *Wayne Morse: a Political Biography*, pp. 15, 59, 65, 92, 103, 121.
20. Ibid., p. 125.
21. Ibid., p. 123.
22. Ibid., p. 123.
23. Ibid., p. 124.
24. Kennedy, p. 798.
25. Ibid., p. 798, 808.
26. "Policy Memorandum prepared by the Research Institute Staff for Executive Members [of WPB]." April 20, 1945, p. 4. Adler House Museum Collections.
27. James T. Patterson, *Grand Expectations: The United States, 1945-1974*, p. 8.

Finding the New Normal

1. Mary Levinger interview, p. 5, 6, 3.
2. Lois Cavallo interview, p. 1-2.
3. "Policy Memorandum prepared by the Research Institute Staff for Executive Members [of WPB]." April 20, 1945, p. 18-19. Adler House Museum Collections.
4. Baker *Record-Courier*, Feb. 14, 1946.
5. Ibid., April 11, 1946.
6. Adler files, Oregon Jewish Museum.
7. Interviews with Bob Young, Mary Levinger, and Lois Cavallo.
8. Bob Young interview, p. 9.
9. Adler files, Oregon Jewish Museum.
10. *Los Angeles Times*, May 31, 1998. In an article titled "Oregon Millionaire Lives on Through Gifts to his Hometown," by Joseph Frazier, Bob Young stated "Leo Adler was a walking advertisement for Old Granddad whiskey and the bars in town kept it on hand for him."
11. Bob Young interview, p. 16.
12. Norma Giles interview.
13. Baker *Record Courier*, Feb. 12, 1948, and Oct. 26, 1948.
14. Baker *Record Courier*, Oct. 28, 1948.
15. Wayne Morse Collection, Box 3A, Leo Adler Folder, April 9, 1949. Special Collections and University Archives, University of Oregon.
16. Wayne Morse Collection, Box 3A, Leo Adler Folder, April 16, 1949. Special Collections and University Archives, University of Oregon.

17. Wayne Morse Collection, Box 3A, Leo Adler Folder, Jan. 9, 1950 letter. Special Collections and University Archives, University of Oregon.
18. Wayne Morse Collection, Box 3A, Leo Adler Folder. Note and attachment, Feb. 24, 1950. Special Collections and University Archives, University of Oregon.
19. Baker *Democrat-Herald*, March 16, 1950.
20. Wayne Morse Collection, Box 3A, Leo Adler Folder. June 2, 1950. Special Collections and University Archives, University of Oregon.
21. Wayne Morse Collection, Box 3A, Leo Adler Folder. June 13, 1950. Special Collections and University Archives, University of Oregon.
22. *Oregon Journal*, May 11, 1950, p. 22.
23. Patterson, p. 214.
24. *Baker Record-Courier*, Aug. 3, 1950
25. Dominic O'Connor and Patrick J. Gaire, *A Brief History of the Diocese of Baker*, Diocesan Chancery, Baker, Ore., 1966, pp. 173-178.
26. Mary Ann Davis phone interview.
27. Patterson, p. 152.
28. Information about Israel bonds came from http://www.us-israel.org/jsource/Economy/bonds.html.
29. Nov. 8, 2002 phone interview with Herschel Tanzer.
30. *Oregon Historical Quarterly*, "Baker County Historical Society," 53 (1952): 210-212.
31. Baker *Democrat-Herald*, May 19, 1953.
32. Baker *Record-Courier*, Feb. 11, 1954.
33. Baker *Democrat-Herald*, Sept. 25, 1954.
34. Adler House Museum Collections.
35. Lois Cavallo interview, p. 8.
36. Telegram from Norman Bay, Adler House Museum.

Airplanes, Fire, and an Ambulance
1. Norma and Ralph Giles interview.
2. Ibid.
3. Gary Hammond interview.
4. Jack Wilson interview.
5. Mary Levinger interview, p. 13.
6. Leo Adler eulogy by Norma Giles.
7. Gary Schmitt interview.
8. Norm Kolb interview, p. 5.
9. *Oregonian*, Nov. 13, 1949, Sunday Magazine p. 6-7. *Oregonian*, Sept. 3, 1978, D10, *Oregon Journal*, Jan. 29, 1960, p. 18.

10. Baker *Record-Courier*, Sept. 25, 1958.
11. Baker *Democrat-Herald*, March 27, 1956.
12. Patterson, *Grand Expectations*, pp. 389, 414-415.
13. Baker *Democrat-Herald*, Jan. 23, 1958.
14. Baker *Record-Courier*, May 1, 1958. Baker *Democrat-Herald*, May 6, 1958.
15. Baker *Record-Courier*, June 5, 1958.
16. Henry Levinger Oral History, p. 13.
17. Norma and Ralph Giles interview, p. 1.*Baker Democrat-Herald*, Dec. 3, 4, and 6, 1958.
18. Henry Levinger Oral History, p. 13. Norma and Ralph Giles interview, p. 1.
19. Norma and Ralph Giles interview, p. 2.
20. Leo Adler Oral History, Oregon Jewish Museum, p. 16-17.
21. Norma and Ralph Giles interview, p. 1.
22. Baker *Record-Courier*, Aug. 27, 1959.
23. *Who's Who in Magazine Distribution*, Ziff-Davis Publishing Company, New York, New York, 1960, p. 9.
24. Baker *Democrat Herald*, April 13, 1951.
25. Ibid., July 7, 1959.
26. Ibid., Feb. 2, 1960.
27. Ibid.
28. Ibid., March 1, 1960.
29. Ibid., April 25, 1961.
30. Ibid., May 12, 1961
31. Baker *Record-Courier*, June 1, 1961.
32. Gene Rose interview.
33. Baker *Democrat Herald*, April 2, 1962, and Baker *Democrat Herald*, April Invitation to Industry supplement. Joining Leo as officers of the corporation were D.E. Clark, a former Ford dealer; R.K. Evans of California-Pacific Utilities Company; John Horton, an attorney; A.C. Lighthall, owner of the Hotel Baker and Builders' Supply; Henry Levinger of Levinger's Rexall Drug; Ken Lockwood, president of station KBKR; County Judge Lloyd Rea; and Rives Waller, manager of the Baker Branch of the First National Bank.
34. *New York Times*, May 4, 1962, p. 16.
35. Baker *Record Courier*, May 10, 1962.
36. Baker *Democrat Herald*, July 27, 1962.
37. Baker *Record Courier*, Aug. 23, 1962.
38. Ibid., July 11, 1963.
39. Baker *Democrat Herald*, Jan. 17, 1964.

An Enduring Love

1. Geoffrey Ward and Ken Burns, *Baseball: an Illustrated History*, Alfred A. Knopf, (New York), 1994, p. 70-73.
2. Baker *Morning Democrat*, March 28, 1913.
3. Ibid., April 4, 1913.
4. Ward and Burns, p. 81.
5. Jules Tygiel, *Past Time: Baseball as History*, Oxford University Press, 2000, p. 83.
6. *Oregon Journal*, Oct. 21, 1924, p. 1.
7. Tygiel, p. 70.
8. Baker *Herald*, Oct. 13, 1972 and *Dictionary of American Biography*, Supplement 7: 1961-1965. American Council of Learned Societies, 1981. J.G. Taylor Spink.
9. Benjamin G. Rader, *Baseball: a History of America's Game*, University of Illinois Press, 2002, p. 152.
10. Tygiel, p. 100.
11. Baker *Democrat-Herald*, June 2, 1937.
12. Ibid., June 4, 1937.
13. Ibid.
14. http://bioguide.congress.gov/scripts/ Norris Poulson. Robert Gottlieb, *LA Weekly*, "Fits and Starts, L.A.'s Struggle for a Great Daily." March 17-23, 2000.
15. *New York Times*, Dec. 22, 1957, p. 100.
16. *New York Times*, Sept. 17, 1957, p. 37. *New York Times*, Oct. 29, 1957, p. 38. *New York Times*, Sept. 26, 1982, p. 44.
17. *New York Times*, Oct. 5, 1959, p. 38.
18. Baker *Democrat Herald*, March 23, 1961.
19. *Oregon Journal*, July 12, 1956, Sec. 3, p. 4. *Oregon Sports*, Chuck Boyce, Aug. 1951. *Oregon Journal*, June 17, 1961, p.6.
20. Gene Rose interview.
21. Baker *Democrat-Herald*, July 14, 1964.
22. Ibid., May 5, 1965.
23. Ibid., Feb. 28, 1966.
24. Ibid., June 22, 1966. *Baker Record Courier*, June 23, 1966.
25. Baker *Democrat-Herald*, Sept. 3, 1966.
26. *Oregonian*, July 3, 1966.
27. Leo Adler funeral eulogy, p. 12. Charles DiGregorio interview with Leo Adler, Nov. 10, 1977, p. 9. *New York Times*, Oct. 17, 1969, p. 1 and p. 60.

Closing the Circle
1. Baker *Democrat Herald*, Feb. 24, 1967.
2. Herschel Tanzer interview, Nov. 8, 2002.
3. *New York Times*, April 10, 1968, p. 95; April 8, 1968, p. 35.
4. Baker *Democrat Herald*, April 15, 1968.
5. Ibid., May 23, 1968.
6. *New York Times*, Aug. 11, 1968, p. D13. *Oregon Journal*, June 27, 1968.
7. Mason Drukman, *Wayne Morse: A Political Biography*, p. 454.
8. Baker *Democrat Herald*, Aug. 20, 1969.
9. Ibid., Jan. 30, 1971.
10. Norm Kolb interview, p. 1.
11. Baker *Democrat Herald*, March 24, 1971.
12. Norm Kolb interview, p. 5.
13. Baker *Democrat Herald*, Oct. 22 and Nov. 8, 1971.
14. Baker *Democrat Herald*, Oct. 27, 1971 and Jan. 23, 1978 "The Adler Times".
15. Ibid., Oct. 9, 1973.
16. Leo Adler correspondence, Adler Family Museum.
17. Baker *Democrat Herald,* June 12, 1974, and July 2, 1974.
18. Norma and Ralph Giles interview, p. 4.
19. Joe Meier interview, Sept. 3, 2002.
20. Baker *Democrat-Herald*, Jan. 23, 1978.
21. Ibid., Jan. 24, 1978.

A Bright Twilight
1. Baker *Democrat-Herald*, Feb. 23, 1980.
2. Norm Kolb interview, *Baker Democrat-Herald*, Jan. 23, 1978, "Adler Times" supplement.
3. Gary Schmitt interview.
4. Roger Ager interview.
5. Ralph and Norma Giles interview.
6. Sister Martha Joseph Rooney interview.
7. *Oregonian*, May 19, 2002, A19.
8. Jonathan Nicholas, *Oregonian*, April 1, 1991, C1.
9. Steve Duin, *Oregonian*, Oct. 14, 1990, D7.
10. Baker *Democrat-Herald*, March 3, 1986.
11. Oregon Elections Division, Official Abstract of Votes: General Election, Nov. 4, 1986, Oregon Secretary of State. 1986.
12. Dr. Chuck Hofmann interview.
13. Chuck Rouse interview.

14. Baker *Democrat Herald*, Nov. 17, 1988, and interview with Norm Kolb.
15. Sister Kay Marie Duncan interview.
16. Norma and Ralph Giles interview.
17. Dr. Chuck Hofmann interview.
18. Norma and Ralph Giles interview.
19. Baker City *Herald*, June 11, 1992, and Dr. Chuck Hofmann interview.
20. Baker City *Herald*, Oct. 13, 1992.
21. Gene Rose interview.
22. Leo Adler's funeral service.
23. Leo Adler's funeral service.

Afterword: Reaping What Was Sown
1. 1993 tax return for Leo Adler.
2. Baker City *Herald*, May 18, 1995.
3. Baker City *Herald*, Feb. 2, 1995. Chary Mires described the gift this way.
4. Chary Mires interview, Oct. 24, 2002.
5. Chary Mires interview, Leo Adler Community Fund Annual reports, 1995-1999, Baker City *Herald*, May 7, 1997.
6. Chary Mires interview, Baker City *Herald*, June 17 and 22, 1998.
7. Chary Mires interview.

BIBLIOGRAPHY

BOOKS AND MONOGRAPHS

Cohn-Sherbok, Dan. *A Concise Encyclopedia of Judaism.* New York: Oneworld, 1998.

Drukman, Mason. *Wayne Morse: A Political Biography.* Portland: Oregon Historical Society Press, 1997.

Editors of Time-Life Books. *Hard Times, the 30s.* Alexandria, Va.: Time-Life Books, 1998.

An Illustrated History of Baker, Grant and Malheur Counties: with a Brief Outline of the Early History of Oregon. Western Historical Publishing Company, 1902

Ingram, Stan. *Anthony Lakes, a Tale of Two Skis.* Baker, Ore., 1971.

Kennedy, David M. *Freedom From Fear: The American People in Depression and War, 1929–1945.* Oxford and New York: Oxford University Press, 1999.

Lowenstein, Steven. *The Jews of Oregon, 1850–1950.* Portland: Jewish Historical Society of Oregon, 1987.

McArthur, Lewis. *Oregon Geographic Names,* 6th ed. Portland: Oregon Historical Society Press, 1992.

Neal, Steve, ed. *They Never Go Back to Pocatello: The Selected Essays of Richard Neuberger.* Portland: Oregon Historical Society Press, 1988.

O'Connor, Dominic, and Patrick J. Gaire. *A Brief History of the Diocese of Baker.* Baker, Ore.: Diocesan Chancery, 1966.

Ohmann, Richard. *Selling Culture: Magazines, Markets, and Class at the Turn of the Century.* London and New York: Verso, 1996.

Patterson, James T. *Grand Expectations: The United States, 1945–1974.* Oxford and New York: Oxford University Press, 1996.

Rochlin, Harriet, and Fred Rochlin. *Pioneer Jews: A New Life in the Far West.*

Boston: Houghton-Mifflin, 2000.

Samuel, Lawrence R. *Pledging Allegiance: American Identity and the Bond Drive of World War II*. Washington , D.C.: Smithsonian Institution Press, 1997.

Scofield, John. *Hail, Columbia*. Portland: Oregon Historical Society Press, 1993.

Scott, Walter L. *Pan Bread & Jerky*. Caldwell, Idaho: Caxton Printers, 1968.

Snyder, Eugene E. *Portland Names and Neighborhoods: Their Historic Origins.* Portland: Binford & Mort, 1979.

Stein, Harry. Salem: *A Pictorial History of Oregon's Capital*. Virginia Beach, Va.: Donning Co., 1981.

Tebbel, John. *The American Magazine: A Compact History*. New York: Hawthorn Book, Inc., 1969.

Toll, William. *The Making of an Ethnic Middle Class: Portland Jewry Over Four Generations*. Albany, N.Y.: State University of New York Press, 1982.

Museum or Library Collections

Adler House Museum
Photographs and ephemera
Baker County Library
Early Baker newspapers and photo collection
Clatsop County Historical Society
Daily Astorian—early articles and advertisements for Carl Adler's Crystal Palace
Oregon Historical Society
Oral History with Leo Adler
Early Baker City newspapers
Oregon Jewish Museum
The Adler Family files
Oral histories with Leo Adler, Elizabeth Baer, Sanford Heilner, Henry Levinger
University of Oregon Knight Library
Correspondence between Leo Adler and Senator Wayne Morse on train schedules and postal rate hikes

Serials

Andrews, Wesley. "Baker City in the Eighties," *Oregon Historical Quarterly* 50 (1949): 83-97.

Carlson, Avis. D. "Dust," *New Republic* 82 (May 1, 1935): 332-3.

Cleveland, Alfred A. "Social and Economic History of Astoria," *Oregon Historical Quarterly* 4 (1903): 138-40.

Current Biography, "Fred Friendly," The H. W. Wilson Company, 1987.

Dielman, Gary "May Live and Die and Miner: the 1864 Clarksville Diary of

James W. Virtue," *Oregon Historical Quarterly*, 105 (2004): 62-95.
Oregon Historical Quarterly, "Baker County Historical Society," 53 (1952): 210-212.
The West Shore, June 1883, Feb. 1885.
Trullinger, Thad S., "The 1883 Astoria Fire," *Cumtux: The Clatsop County Historical Society Quarterly*, 9 (1989): 15-23.
Samuel Suwol, *Jewish History of Oregon, 1958*. Found at Congregation Neveh Shalom Feldstein Library, Portland. Pamphlet.

Newspapers
Baker City *Herald*
Baker *Democrat-Herald*
Baker *Morning Democrat*
Baker *Record-Courier*
Daily Astorian
Eugene *Oregon State Journal*
Los Angeles Times
New York Times
Oregon Journal
Oregonian
Salem *Oregon Statesman*

Interviews
Ager, Roger—Sept. 26, 2002
Cavallo, Lois—Aug. 20, 2002
Davis, Mary Ann—Oct. 12, 2002
Duncan, Sister Kay Marie—Sept. 11, 2002
Fleetwood, Johannah—August 22, 2002
Frank, Gerry—Sept. 4, 2002
Giles, Norma and Ralph—Sept. 11, 2002
Hammond, Gary—Oct. 24, 2002
Hofmann, Dr. Chuck—Oct. 23, 2002
Jones, Pearl—Sept. 11, 2002
Kolb, Norm—Oct. 24, 2002
Levinger, Mary—Aug. 20, 2002
Joseph Meier—October 2002
Mires, Chary—Oct. 24, 2002
Rooney, Sister Mary Joseph—Oct. 16, 2002
Rose, Gene—Oct. 24, 2002

Rouse, Chuck—Nov. 22, 2002
Savitt, Ron—April 16, 2004
Schmitt, Gary—Sept. 26, 2002
Sturgill, Barbara Anne—June 22, 2002
Tanzer, Herschel—Nov. 8, 2002
Vaughan, Tom—Sept. 17, 2002
Wilson, Jack—Sept. 9, 2002
Young, Bob—June 22, 2002

ORAL HISTORY
Adler, Leo. Oregon Historical Society.
Adler, Leo. Oregon Jewish Museum.
Baer, Elizabeth. Oregon Jewish Museum.
Heilner, Sanford,
Levinger, Henry. Oregon Jewish Museum.

OTHER
1880 United States Census
Baker City Directory, 1893
Baker High School Rosemary, 1914
Laura Adler Will and Probate. Baker County Circuit Court Records
Norma Giles Eulogy for Leo Adler
"Of Fraud and Force Fast Woven: Domestic Propaganda During The First World War" by Aaron Delwiche. Found on http://www.firstworldwar.com/features/propaganda.htm.
Our Teams, Curtis Publishing Company, June 1910, p. 5, 8, and 9.
"Policy Memorandum prepared by the Research Institute Staff for Executive Members [of WPB]." April 20, 1945.

INDEX

Editor's Note: All illustrations and photographs are bold italic.

Adler, Adelaide (sister of Carl Adler). *See* Hirsch, Adelaide Adler.
Adler, Anna (sister of Carl Adler), 2, 10, 83
Adler, Bertha (sister of Carl Adler), 2, 15, 30: letter from, *18*
Adler, Carl (father of Leo), xiii, 10, *26*, *35*, *63*, *79*, 146, 209: in Astoria, Ore., 24-44, 70-71; Crystal Palace, 43-44, 55, 59, 61, 65-66; death of, 83-4, 162; early business of, 24-25, *26*, *27*, 30, 32; family of, 1-2, 10-11, 15-19, *17*, 44, 54, 58-59, *60*, 61, 81; in fire company, 26, 28, 70, 128; German language classes, 63, 72-73, 80; in Germany, 1-3; homes of, 34, *36*, 40, 61-62, *62-63*; letters, 4, 11, 13, 15-19, 28-30; marriage of, 30, 32-34, 36; religious practices of, 15-17, 55, 58; in Tennessee, 3-5. *See also names of family members.*
Adler, Jacob (father of Carl Adler), 1, *14*, 18, 64, 81: letters from, 11, 13, 15-17, 28-29
Adler, Jerome J. (brother of Leo), 55, 58: death notice for, *56*
Adler, Josne (brother of Carl Adler), 2, 16
Adler, Laura Hirsch (mother of Leo), 8, *34*, *44*, 44-45, 47, 54, 58, *63*, *79*, 83, 85, *99*: death of, 99-100, 162; marriage of, 32-34, 36
Adler, Leopold "Leo," xi-xiii, *61*, *62*, *63*, *79*, 81, 82, 84, *109*, *129*, *133*, *143*, *145*, *167*, *173*, *183*, *202*, *203*, *204*, *205*, *207*, *210*, *213*, *216*, *222*, *224*, *228*, *235*, *237*, *238*, *241*, *242*, *244*: accounts of, 117-18, 119, 142, 145, 159, 161-62, 163-64, 226-27, 232, 239-40; and air service issue, 172-73, 175, 177-82, 217, 219; awards to, 89, 158-59, *160*, 182, 209, 211-12, 244-45; Baker Flood-Lighting Corporation, 112, 118, 126, 193-94; and baseball, 185, 190-94, 197-98, 201-08; birth of, 61; business reputation of, 102-03, 112-13, 118, 159; civic duties of ("Mr. Baker"), 71, 91, 97, 101-02, 112-17, 130-33, 142-43, 147, 152, 154, 157-58, 165-66, 172, 174-75, 181, 193, 217, 234; death of, 245-46; in the Depression, 97-104; and desegregation issue, 166-67, 176-77; drinking by, 144-47, 169-70, 242; education of, 64, 72-73, 80; essay by, 64-65; final years of, 240-45; and fire department, 146, 168, 183-84, 200, 216, 222-23, 237, 243; friendships of, 127, 154, 163, 242-43, 245; health of, 103, 242, 245; home of, 62, 162-63, 240-41, 249-54; and Hotel Baker, 91-92, 94-97, 163; investments of, 164, 230-31, 248; and Oregon Trail, 130, 132, *134*, 156, 182, 234-35, 237-39, 243-45; as paperboy, 65-66; politics of, 133-35, 147-52, 158, 220-22; religion of, 62-64, 72-73, 83, 154-56, 210-12, 232-33; retirement of, 220, 223-27, 229; romantic relationships of, 90, 163; WWI efforts of, 81-83, 85; WWII efforts of, 125-26, 128-31, 138-40, 142, 150. *See also* Leo Adler, Magazine Specialist; Leo Adler Trust.
Adler, Mary Louise Weiden (Mrs. Sanford), 89-90, *129*, 134, 232-33, 233
Adler, Mathilde (sister of Carl Adler). *See* Friendly, Mathilde Adler.
Adler, Moritz (brother of Carl Adler), 2
Adler, Recha (sister of Carl Adler), 2, 18: letters from, 19, 29-30
Adler, Rosalie (sister of Carl Adler), 2, 18, 29

Adler, Sanford (brother of Leo), 55, *60*, 61, *62*, *63*, 65, 73, 79, *81*, 82, 83, *87*, 100, 114, *129*, 134, 146, 154, 225, 226, *228*, 231: career of, 75-76, 85-86, 99, 182; death of, 232-33; marriage of, 89-90
Adler, Therese Gutmann (mother of Carl Adler), 1, 11, *12*
Adler, Theresa (sister of Leo), *44*, 44-45, 55, *60*, 61, *62*, 73, 79, 83, 85, *87*, 100, 113, *113*, 253
Adler House Museum, xii, 250-54, *251*
Adler's Book and Music Store (Crystal Palace), 75-76, 86: ad for, *77*
Adler Scholars, 248-49, 255
Ager, Roger, 230-32, 248
Alert Hook and Ladder Co. No. 1 (1877), 26, 28, 33, 70
American Pioneer Trails Association, 182, 245
Anti-Defamation League of Oregon, 156, 204
Astor, John Jacob, 22
Astoria, Ore., 21, 25, 23, *43*: 1883 fire, 37-43, *38-39*; fire department in, 26, 28, 33, 37, 40, 41, 70; industry of, 22-25; Jewish community in, 24-25; shipping routes to, 24-25
Astoria *Daily Astorian*: on business growth, 24; on Carl Adler, 25, 30, 32, 43, 44-45
Astoria *Daily Budget*: Carl and Leo in Astoria, 70-71
Astoria *Daily News*: 1883 Astoria fire, 37-40
AuCoin, Les, 238

Baer, Bernhard "Bernie," (son of Sallie and Sam), 55, *60*, 114
Baer, Elizabeth (daughter of Sallie and Sam), 55, *60*, 64, 73, 114, 163
Baer, Peter, 250
Baer, Rosa Hirsch (first Mrs. Sam), 8, 47, 54
Baer, Sallie Hirsch (second Mrs. Sam), 8, 32, 54, 58
Baer, Sam, 47, 55
Baer Mercantile Company (Baer and Ottenheimer General Store), 47
Baker, Edward Dickinson, 52-53, 156-57
Baker, Ore. *See* Baker City, Ore.
Baker Airport, 131
Baker City, Ore., *50*, *54*, *102*, 116-17: air service to, 98-99, 172-81, 220; baseball in, 186-90, 193-94, 198-201, *202*, *203*, 203-07; City Council, 175; Depression in, 96-98, 101; economic decline of, 235-37; entertainment in, 115-17; fire department in, 128, 144-46, 153, 167, 168, 183-84, 216, 222-23, 225, 243; hotels in, 91-96; Jewish community in, 51-52, 62-64, 232; movie made in, 214-15; naming of, 52-53, 157; and Oregon Trail, 156-57, 237, 243; resources of, xi, 53; tourism in, 98, 113, 157-58, 174; WWI efforts in, 81-83; WWII efforts in, 125-26, 128-33, 139-40. *See also* Baker County Chamber of Commerce.
Baker City *Democrat Herald*: "The Adler Times," 225-26
Baker City *Morning Democrat*: on baseball, 186-88; on Hotel Baker, 94; on Leo Adler, 77, 218; Leopold Hirsch obit., 58-59; on WWI, 78, 80, 82-83; on youth smoking, 66
Baker City *Record-Courier*: on desegregation, 166-67; on Mining Jubilee, 115-16; on War effort, 139
Baker Community Chest, 132-33, 147
Baker County, 52-53, 76, 166, 243: economic decline of, 235-36

273

Baker County Baseball Association, 196-97
Baker County Chamber of Commerce, 91, 95, 97, 117-18, 165, 168, 225: Aviation Committee, 173, 175, 219; baseball, 193; on desegregation issue, 176-77; programs by, 114, 116; and tourism, 98; war efforts by, 130-31
Baker County Defense Bond Group, 123, 125
Baker County Historical Society, 249
Baker County Museum Commission, 249
Baker Democrat-Herald: on Depression, 97-98; on Fred Soll, 94-95; Hotel Baker ad, 94; on Leo Adler Field, 201
Baker Economic Development Commission, 236-37
Baker Flood-Lighting Corporation, 112, 116, 118, 193
Baker Gold Diggers, 189
Baker Hotel. *See* Hotel Baker.
Baker Industry and Resources Corporation, 181
Baker Little League, 199-201, 206
Baker Loggers (baseball team), 199
Baker Miners (baseball team), 193
Baker Motel Association, 157-58
Baker News Industry. *See* Leo Adler, Magazine Specialist.
Baker War Industries Inc., 128-30
Barber, Red, 191
Barr, Louis D., 92, 94
Bartlett, Dr. C.J., 99
Baseball: in Baker City, 186-90, 193-94, 198-208; national, 185-86, 194-98; night games, 192-93; radio broadcasts of, 191-92
Bay, Norman, 159
Beck, Charles Clarence, 110
Ben-Gurion, David, 155
Benton, Doug, *183*, 184
Berg, Bill, 180
Black Sunday, 103-04
Boit, John, 21-22
Bowron, Fletcher, 195
Brandenthaler, Anthony, 211, 219
Brooks, Colleen, 249-50, 252
Brown, Joe E., 196
Browning, W.H., 92
Bureau of Independent Publishers and Distributors, 143-44
Butterfield, Henry, 32
Butterick, Ebeneezer, 106-07

Calkins News Company (Spokane), 110
Campbell, Don, 177
Captain Billy's *Whiz Bang*, 108-09
Carl Adler's Stationery Store, 24, *26*: advertisement of, 25-6; ledger, *27*; success of, 30, 32
Cavallo, Lois, 142, 159
Chandler, Norman, 195
Chatfield, Eva. *See* Meyer, Eva Chatfield.
Chaves, Art, 200
Chaves, Francis, 200
Cholera epidemic, 4-5
Civil Aeronautics Board (CAB), 173, 175, 212: hearing, 177-80
Civil Service Board, 168
Civil Service Commission, 174-75, 183
Clarke, S.A., 6
Colburn-Sorenson Rodeo, 116
Cole, Brian, 238
Columbia Rediviva (ship), 21
Compton, Leo, 174
Congregation Beth Israel (Portland), 10, 55, 83, 99-100: membership of, 57. *See also* Temple Beth Israel.
Cornucopia Mine, 76

Council for Independent Distribution, 166
Cramer, Ted, 97
Crystal Palace: in Astoria, 43-45; in Baker City, 55, 59, 61, 65, 75. *See also* Adler's Book and Music Store.
Curtis, Cyrus H., 66-68
Curtis Publishing Company, 71, 76-77, 86, 105, 147, 158-59, 212

David, Herman, 154
Davis, H.L., 157
Davis, Mary Ann, 154
Defense Savings Bond and Stamp program, 123-25, 130
Desegregation, 166-67, 176-77
Development Corporation for Israel, 155
Dodgers (baseball team), 195-97
Donald, James T., 130-31
Douglas, William O., *116*, 117
Driggs, Howard R., *143*, 156-57, 182
Drown, Jack, 221

Eastern Oregon Light and Power, 193
E. Butterick & Co., 106-07
Eccles, David, 88
Eisenberg, Theresa, 83
Eisenhower, Pres. Dwight, 166
Elks club, 91, 209
Elks Park, 199. *See also* Wade E. Williams Park.
Empire Theatre, 171
Erautt, Eddie, 199
Erautt, Joe, 199
Erickson, Dennis, 201

Faubus, Wayne, 166-67
Fawcett, Roscoe, 108-10, *109*
Fawcett, Wilford H., 108-10
Fawcett Publishing Company, 100-01, 106, 108
Fernald, Jane, 132
First National Bank of Baker City, 51, 101, 112, 118, 168
Fleetwood, Johannah, 110-12, *118*, 131-32, *137*, 138
Fort George. *See* Astoria, Ore.
Fossum, Helma, 119
Fred Meyer stores, 164-65
Freedom Rides, 176-77
Friendly, Carrie (daughter of Mathilde and Sam), 16, 30, *31*
Friendly, Fred (Ferdinand Friendly Wachenheimer), 10
Friendly, Mathilde Adler, 2, 5, 8, 9, *10*, 10-11, 16, 59
Friendly, Rosa (daughter of Mathilde and Sam), *31*
Friendly, Sam, 10, 24, 28
Friendly, Theresa (daughter of Mathilde and Sam), 16, 30, *31*
Froehlich, F., 3-5
Frontier Airlines, 173
Fuller, Walter D., 147-48

Gabrielson, Guy, 152
Geiser, Al, 92
Geiser Grand (Baker City), 92
German Americans: culture of, 81-82; discrimination against, 78-82
German Verein, 72, 78, 79
Giles, Norma, 161-62, 170, 223, 224-25, 230, 242, 245-46, 247
Giles, Ralph, 161-62, 163-64, 168-69, 230, 242, 243, 245
Goldman, Alise (Lizzie), 8
Goldschmidt, Neil, 236, *238*, 244
Goldsmith, Bernard, 49, 51
Goldsmith, Isaac, 49
Gray, Capt. Robert, 21

Great Depression, 96-98, 101, 107
Griffin, Henry, 52
Gruening, Ernest, 115

Harris, Phil, 117
Haskell, Scotty, 252
Hatfield, Mark O., 205, *207*, *227*, 238
Hauser, Eric Jr., 91-92
Hawes, Oden, 174, 219
Hazeltine Photo Studios (Baker City), 55
Heilner, Aron (father of Sigmund), 47: letters from, 48-49
Heilner, Clara Neuberger (Mrs. Sigmund), 51
Heilner, Marian (Mrs. Sanford), 163
Heilner, Sanford (son of Sigmund), 48, 63-64, 126, 163, 209, *210*
Heilner, Seligmann (brother of Sigmund), 47-48, 49: murder of, 53
Heilner, Sigmund, 47-49, 55, 63, 209: diary entry, 51; house of, 51, *52*
Heilner Commercial and Commission Company, *46*, 51. *See also* First National Bank of Baker City.
Hiatt, George, 225
Hirsch, Adelaide Adler (sister of Carl Adler), 2, 5, 7, 8, *9*, 16, 32
Hirsch, Edward (brother of Leopold), 6, 58
Hirsch, J.B. (brother of Leopold), 6
Hirsch, Laura. *See* Adler, Laura Hirsch.
Hirsch, Leopold (father of Laura Adler), 5-6, 8, 28, 32, 34, 61: obit., 58-59
Hirsch, Mayer (brother of Leopold), 6
Hirsch, Rosa (sister of Laura Adler). *See* Baer, Rosa Hirsch.
Hirsch, Sally (sister of Laura Adler). *See* Baer, Sallie Hirsch.
Hirsch, Solomon (brother of Leopold), 6, *6*, 8
Holden, E.G., 41
Holiday (magazine), 157
Holman, Rufus C., 135-36
Hoskins, Jessie, 110
Hoss, Hale E., 97
Hotel Baker (Baker Hotel), xiii, 91-92, *93*, 94-96, *102*, 117, 118, 163: conventions in, 102
House Committee on Un-American Activities, 151
Hughes Air West, 219
Hutton, Jane, 252

Inland Empire Periodicals, 225
Israel, 154-55, 210-11
Israel Bonds, 155-56, 210

Jewett, Stanley, *116*
Jews, 51-52: in Astoria, 24-25; discrimination against, 2-3, 47, 64, 72-73, 114-15, 127, 136, 154, 156; education of, 33; German Period, 3; and Israel, 154-56. *See also* Congregation Beth Israel; Judaism; Temple Beth Israel.
Johnson, Bard, 177, 180
Johnson, Pres. Lyndon Baines, 180
Joslin, Harold, 99
Judaism, 16-17: mourning practices, 13, 15, 83

Kable, Harry, 107
Kable News Company, 106, 107
Karg, Otto, 128
Kennedy, Robert, 214
Kiwanis Club, 91, 130
Klevansky, Mrs. B., 77-78
Kolb, Norm, 217-18, 229, 240, 248
Knights of Pythias, 91: Lodge, 170-71, 217, *228*, 229
Krupeka, Martin, 222

Ladies Home Journal, 66-67, 71

La Grande, Ore., 97-98, 101
Lambert, Francis, *116*, 133
Landeen, William, 114, 115
Lane, Harry, 80
Lawrence, Lyle. *See* Levinger, Lyle Lawrence.
Leipzig, Frances P., 66, 153-54, 184, *195*, 206, 211, *213*, *222*, 226: and athletics, 174, 200, 201, *204-05*, 206; tribute to, 219-20
Lend-Lease bill, 120-21
Leo Adler Community Fund, 247, 250-51, 254
Leo Adler Field, xi-xii, 201, *202-05*, 203-07
Leo Adler Foundation, 247
Leo Adler, Magazine Specialist: advertising for, 72; beginnings of, 65-73; business practices of, 88-89, 110-12, 119, 131-32, 172, 217-18; conventions, 102, 105, 113, 143-44, 147, 158, 166, 212; distribution accounts of, 66-68, 71, 86, 88-90, 100-01, 106-10, 164-65; handbill for, *134*; offices of, 75, 88, 110, 168-71, 217-18, *228*; postal rate issue, 147-51, 167, 216-17, 220, 223; reputation of, 102-03, 118, 159; sale of, 223-25, 229-30; sales awards, 76-77, 158-59, *160*, 182-83; staff of, 87-89, *106*, 106, 110-12, *111*, 117, *118*, 119-20, 131-32, *137*, 137-38, 142, 159, 162-63, 218, 230; territory of, 76, 86-87, 103, 105
Leo Adler Memorial Parkway, xii
Leo Adler Theater, xii, 245
Leo Adler Trust, 247: disbursements, 248-49, 250-51, 254-55
Leovich, Johnny, 199
Levinger, Henry, 126-28, 141, 161-62, 163, 168-69, 171, 199, 234, 242, *242*, 248
Levinger, Louis, 126-27
Levinger, Lyle Lawrence (Mrs. Louis), 126-27
Levinger, Mary (Mrs. Henry), 141, 163, 234, 242
Levinger Drugstore, 126, 128, 141: fire in, 168-71
Lewis, Freeman, 149
L. Fleischner and Co. (Portland), 6
Logsdon, Aaron, 203-4
Lorimer, George, 68

MacPhail, Larry, 192-93
Mathewson, Christy, 185-86, 190
May, Rabbi Mayer, 10
McCarthy, Joseph, 151
Meacham, Walter, *133*, *143*
Meeker, Ezra, 182
Meier, Joe, 224, *224*, 225, 229-30
Meier, Julius, 97
Meir, Golda, 155, 211, *211*
Merrick, LeRoy, *204*, 206
Meyer, Eva Chatfield, 164
Meyer, Fred, 164-65
Miller, Harry, 81
Mining Jubilee Dance and Rodeo, 105, 115-17, 126, 132
Mires, Chary, 249-50, 252-54
Mitchell, Joseph, 158
Moffett, Charles, 32
Morgan, Don, 245-46
Morgenthau, Henry, 123-25
Morse, Wayne Lyman, 134, *135*, 151-52, 158, 180, 215, *215*, 223: campaign of, 135-37; postal rate issue, 147-50, 167, 182
"Mr. Baker." *See* Adler, Leopold.
Multnomah Hotels Corporation, 91, 94

Nelson, Donald, 128
Nelson, Mike, 236, *238*
Neuberger, Bert, 154
Neuberger, Clara. *See* Heilner, Clara Neuberger.

275

Neuberger, Gerson "Gert," 154
Neuberger, Hans, 154, 242
Neuberger, Julius, 115
Neuberger, Maurine (Mrs. Richard), 182
Neuberger, Richard "Dick," 114-15, 158
Neuberger Heilner Banking Company. *See* First National Bank of Baker City.
Neuberger-Heilner store (Baker City), *114*, 115, 209
Newbry, Earl, 157
Nixon, Pres. Richard, 215, 220-21, 223
Nobach, Ewald, 79

Old Oregon Trail Centennial Commission, 130, 132, 143
O'Malley, Walter, 195-96
Optimist Club, 91
Oregon Council of American Pioneer Trails Association, 156
Oregon Democratic Party, 136
Oregon Historical Society, 157
Oregon Horse and Land Company, 53
Oregon Lumber Company, 88
Oregon Railroad and Navigation, 40-41
Oregon State Community Chest, 154
Oregon State Federation of Young Republicans, 152
Oregon Trail, xi, *143*: commemoration of, *129*, 130, 143; guide to, 98; preservation of, 182. *See also* Oregon Trail Interpretive Center.
Oregon Trail (ship), 132
Oregon Trail Interpretive Center, xii, xiii, 237: funding of, 238-39; dedication of, 243-45
Oregon Trail Regional Museum, 234-35, 239, 250
Oregon War Chest, 142-43
Our Teams (Curtis Co. publication), 71

Pacific Coast Magazine Wholesalers Association, 105, 112, 113, 144
Packwood, Robert, 215-17, *216*, 223
Paint Your Wagon (film), 214-15
Palmer, Charles, 92
Parker, Bill, 110
Parrish, Philip, *133*, 143
Pasadena Tournament of Roses Band, 115-16
Patrick, Sister Mary: letter from, 33
Patterson, Paul L., 157
Paulus, Norma, 236
Penney, James Cash, 92
Perkins, Frances, 134-35
Pesky, Johnny, 199
Pesky, Vince, 199
Pictorial Review Company, 88-89
Pierce, Walter, 99
Portland *Oregonian*, 68, 70: on 1883 Astoria fire, 40-41; on Leo Adler Baseball Field, 207
Portland *Oregon Journal*: on Hotel Baker, 95-96
Postal rates: debate over, 147-51, 167, 216-17, 220, 223
Poulson, Norris, 66, 194-97, *195*, 226

Rachoi, Albert, 227
Rayburn, Sam, 180
Reader's Digest, 182-83
Reens, Louis, 82-83
Regional Strategies program, 236. *See also* Oregon Trail Interpretive Center.
Reynolds, Charles, 133
Rooney, Sister Martha Joseph, 234
Roosevelt, Pres. Franklin D., 101, 120, 125, 138, 193
Rose, Gene, 245: CAB hearing, 177-81; Leo Adler Field, 200-01, 203, *204*, 205-06
Roske, Nedra, 88, *118*, 217-18, *218*, 230

Ruth, Babe, 190-91

Salmon industry, 23, 25: in 1883 Astoria fire, 42-43
Sanford and Mary Louise Adler Scholarship, 233
Saturday Evening Post, 67-68, 71, *74*, 216
Savitt, Ron, 144
Schmitt, Gary, 230-31, 237
Sheehy, Dick, 201, *202*
Sherreib, Carolyn, 250
Sinovic, Dick, 199
Smurthwaite, Zella, 87-89, 110, 112, *118*, 127, 131, 132, 137, 137, 169-70, 217, *219*, 223, 230: death of, 242-43; Leo, personal relationship with, 90, 119, 146, 162, 243
Soll, Fred, 92, 94-95
Spink, J.G. Taylor, 192, 207
The Sporting News, 192
Sprague, Charles, 142
St. Elizabeth's Hospital, 234, 254
St. Francis Academy, 200
St. Francis Cathedral (Baker City), 153-54
Straub, Bob, 227
Stuchell, J.W., 92
Sturgill, Barbara, *118*, 119-20, 132, 137-36, *137*

Tanzer, Herschel, 156
Tanzer, Shirley, 225-26
Taylor, Ed, 40
Temple Beth Israel, 64, 113
Thompson, Emily, 248-49
Thompson, Michael, 248
Trullinger, Thad, 42-43
Truman, Pres. Harry, 138, 152

Ullman, Al, 182, 219, 223, 227
Unander, Sig, 157
United Airlines, 178-79
University of Oregon, 10

Vancouver, Capt. George, 21
Vaughan, Thomas, 226-27
Vermillion, Cam, 167

Wachenheimer, Ferdinand Friendly (Fred Friendly), 10
Wade E. Williams Park, 199-200
Wallowa Whitman National Forest, 214
War Advertising Council, 150
Ward, Pete, 199
War Labor Board (WLB), 135
War Production Board, 128-29, 138-39, 142
Warshauer Brothers, 92
Weiden, Mary Louise. *See* Adler, Mary Louis Weiden.
Welch, Nancy, 32
West Coast Airlines, 173, 175, 178-79
Western Tri-State League, 186-99
Whiz Comics, 110
Wilhelm, Rudie, 191
Williams, Wade, 188-89, 199-200, 201, *202*
Wilson, Pres. Woodrow, 80
Witham, Harvey, 169
Woodman, Don, 201
Woods, Rose Mary, 220-21
World War I, 75, 84, 190: anti-German sentiment, 78-81
World War II, 114-15, 120, 127-28, 138-39, 154: defense bonds, 123-26, 130, 133; war work, 128-31
Wrenn, Thomas, 178-80

Yeakley, Karen, 253
York, Carl, 193
Young, Bob, 128, 145-46, 225, 235, 240, 242